GREEK ENTANGLEMENT

The original party of British officers and men who were dropped into
Greece in the autumn of 1942

Left to right, standing: Themie Marinos, Denys Hamson, Nat Barker, Chris Woodhouse,
Inder Gill, the author, John Cook, Arthur Edmonds and Tom Barnes;
Kneeling: Sergeants Len Wilmot, Chittis and Phillips.

GREEK ENTANGLEMENT

BRIGADIER

E. C. W. Myers

C.B.E., D.S.O.

Commander of the British Military Mission to Greece 1942–1943

"Anthony and I are going out to see what
we can do to square this Greek entanglement."
WINSTON S. CHURCHILL.   *Triumph and Tragedy*

ALAN SUTTON
1985

Alan Sutton Publishing Limited
Brunswick Road · Gloucester

Copyright © 1985 E.C.W. Myers

First published 1955
This revised edition published 1985

British Library Cataloguing in Publication Data

Myers, E.C.W.
  Greek entanglement.
  1. Great Britain. Army. Special Operations
  Executive   2. World War, 1939–1945—Campaigns
  —Greece   3. World War, 1939–1945—Personal
  narratives, British
  I. Title
  940.54′86′41   D766.3

  ISBN 0-86299-212-5

Cover picture: mule-tracks in the mountains; inset: Chris Woodhouse, the author and his brave guide, Yani Pistoli, outside the cave near Stromni in 1982 (photograph courtesy of C.J. Riley, BBC Television producer).

Printed and bound in Great Britain

Contents

	ACKNOWLEDGMENTS	10
	PREFACE	11
I	*Into Enemy-Occupied Greece*	13
II	*In the Mountains Around Giona*	31
III	*We Gather Strength*	49
IV	*The Gorgopotamos Operation*	69
V	*No Evacuation*	88
VI	*Stormy Political Horizon*	97
VII	*Plans for Expansion*	110
VIII	*EAM/ELAS Bid for Power*	125
IX	*Volte-face by Saraphis*	133
X	*Progress In Spite of EAM/ELAS*	151
XI	*The Asopos Operation*	169
XII	*'National Bands' Agreement*	187
XIII	*Widespread Sabotage*	202
XIV	*Politics Predominate*	210
XV	*Andarte Joint GHQ*	218
XVI	*Delegation in Cairo*	228
XVII	*Cairo and London*	246
XVIII	*More EAM/ELAS Bids for Power*	266
XIX	*Retrospect*	274
	APPENDIX	285
	INDEX	295

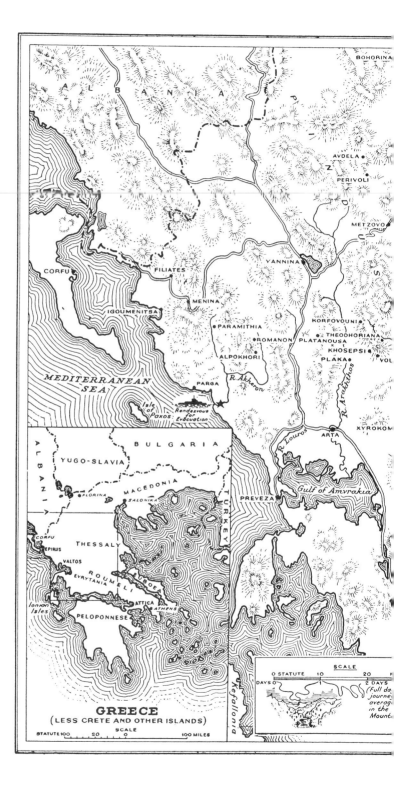

GREECE
(LESS CRETE AND OTHER ISLANDS)

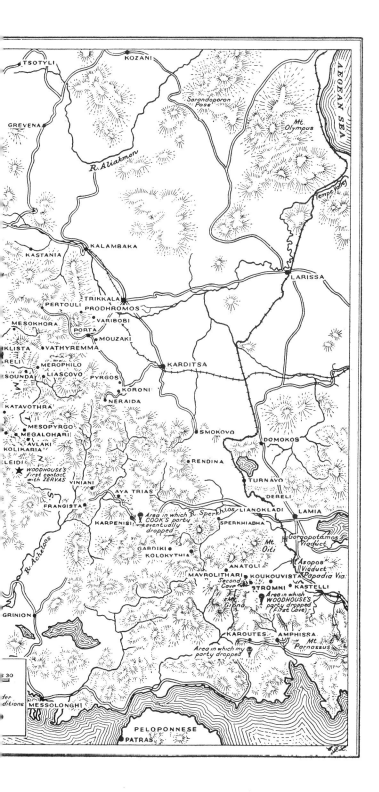

Acknowledgments

I am greatly indebted to my brother-in-law, Bickham Sweet-Escott and to my late second-in-command, Colonel the Hon. C. M. Woodhouse, D.S.O., O.B.E.—both of whom are well known authorities on Greece—for their help in checking the manuscript of this book. I would also like to record my thanks to Mr. Milton Waldman for his invaluable and most painstaking professional advice, to Messrs. Hutchinson & Co. Ltd. for permission to quote from C. M. Woodhouse's *Apple of Discord* and to Messrs. Cassell & Co. Ltd. for permission to quote from Sir Winston Churchill's *Triumph and Tragedy.*

E. C. W. M.

R.A.F. Staff College
Dec. 1954

Preface to 1985 Edition

THIS is the story of my experiences in enemy-occupied Greece in 1942 and 1943, of the bearing of contemporary events upon the Greek war of resistance and, in particular, upon the outbreak of civil war in December 1944. When I first wrote it shortly after the end of World War II, in order to obtain permission to publish it I should have had to delete certain passages in the later, controversial, part of the book. At the time I did not feel able to do this without detracting from any historical value the book might have. After a lapse of nearly ten years I found that it was possible to publish in all essentials the story I had already written. But copies of the 1955 edition have been virtually unobtainable on the open market for some years. It is republished now as a result of renewed interest generated by the recent BBC documentary series on SOE's activities in World War II. In this edition I have been able to take advantage of the fact that a number of documents in the Public Records Office have now been released for public scrutiny. As a result I have been able to include as an appendix to Chapter XVII more detailed accounts, recorded at the time, of my visits to Buckingham Palace, the Foreign Office and Chequers in the autumn of 1943. Some of these details may be of historical importance.

My story was published in 1955 partly because in it there might be a small unrecorded contribution to history, and partly in belated tribute to those under my command and to the many gallant andartes* in the Greek Resistance. But it was published mainly in tribute to the other, perhaps the greatest, heroes of the Greek war of resistance, the unarmed people in the mountains; the people who endured the full terror of enemy reprisals; who produced no traitors; among whom we always moved freely and by whom we were provided with food, shelter, guides and information about the enemy. It should not be forgotten that, without their loyal support and almost incredible fortitude, there could have been no effective resistance.

Broadwell, Gloucestershire   E.C.W.M.
  Feb. 1985

---

* Andarte is the Greek name given to an 'irregular or guerilla fighter' (Greek *andartis* literally means 'rebel').

CHAPTER I

Into Enemy-Occupied Greece

20TH SEPTEMBER, 1942. I vividly remember that hot evening. The enemy, a little over a hundred miles away, was facing us in front of El Alamein. Acting as Brigadier in the Combined Operations branch of General Headquarters in Cairo, I was sitting in my office working on a problem connected with the reinforcement of Northern Syria should the enemy violate Turkey's neutrality and break through Thrace and Anatolia into the Middle East from the north. In spite of the cool draughts intermittently sprayed on me by the buzzing fan as it groaned from side to side, I was perspiring freely when the door opened and in walked a friend of mine, Lieut.-Colonel Hamilton, whom I had not seen since we had been students together at the Middle East Staff College in Haifa six months before.

Hamilton sat down beside me and told me that he had rather a confidential matter to discuss and that he wanted my advice. He said he was on the staff of an organisation which directed operations behind the enemy lines and which I subsequently discovered was called the Special Operations Executive.* He wanted to know whom he should see in order to get three parachute-trained sapper officers to jump into enemy-occupied territory to blow up a bridge somewhere in the Balkans.

I had recently been concerned with the training of the first RE

---

* This organisation had many different names. It will be referred to hereafter as SOE; its headquarters in London as SOE (London) and that in Cairo as SOE (Cairo).

contingent of Airborne troops in the Middle East. But they had not yet started their training. They had not even been earmarked, and I told Hamilton that there was no pool of parachute-trained sapper officers in the Middle East from which he could select volunteers. I knew of no parachutists other than those few who were already actively employed in the SAS—Special Air Service under the command of Lieut.-Colonel David Stirling, in raiding aerodromes and other installations far behind the enemy lines in the North African desert.

Hamilton looked at me. "But what is that badge you are wearing?" he asked. "I see you are a parachutist."

"Oh, yes," I replied. "But I am not a proper one," and I told him how I had learnt to jump in my spare time when I was the senior Army instructor at the Combined Operations School on the Suez Canal and had been partly laughed into it by the instructors at the SAS Training Centre alongside us. I had made my first jump chiefly for the sake of propaganda, in order to get students at the Combined Operations School to realise that one of the future roles of airborne troops would be to assist seaborne forces in an assault landing. Having done one jump, I could think of no adequate reason for not completing the remainder, a course of five, which would entitle me to wear the parachute badge, a standing advertisement for my purpose; and I had done so. "I am just completing my seventh year in the Middle East," I added, "and I am going home in a fortnight's time. Anyhow, I don't speak any Balkan language, and my knowledge of that part of the world is limited to a few hours in Athens and Dubrovnik."

Hamilton's eyes opened wide. "But that doesn't matter a bit! You are just the sort of chap we are looking for. How would you like to take command of this show? It is frightfully important. You would be back in a few weeks, and you could then go home on the crest of a wave."

I said I was not really interested. It was not my line. I was a regular soldier. I had spent long enough in the Middle East and I wanted to have something to do with the Second Front.

"A regular soldier! That's just why you are so suitable for this particular job," he replied. "We want somebody who is a trained staff officer, who could impress the guerilla leaders, and who could organise their forces for a concerted attack."

I asked him if he really meant this. He replied more than once, "Yes, I do."

Still quite undecided whether I would accept such a mission, I said light-heartedly: "Well, come in next door and let's see what my boss, Admiral Maund,* has got to say about it"; and we went into his office.

Admiral Maund in due course said that he didn't mind. It was up to me. He was losing me anyway in a fortnight's time.

I didn't know what to say to this, and rather sheepishly I dragged Hamilton out again, telling the Admiral that we would talk it over outside.

I gave Hamilton the name of a brother officer on the Engineer-in-Chief's staff. I suggested that he should first of all seek his help, and then come and let me know how he had got on.

He agreed and left me. His visit, which I had not taken really seriously, soon passed from my mind and I went on with my work.

The next day Hamilton came back into my office and said that he had had a talk with the Engineer-in-Chief's branch. They had been most helpful. In addition, he said, he had had a talk with his own people, and they had confirmed his view that I was just the chap they were looking for to take charge.

I thought rapidly. I came to a rather hazy conclusion that, if I was really wanted, I ought to go, and I told him that if there was nobody to take my place, I was prepared to take the job on, but that I was not going to move a hand's turn about going. He must

* Now Rear-Admiral L. E. Maund, C.B.E., R.N. (retd.).

get permission for me to go. I presumed that his own command-ing officer, whoever he was, would have to see the Chief of Staff about it.

"Grand!" Hamilton replied. "But, because of the waning moon, bear in mind that you will have to drop within the next week. Otherwise it means postponing the operation until the next moon, and that might be too late for our purpose. I will let you know tomorrow whether I can get permission for you to go"; and we left it at that.

Two days later, having heard no more, I rang up Hamilton and asked him what the position was. He said he thought it would be all right, but he had not yet finally heard. He would let me know in the evening.

Things were slack for me that day, and I had the offer of a trip to Alexandria in a friend's aeroplane. As I had a small job of work to do there, I decided to go. I finished my work in Alexandria quite quickly; I had a luxurious lunch at the Cecil Hotel, and then, with a good hour to spare, I decided to take a walk along the esplanade. I was far from fit. I had spent the last four months in an office and, apart from an occasional swim in the Suez Canal, had had little exercise. I walked hard for an hour, and in due course met my friend who had flown me down. We returned to Cairo uneventfully. Immediately I got back I again rang up Hamilton.

"It's all right," he said. "We have got you. The C.-in-C. says: 'You will go'."

"That's all very well," I answered, "but this is surely a job for volunteers, and not a question of ordering people to go."

"Oh, yes," Hamilton replied. "I meant that, but the C.-in-C. is very keen that you should go. You have been personally selected."

Many thoughts—of home, parents, duty and of my longing to return to England—rushed, all jumbled up, through my mind.

But I replied, I hoped calmly: "All right"; and we arranged that I should go round to his office first thing the next day to be briefed.

The following morning I was shown into the offices of SOE (Cairo) and was told that the operation would take place in four days' time. A party of fourteen volunteers had by then been ear-marked. Some of these were already at the Parachute Training School beside the Suez Canal, only now learning to jump.

The task was explained to me. The Middle East Command was planning the break-out of the El Alamein line. It was most important to hinder the enemy in every way we could in his efforts to bring supplies by sea from southern Europe to his bases along the North African coast. One of the routes, which it was very difficult for our Air Force and Navy to prevent him from using because of enemy air cover based upon the Greek islands, was from Piræus, the port of Athens, via Crete. From Crete a con-siderable number of enemy ships were able to slip across to Tobruk and Benghazi each night. Piræus was served by a single-line standard-gauge railway, which hugged the coast south of Salonica, then meandered southwards across the plains of Thessaly and eventually wound its intricate way through the steep mountains of Roumeli and Attica down to Athens and the coast.

In Roumeli there were three large railway viaducts situated on the north-eastern edge of the mountain group of Giona, the demolition of any one of which would cut the railway line for many weeks, possibly months. These were, in order from north to south, the Gorgopotamos, the Asopos and the Papadia viaducts. Our task was to blow up any one of them. The Papadia viaduct had already been blown up once, during the withdrawal of the Allied Forces in 1941, but it had since been repaired.

It was explained to me how, during our hurried withdrawal in April, 1941, we had had little time to arrange for any patriots to carry out sabotage behind the enemy lines. At the last minute, however, a few Greek volunteers had been obtained to act as agents on our behalf in Athens. One or two of them were now in communication with us by wireless and we were able to direct them and, through them, other groups of patriots on to particular sabotage targets. These few agents of ours had already proved their ability and their bravery. A considerable number of ships had been sabotaged by being either holed or sunk at their moorings both in Piræus and in other ports of Greece. Our chief co-ordinating agent in Athens was a young Greek naval officer called Koutsoyiannopoulos, who went under the pseudonym of Prometheus. At that time, owing to the weakness of his set, wireless messages to him had to be re-transmitted through a relay station in Turkey and were therefore sometimes delayed.

Through Prometheus, contact had been obtained with certain small andarte bands, which had recently been formed in the mountains, and we had been able to drop a limited amount of explosives and small arms by parachute to assist them in sabotage work. As a result, these bands had carried out a few small but successful raids against detached parties of Italian troops and isolated targets.

On 4th September, 1942, SOE (Cairo) had sent Prometheus a message telling him that the C.-in-C., Middle East Forces, General Alexander,* considered it vital to destroy the railway line between Salonica and Athens, and inquiring if any of the bands of andartes with which he was in contact in the mountains would blow up the Papadia viaduct. Prometheus was told that we were prepared to drop the necessary explosives on to the nearest band in the Mount Giona area. He was asked to inform us quickly if he considered this job feasible.

On 21st September the reply was received. This stated that in order to carry out successful sabotage of any of the viaducts in

* Now Field Marshal the Rt. Hon. Earl Alexander of Tunis, K.G., G.C.B., G.C.M.G., C.S.I., D.S.O., M.C.

the Giona area the local andartes would require the assistance of a party of about ten British parachutists, including at least two sabotage experts with the necessary explosives, which would have to be dropped by night between 28th September and 3rd October. Some patriots under a lawyer called Seferiades would be waiting for them near Giona. To indicate the exact dropping ground, each night between the above dates Seferiades' men would light bonfires laid out in the form of a cross.

At the same time we were asked to drop an additional officer with a wireless set on to another andarte leader called Colonel Zervas, last heard of in the Valtos area, in Western Greece. He was to act as liaison officer between Zervas and SOE (Cairo). Unfortunately the name of the place where he was to be dropped was indecipherable in the signal.

On such data the details of our operation were evolved. It was decided that three Liberator aircraft, out of the total of only four then available in the Middle East for Special Operations, would drop a party of nine officers and three wireless operators on to andartes in the mountains. I was to command the operation. Major—later Colonel—Chris Woodhouse,★ who had already spent some time in enemy-occupied Crete, was to be my Second-in-Command. Eight of our party, including myself, were to be taken in two Liberators to Seferiades' bands near Giona. The remaining four, under Chris, were to go in the third aircraft to Zervas.

In our search on the map of Greece for a name anything like that which the corrupt group of letters in the message made, we eventually discovered an almost identical name—that of a village near a mountain called Timfristos in Central Greece, about thirty

★ Now Colonel the Hon. C. M. Woodhouse, D.S.O., O.B.E. He subsequently succeeded me as head of the Mission to Greece. Shortly after the war he wrote *Apple of Discord*, a detailed and brilliant survey of Greek politics, largely based upon his war time experiences in Greece.

miles north-west of Giona. There was insufficient time to check with Prometheus that this was the correct place, because our indirect means of communication with him at that time took several days. SOE (Cairo) assumed that Zervas had moved eastwards to this area.

We were all to be dropped in uniform. As soon as possible after our arrival my own and Woodhouse's party were to join up with our respective andarte forces for a concerted attack upon one of the three railway viaducts. After the successful destruction of one of them, all of us, with the exception of Chris, a young Greek second-lieutenant called 'Themie' Marinos (who held a British commission and who spoke English fluently), and two wireless operators, were to be evacuated from the west coast of Greece by submarine. We were to signal the exact point at a later date. After our departure, it was intended that for the time being there should be no more major activity by the andartes in the mountains and that operations should be confined to sabotage by clandestine groups in Athens and other towns. Chris would act as an observer with the andartes and as a link with any other party which might have to be infiltrated in the future. With this object in view, he was instructed to stay with Colonel Zervas, under whom SOE apparently considered that the Greek Resistance Forces in the mountains might be united. Only if it proved impossible for Chris to stay with Zervas was he to look around for an alternative leader.

During those last four days in Egypt there was a tremendous lot to be done. I had to get myself briefed about the situation inside Greece at that time, prepare a plan and brief everyone else. In addition I had to collect personal equipment and clothing.

For the first two days I worked continuously in Cairo, mostly in the offices of SOE. I asked for drawings of the bridges. Plans of the Papadia and Gorgopotamos viaducts were immediately available and given to me to study. Those of the Asopos viaduct were expected to arrive from London within the next two days. I studied the drawings as best I could. I got the advice of a capable officer in the Royal New Zealand Engineers; I then went across to our Engineer-in-Chief's branch and saw General Tickell,★ whom I knew personally, and asked his advice, having got permission to do so in both cases. When I had evolved the simplest possible demolition plan for each viaduct, I calculated the explosives and accessories required; I multiplied by three in order that there should be sufficient in any one aircraft to blow up one of the three viaducts; and I handed in my requirements.

In the evening of the second day I motored down to the Canal area, a two-hour journey, to meet the remainder of my party—which included two reserves—under training and to select those who were to come with me. On arrival I discovered that one of them had only joined that afternoon and that the remainder, after two days' preliminary training, had carried out their first practice parachute drop that morning. They were to do their first and only practice night drop that evening. Although I had done two night drops myself during my initial training, I decided to do the jump with them. The officer who had just joined that day also volunteered to do his first jump in the darkness with us.

Parachute training at that time was very much impeded. The aerodrome from which the training aircraft were operating was crammed full of bombers which had been forced to withdraw from our forward desert aerodromes by the German drive right up to the El Alamein line. They were operating throughout the twenty-four hours in a more or less continuous shuttle service, bombing the enemy only two hours' flying away.

We eventually got off the ground a little before midnight and did our drop. All had a successful landing, and none was the worse for wear. Immediately afterwards, as Chris had seen something of these people during the past two days, I led him aside to

★ Now Major-General Sir Eustace F. Tickell, K.B.E., C.B., M.C. (retd.).

help me make my final selections. He, I and Major John Cook, a Commando officer, had already been selected by SOE (Cairo) to be the leaders, one in each aircraft. We had to take the three wireless operators, Sergeants Wilmot, Phillips and Chittis, one for each aircraft party. Chris wanted second-lieutenant Themie Marinos to stay behind with him in Greece after the rest of us had been evacuated. Captains Denys Hamson and Nat Barker (Commando officers, trained in the use of explosives) spoke Greek. We might need both of them as interpreters. That left the five sapper officers, from whom to select three. I asked Chris whom he recommended we should leave out.

Chris thought that they were all first-class, but that one had slightly less stamina than the rest of them, and that another, although frightfully keen, appeared to be a bit too highly strung; and we selected the remaining three: Captains Tom Barnes and Arthur Edmonds, both of them Royal New Zealand Engineers, and Lieutenant Inder Gill, Royal Engineers.

The other two were bitterly disappointed. I told them that they would have to stand by, in case anybody became a last-minute casualty, and that I would ask for them to be sent on to me later if I found that I could take them. After a few hours' sleep we all returned to Cairo to make final preparations for our departure the following evening.

During our last day, 28th September, Chris and I arranged to distribute our party of twelve amongst our three aircraft as follows: Tom Barnes, Denys Hamson, Sergeant Wilmot and myself in one aircraft; Chris Woodhouse, Arthur Edmonds, Themie Marinos and Sergeant Chittis in the second; John Cook, Inder Gill, Nat Barker and Sergeant Phillips in the third. We went over our briefing again. Chris met one or two Greek authorities in Cairo—the Greek King and Government were still in London—and he got a little more information from them about the people whom he might eventually meet in Greece. As my task was limited to the specific operation of destroying one of the three railway viaducts, I had no such interviews, and confined myself purely to our immediate task.

About tea-time we left Cairo by car for our aerodrome in the Canal zone. We arrived some two hours later, and almost immediately started changing out of our thin tropical clothes into warm winter suits of thick battledress, which we were told we would need upon our arrival in the mountains of Greece. Leather money-belts were given to us, and I distributed several hundred gold sovereigns amongst each of the party, for use by Chris and me, at our discretion, the other end. We all felt suffocatingly hot in these heavy clothes, which were so unsuitable for an Egyptian summer evening. At about eight o'clock we had a hurried final meal in the RAF Mess adjoining the aerodrome. We then completed our dressing with still warmer overalls, and lastly had our parachute harnesses fitted on top of everything.

Besides explosives we were taking with us rifles, light automatics, ammunition and hand grenades for the andartes whom we expected to meet on arrival, and a little personal clothing and food. All the stores had been packed into metal canisters that afternoon. Twelve containers, each holding three canisters, had been subsequently loaded on to the bomb bays of each of the three aircraft. Our wireless sets and their batteries, which did not fit conveniently into canisters, were prepared in such a way that they could be dropped with some of us, by means of a special attachment to our parachutes.

With the normal type of parachute all one had to do was to sit over a hole in the fuselage of the aircraft and, on the signal to jump, slip down through the hole. Shortly before jumping, a line known as the 'static line' was securely fixed from a 'strong point' inside the aircraft to the top of the parachute packed away on one's back. After one had fallen a few feet, the static line began to tauten and pulled one's parachute out of the pack. When it had completely pulled out the parachute, some string which attached it to the parachute broke, leaving the latter free to open out above one. A modification was arranged so that, between parachute and man, attached to his harness a few feet above his head, an additional and quite heavy package could be carried down to earth. The procedure here was exactly the same so far as the parachutist was concerned. But immediately after he had jumped, a 'despatcher', who travelled in the aircraft, bundled out the additional package behind him. The parachute, which was attached to the package, was pulled out of its pack in the ordinary way by the 'static line'.

None of us had previously jumped with this modified arrangement. It was by no means a desirable contrivance because, as soon as one landed, one was liable to be hit on the head by the package, and during the descent one swung like a pendulum below it, with no control whatever either upon swaying or upon direction, both of which to a certain extent one could control with the ordinary parachute. In due course this contrivance became obsolete because of this. Two of the four of us in each of the three aircraft had to wear it, one to carry a wireless set, the other to carry two heavy batteries. I took a wireless set.

It was already dusk when, sweating at every pore, we eventually walked—or, to be more accurate, waddled—out of the dressing-rooms and across to the waiting aeroplanes not far away. We parted, each to our own aircraft, in the hope that we would meet again in Greece in a few hours' time. I vividly remember my final conversation with Derek Lang,* the Staff Officer who had travelled down with us from Cairo to see us off; our anxious wait outside our aeroplane, as first one engine and then another of the huge aircraft was started up, the flashes from the exhaust showing up in spurts of blue flame in the failing light. Eventually all four engines were ticking over smoothly, and we

* Now Lieut.-Colonel D. B. Lang, D.S.O., M.C., Camerons.

were told to climb in. We duly did so through a small opening underneath the fuselage of the aeroplane, the hole through which we were destined to drop. A board was put down over it, and after a short wait we departed, each aircraft taking off after a quarter of an hour interval. We were the first.

The four of us were crouched together in the cockpit of the Liberator, where we had been gathered so as to keep as much weight as possible off the tail of the aircraft during the take-off. I anxiously waited during what seemed to be an interminable race down the runway. But we took off perfectly, and after gaining height our pilot set a course which would carry us clear of the east coast of Crete.

Not long after the take-off we clambered back along the open gangway of the Liberator, alongside which our containers were stacked on the bomb bays, and we settled down for a four to five hours' journey. We took off our harness and hot overalls and made ourselves as comfortable as we could.

We had soon left the African coast far behind us and our journey became monotonously uneventful. Only once, some two hours later, did we have to do what appeared to be a rapid turn, in order to avoid a few sporadic bursts of flak coming up from an island on our flank. Little over an hour later we looked down and saw below us, standing out clearly in the moonlight, the beautiful but rugged mountains of Greece. It was now about one o'clock in the morning. I went forward and had a talk with the pilot. I learnt that, all being well, we would be over the dropping-ground in about twenty minutes. I returned and ordered everyone to put on their parachutes.

We were quickly muffled and trussed up again, all ready to jump. I managed to get into a position where I could put on some inter-communication head-phones, in order to listen and speak to the pilot.

Soon we began circling over what I presumed to be the area

where we expected to find the bonfire signals to greet us. Alternately through a small window or through the now open hole in the floor of the fuselage I caught glimpses here and there of quite a number of bonfires scattered in the valleys. But I saw no group of them resembling a cross. We circled the area for several minutes and then flew westwards towards Timfristos, to see if we could find any signals there. Seeing none, we flew right on to the west coast of Greece, keeping a look-out and circling frequently as we went. We turned back and, when over the Giona area again, circled afresh.

After a further quarter of an hour the pilot called for me to join him in the cockpit. The despatcher disengaged my parachute from the static line and I went forward. The pilot said that he had seen absolutely nothing like the signal which we expected to find on the ground, and that there was no alternative for us other than to return to Cairo, in accordance with our instructions should there be no signals. I could but agree. I went back and informed the others of our decision. The anti-climax was great. We took off our parachute harness and rolled ourselves up—now gladly because of the cold at the great height at which we were flying—in any and every blanket which we could find in the aircraft, and I think we all went soundly to sleep.

As dawn was breaking we re-crossed the coast of Egypt, and not many minutes later we landed at the same aerodrome as that from which we had taken off some eleven hours earlier. We clambered out and were greeted by an RAF officer, who informed us that already one of the other two aircraft had returned for the same reason as we had. We had hardly started our breakfast in the station Mess when the third and remaining aircraft crew and party joined us. They, too, had seen no signals. After breakfast we learnt that the aircraft in which we had just flown could not be serviced in time for another sortie that night. As there were no others available, our departure would have to be delayed a further twenty-four hours. We got into cars and motored up to Cairo.

We slept most of the remainder of that day. The following day some only partly satisfactory plans of the Asopos viaduct belatedly arrived from England and I studied them intensively. We were told that if we did not drop that night—the night of 30th September—we would have to wait three weeks for another suitable period of moonlight. This might mean the cancellation of the project. Chris and I were determined not to come back again. We arranged that should there be no signals, the aircraft with John Cook in it would drop its party at a suitable point, as near as possible to Mount Giona, and if, on dropping, the ground was found to be safe, this party would light red flares to guide the remainder of us down.

That evening we again motored down to the Canal area and went through the same procedure as two nights before. Themie Marinos and Nat Barker changed aeroplanes. Otherwise our teams were unaltered. We set out almost nonchalantly, as if we had done this sort of thing every day of our lives: at least, that was my feeling as we taxied towards the end of the runway. Soon after we had taken off we were settled in the most comfortable places in the aeroplane, the inside of which we by now knew well.

It appeared no time before we reached Greece and were over Mount Giona. Again there were several single and sometimes pairs of bonfires. But nowhere could we see a cross. We flew to the west coast and back again. Still nothing. But on returning to the Giona area I spotted a group of three fires in what appeared to be a reasonably flat valley. I spoke to the pilot on the inter-communication telephone and said that I was prepared to have a go there if he agreed.

The pilot, a New Zealander, replied that it was up to me. He thought it was just good enough.

"O.K. Let's go," I decided.

27

We got into a position to drop, and the pilot made a big circle and came down as low as he dared. We were flying, I should say, some three thousand feet above the deep valleys beneath us, although much less above the mountain tops, when I, who was to go first, got the signal to jump.

When my parachute opened, my harness slipped off the rucksack of personal equipment strapped on to my back underneath my overalls. As a result the two main supporting straps, by which I was suspended below the wireless package, soon squeezed painfully against both sides of my face. I could only move my head by taking the weight off my heavily laden body with my hands on the straps.

As I floated down through the cool air, it was hard to realise that this was Greece spread out below me, with rugged mountains and steep valleys all round. I looked for the valley with the triangle of fires in it, but could see neither anywhere. I saw several parachutes, with their lighter loads of containers with our stores, disappearing to leeward of me.

On this run-up on to the target one other officer, Tom Barnes, had jumped immediately behind me. I thought that he might be close to me in the air, and that I couldn't see him because he was above me. I shouted to him; but got no reply. I took a torch out of the big pocket of my overalls and flashed it on to my parachute thinking that he would see it when lit up and that it would show him where I was and where the wind was taking me. I shouted again. But I heard nothing except the aeroplane circling in the distance. I put the torch back in my pocket and, raising myself again on my arms, I glanced down to the ground to see what awaited me below.

I was being carried by the wind at a considerable speed above the mountains and across valleys. It seemed that I had travelled laterally nearly a mile before I was sufficiently low to realise approximately where I was going to land. Still several hundred feet above the ground, it appeared to be covered with masses of small shrubs. But, as I floated down closer, these shrubs turned out to be pointed trees—fir trees: a huge, black and apparently interminable forest of them. I looked for an open space. There was none. Anyhow, had there been one, I couldn't have directed my parachute towards it. I realised that I was bound for a tree, one of thousands, and in a second or two they appeared to come up at me with an alarming speed.

I fell into the middle of a tall mountain fir, which opened and parted its arms and had some rudely broken as I crashed through it. I hit my head against its stem, but was fortunately to a large extent protected by my helmet. The next thing I knew I was sitting on the ground, on an extremely steep slope, with my parachute caught up above me. A few feet above my head the wireless set was dangling from it. I automatically slipped out of my harness and, out of control, rolled head first several feet down the steep slope, until another friendly tree arrested my fall. The lovely warm smell of fresh and rotting pinewood greeted me. In the distance above me I heard the throb of the engines of the aircraft which I had so recently left, partially drowned by the noise of the wind swishing through the fir trees all round me.

I carried six red flares in the pockets of my overalls. I took one out, lit it and threw it up in the air, trying to get it above the tops of the trees. I waited, ready with my others, until I heard the aeroplane approaching for a second time to drop the remaining two of our party, and then, in quick succession, I lit three of them. There was no gap in the densely packed trees, so I could not see whether anyone else was coming down near to me. I waited and listened. I lit another flare and threw it up above the trees. Then I lit my remaining one and threw it up. I blew my whistle and shouted, and at intervals again and again. But I got no reply. I peered through the darkness and across the steep valley for any answering signal. I saw none. In a few minutes the aeroplane disappeared behind a mountain and, except for the gentle noise of the wind through the trees, all became suddenly quiet. I realised that, for the moment anyhow, I was alone in the mountains of Greece.

What a contrast to the busy, sand-swept desert aerodrome which I had so recently left in Egypt. What a stillness after five hours in the noisy aircraft. What peace! But, suddenly, what utter loneliness!

CHAPTER II

In the Mountains Around Giona

I SCRAMBLED BACK to my parachute harness. In the darkness, and alone, I realised that it would take me a long time to disengage the wireless set, which was entangled in a mass of boughs, several feet from the ground. A few moments earlier, as I was floating down the last few hundred feet to earth, I had noticed that I was passing over a narrow ridge. I had landed some two hundred yards from its knife-like edge. I thought that I might get a better view from this ridge. So I took off my overalls and, with them under my arm, I clambered up the steep and slippery slope. By the time I reached the top I was panting heavily. I realised that, as a result of the frantic rush and the excitement of the past few days in Cairo, I was not only far from fit, but also extremely tired.

From the top of the ridge I found that I could see something of the countryside, but nothing of the main valley below me. Walking down the edge of the ridge, I found an open space. The moon was fast disappearing behind the mountains, but it was still sufficiently light for me to see a huge and deep valley in front of me. It was covered throughout with fir trees. Behind and ahead of me, the ground sloped steeply up into a vastness of black mountain-sides, whose sky-lines were outlined against the still moonlit clouds. In the open now, the wind was blowing quite strongly. I had no red flares left and, after I had listened for some minutes, at the same time keeping a sharp look-out for anybody else's signals, I gathered together some small sticks and lit a bonfire. I kept it going for some few minutes. But there was no response to it. Then, in the distance, in the valley below me, I heard some sheep bleating, and a few moments later I distinctly heard a man's voice call out. No longer was I all alone.

It appeared to me that the most sensible thing to do was to go down into the valley and, if this voice turned out to be that of a Greek shepherd, to get him to help me find the remainder of my party, who, for all I knew, might not have escaped unhurt in their drop. I took off my heavy pack and dumped it with my overalls beside a large rock in a small clearing close to the ridge. I reckoned I should be able to find the place again without difficulty. Then I descended the mountain-side. 'Descended' was hardly the word for it. The slope was almost precipitous. I alternately fell and skidded as I dropped down the best part of a thousand feet to the valley below. Occasionally I stopped, to listen for the noise of the sheep, to make sure that I was keeping my direction. Reassured, I slid on downwards.

After about twenty minutes I realised that I was approaching the bottom of the valley. I now moved more cautiously. Someone called out again. Another voice answered. The language was definitely Greek. Satisfied that ahead of me were neither Italians nor Germans, but in all probability merely shepherds, I called out at the top of my voice. I knew only two words in Greek, "Imi Inglésos"—"I'm English". So I just shouted "Hoy!" I got no reply. I walked on slowly in the direction of the voices and, as I came to a clearing in the trees, I spotted a small bonfire ahead of me. Two people were standing beside it. From my position of cover I decided that it would be better if I waited there and managed to get them to approach me, in case they turned out to be some mountain police in the pay of the enemy. So I called out again. This time I got an answer. I stood still, and the two people moved towards me. I undid the clip of my revolver holster. As they came closer I saw, in the waning moonlight, that they were neither wearing hats nor carrying rifles. So I called out again and, with my hand on my revolver, came out of my hiding-place to meet them. Immediately they saw me they stopped. I approached deliberately, calling out, "Imi Inglésos". They still did not move, and I walked the few remaining paces up to them, repeating my only two Greek words. They were shepherds.

They looked me up and down, and, apparently reassured that I, in turn, was not a member of the Italian Police, but perhaps really an Englishman, they started to talk to me rapidly in Greek. I did not understand a word they were saying. I pointed to myself and then up the mountains, and counted three on my fingers, trying to indicate that there were three others up there. Eventually I think they understood what I was trying to tell them. After a roundabout sort of deaf-and-dumb conversation, including a lot of pointing to the sky, we mutually agreed that we would stay where we were for the next three hours, until dawn broke. It would have been useless looking for the rest of my party in the moonless part of the night. The shepherds invited me to rest by their fireside. I was soon fast asleep, a sleep more or less of exhaustion.

In what seemed to be only a few minutes I was woken up by one of the Greeks. Dawn was breaking. He pointed up the mountain-side, and I nodded in assent. One of them handed me a few black olives, which I gladly ate. Then we started off, this time by a pathway. Even so, our journey was long and steep, and it was well over an hour before we approached the place, to which I deliberately led them, where I had left my pack. When we reached the actual point, which I was able to confirm by the ashes from my bonfire near by, my kit was gone. There were only two possible explanations. Either another member of our party had come that way and discovered it, or else the younger of the two shepherds, a mere boy who had been travelling ahead of us, had found it before I reached the place and had quickly hidden it for himself. But my lack of Greek made it impossible for me to pursue the matter. In case one of my own people had picked it up, I got out a piece of paper from the message-pad in my pocket and wrote a short note to the effect that anybody finding it should stay here, as I would be coming back. I pinned it visibly to the nearest tree. I had hardly done this when, from a parting in the trees, emerged Tom Barnes, the New Zealander.

We were both relieved to find each other unhurt. He had landed about a quarter of a mile away, the other side of a subsidiary valley further up the mountain, and was wandering about, like me, trying to find the others. He said that he knew where the wireless operator, Sergeant Wilmot, was, but that he had not seen anything yet of Denys Hamson, the fourth member of our party. I asked him if he had picked up my pack. He replied that he hadn't. But he, like me, knew no Greek; so we went on with the more important task of trying to find Denys.

Tom Barnes said that the wireless operator needed assistance to get the batteries off his parachute, which, like the wireless set which I had brought down with me, had also got entangled up in the trees. After showing him where my 'chute was, and agreeing to return there in due course, I sent him off with one of the shepherds. I took the other one with me to look for Denys and for any of the parachutes with our stores attached to them.

After two hours of fruitless searching I came across a Greek who had apparently come up from a village in the valley below to see what had been dropped from the aeroplane the previous night. I returned to the rendezvous at my parachute, while the two Greeks continued the search. Towards midday one of them returned with Denys.

We were now in a much stronger position, because Denys spoke Greek. We discovered that we were about a mile from a village called Karoutes, some ten miles south of the point where we should have dropped. We learned that there were no Italians or

Germans in the village, and that their nearest garrison town, where there was a battalion of them, was about an hour's walk away. The villager, who had returned with Denys, volunteered to go back to Karoutes and to bring up to us an ex-army officer, who, he said, would probably be able to organise assistance for us. We agreed to this, and asked him to bring up some food as well. In the middle of the afternoon Tom Barnes and Sergeant Wilmot, with his batteries, joined us, thereby completing the party from our aircraft.

From the direction in which the wind had been blowing when we had dropped, I realised that most of the lighter parachutes bearing our stores had been blown further up the mountain-side, and that it would take us many hours, possibly days, to find them all. In the process we would probably get lost in the forest. As it was already late in the afternoon, I decided to wait until we had got enough daylight and assistance to organise a thorough search. So we stayed where we were and rested.

In due course the villager returned with some goat's cheese, brown bread and a bottle of local wine. He informed us that the officer was on his way up to us. We had finished our late and meagre lunch, washed down by a little of the welcome wine, by the time the latter arrived. He turned out to be a young Greek officer called Katsimbas. He was extremely polite, even though excited to be talking to British officers again. He told us that he was afraid to take us back to his village because, with an Italian garrison so near, it would be too dangerous for the villagers. If we would go with him, however, he would show us a safe hiding-place nearer the village and more convenient for bringing us food. We agreed to do this. He led us about half a mile towards the valley which I had already descended once, to a reasonably comfortable nook. Here he left us, saying that he would return later in the evening. Just before dark he did so, bringing with him more bread, cheese and black olives, and a little more of the Greek wine.

He told us he had heard that an andarte called Karalivanos and a small band had arrived that afternoon on the other side of the valley and wanted to meet us. Katsimbas had been instructed to take us to meet him the following morning, and recommended that we should start in the half-light of dawn, when it would be safe for us to cross the road which ran along the bottom of the valley.

Karalivanos was the name of one of the andarte leaders whom we had been told in Cairo that we might possibly meet in the Giona area. Our hopes were raised considerably at the thought of meeting him on the following day, for we had been led to believe that he controlled a band of about a hundred andartes. After our evening meal we wrapped ourselves up in our parachutes and went to sleep, our first proper rest since we had left Egypt.

True to his word, Katsimbas returned to us whilst it was still dark the following morning. We rolled up our parachutes and, with three or four villagers who had come to help us, we carried our personal equipment, wireless set and batteries down into the valley, across the road and up the opposite side. After half-an-hour's clambering up a steep, rocky pathway, we rounded a corner, to be greeted by our first andarte.

Above us, in a parting in the trees, there stood a little, squat man in a grimy black Evzone uniform. He wore three bandoliers full of ammunition, one round his waist and one over each of his shoulders. He carried a rifle at the ready. Several knives with beautifully engraved handles, protruding from various parts of his waist, completed his equipment. The smile which spread over his shaggy, uncouth face revealed an almost toothless jaw. He slid nimbly down the few yards which separated us, on to the pathway in front of me, and in turn shook each of us heartily by the hand. He then led us off the pathway, and we soon found ourselves in front of four other similarly dressed people, one of whom, distinguished by a red fez on his head and a tommy-gun in his hand, was introduced to me as their 'Capitanos', or leader, Karalivanos.

Using Denys as my interpreter, I explained that we had arrived in the aeroplane the previous night, that we had been specially sent by the C.-in-C. Middle East, and that we wished to get in touch with the andarte bands in that area. I asked him where the rest of his band was. I was rather taken aback when he told me that these men were all he had, a total of five. I left it at that for the moment, and told him that the next most important thing was to collect our stores, which were presumably scattered about on the mountain slopes on the opposite side of the valley. He agreed to do this.

Karalivanos selected a small plateau on which to make our temporary headquarters. From the edge of it we could get an excellent view of the valley and of all the approaches from below us. There was sufficient cover for a bonfire on it to be invisible except from a small area on the opposite side of the valley. He left us there to organise the search for our stores. Meanwhile all hands set to, to establish wireless contact with Cairo. But we soon discovered that the set had been damaged by the drop. Until a canister with spare parts was retrieved from the forest on the mountain opposite us, we could do nothing.

Towards evening Karalivanos returned, but with nothing. Denys assured me, however, that he had taken all possible steps, and that parties of villagers were scouring the forest on our behalf. The following morning, with all his band except one, he left us again to continue the search. Towards midday a villager with a mule laden with two canisters clambered up to our plateau. We undid them carefully. They were full of hand grenades and various demolition accessories.

When Karalivanos returned that evening, Denys and I had a long talk with him. I gathered that, as fast as the villagers were finding our stores, they were hiding them for themselves, and that he was having great difficulty in getting them to hand them over. Karalivanos said he would have to use sterner measures to induce them to give them up. Before resorting to punishment of the next villager caught red-handed we agreed that he should bring the village President up to us for an interview.

The following morning he produced for us not only the President of Karoutes, but two Greek policemen as well. The President, obviously frightened, promised to do all he could for us. By way of indicating what would happen if he did not, Karalivanos seized hold of the two policemen and explained to him that these men were an insult to Greece, because they were in Italian pay. With one of his knives he slashed the buttons off their tunics, and said that if all our stores were not brought up within the next twenty-four hours he would cut their throats. Meanwhile he would keep them as hostages.

The village President asked to talk privately with Denys and myself. He said that, although he was willing, and in fact wanted, to help us in every possible way, he was pretty sure that the Italian garrison nearby already knew that our aeroplane, which they would have heard three nights previously, had dropped stores in this neighbourhood, and that, unless he soon reported something to them, they were likely to send a patrol to his village to find out for themselves. If they found anything, he would be arrested. He therefore wanted us to clear out. We explained that we could not do this until we had gathered all our stores and had put them in a safe hiding-place. He promised to do his utmost to get them for us within the next forty-eight hours. If he did so, we told him, we would then move away from his village, and he could report to the Italian garrison that only a few parachutes with stores, but no men, had been dropped.

Karalivanos' threats and the village President's wish to see the last of us now began to bear fruit, and during the day some half a dozen mule-loads of canisters containing arms, ammunition, explosives and clothing were brought up to us on our little plateau. No food was brought and, what was strange, no single canister which we spotted as definitely coming from our own aircraft. This made me feel that somewhere in the district there was at least one more party of four, who had dropped from one of the other two Liberators.

After a further delay of twenty-four hours, during which a few more canisters were brought up to us, the village President said that he could find no more, and he pleaded with us to leave the precincts of his village, because he simply must go the next day to the Italians to report something.

Unsatisfactory as the position was, I calculated that we had just enough explosives to blow up a bridge. With the help of Katsimbas, the Greek officer, we stealthily hid everything which we did not immediately require. At dawn the following day we loaded three village mules with our wireless set, batteries and such clothing as we had gathered. We set off with Karalivanos in a north-westerly direction towards the area, some ten miles away, in which we should have been dropped, and where we expected to find Seferiades and bands of andartes several hundred strong awaiting us.

It poured with rain all that day. We made some five or six hours' progress. Clambering up and down the stony mountain pathways, I again realised that I was far from fit, and towards evening, when we rested for the night, I was weary and footsore. To protect ourselves from the pouring rain which, even under the fir trees, dripped heavily down upon us, Karalivanos' men built two small shelters out of broken fir branches, one for themselves and one for us. They built them like wigwams, each with a tiny entrance. With bracken floors, they made dry and snug resting-places. One of Karalivanos' men, called Yorgo, disappeared in search of meat. In about an hour he returned with a live sheep across his back. This was quickly despatched and expertly skinned.

Part of it was roasting on our open fire within a few minutes of its throat being cut. The gut of the animal's stomach was carefully packed with chopped-up kidney, heart and liver. It was then wound round a thick stick which served as a spit on which to cook it over the fire. With a little brown bread, which we had brought with us from Karoutes, it made a delicious 'hors d'œuvre', which the Greeks call *kokoretsi*. There was an abundance of water, for every valley possessed a cool, clear stream of water.

Later, Sergeant Wilmot announced that he thought he had at last got the wireless working. We clambered up to the nearest open ground and set up an aerial for him. He tapped away for a couple of hours, but got no reply. After a further attempt the following morning we glumly took the set to pieces again, re-packed it on to one of our mules, and set off once more, still heading north-westwards towards Mount Giona.

After a few hours we came across a lonely shepherd with his flock. He told us that, not an hour away, on the other side of the nearest mountain, there was another party of Englishmen. We were greatly heartened by this news. I immediately sent off Denys with one of Karalivanos' men, who knew where we were going to spend that night, to see if they were any of our people. At our night's resting place Denys rejoined us with the excellent news that he had found Chris Woodhouse's party, all safe and sound, together with their stores, on a plateau called Prophet Elias, not two hours away from where we were. Chris himself was away, trying to contact someone in a nearby village, but he was expected back the following day. As Denys said that they had found an excellent cave in which to store everything, we decided to join up with them there the next day.

That night, as we were sitting around our bonfire, trying to get its warmth to reduce the effects of the rain dripping on to us through the trees, a little old Greek who had been passing near by was brought by our sentry to the fireside. He was armed with an

The Gorgopotamos Viaduct under construction. This was the only photograph available in Cairo when the operation was being planned in September 1942.

Barba Niko, M.B.E.

The Gorgopotamos Viaduct.

ancient musket and a rusty revolver, and was apparently no stranger to Karalivanos and his men. He spoke in broken English with a strong American accent. To begin with he was very reticent about himself. He did say, however, that he had recently visited Koukouvista. This made me prick up my ears, because Koukouvista was the nearest village to the actual place where we should have been dropped. Presently he told us that, the day before we arrived, Koukouvista had been raided by the Italians, and that every male member of the village over sixteen years of age had been taken away by them. But the most important piece of news which he gave us was that, included among the men-folk of the village who had been taken away, was a lawyer called Seferiades. This made things look rather black for us, because it indicated that the Italians had been forewarned of our arrival. Moreover, it accounted for the fact that we had seen no signal flares when we flew over Greece on our second attempt.

The new-comer told us that his name was Nikolaos Beis, and that he was usually known as "Barba Niko", which is the Greek for Uncle Niko. His English was barely intelligible until one got used to it. But he understood it better. As the evening wore on, he told us that he had spent many years of his life in America. In the flickering light from our fire, as he puffed away at the cigarettes we offered him, I studied him closely. When he took off his grimy cap I noticed that his hair was thin and grey; I guessed that he was in his middle fifties. He had twinkling, humorous eyes, a big walrus moustache and a large bulbous nose. He was dressed very poorly. In fact his clothes were almost rags, and one of the Greek country shoes protecting his bare and dirt-encrusted feet had practically no sole to it. He said he didn't know why we had been sent to Greece, but, if there was any way in which he could help us, he would willingly do so, and he agreed to come with us the following day when we joined Chris Woodhouse.

Until then I had given Karalivanos only the barest information regarding our actual task. I had told him that I wanted to get into touch with other andartes in the Giona district with a view to carrying out general sabotage from there. When he learnt that the village of Koukouvista had been raided by the Italians, he became extremely depressed. Apparently he had also anticipated that in this village he would be able to get in touch with other andartes. But when I told him that in two nights' time we were expecting an aircraft with additional stores, and possibly food, he cheered up somewhat and took more interest in us once again.

After a two-hour trek, the next day towards noon we clambered over a rocky ridge from which we suddenly looked down on to a stony plateau over a thousand yards in diameter, on the edge of which we could clearly see, through our field-glasses, a small tent rigged from parachutes. A few minutes later we were greeted by the three members of Chris Woodhouse's party, Nat Barker, Arthur Edmonds, Sergeant Chittis, and by two escaped Cypriot prisoners of war called Yani and Panioti * whom they had found on landing. Chris was still away. I was soon shown their cave. Through a narrow entrance, one wriggled one's way into quite a wide expanse, some twenty feet square and four to six feet high, in which all their containers and stores were neatly packed. As Sergeant Chittis had also been unable to get wireless contact with Cairo, our two operators now pooled their resources to try to make one set work. Late that night Chris returned, and I learned his full story up to date.

As from our aircraft on the night of 30th September, his party too had seen no signals resembling the ones expected. They had eventually spotted a definite triangle of fires on this plateau and had dropped on them. On landing they had been met by a Greek who said he was an independent agent of ours, expecting some explosives from Cairo to blow up one of the retaining walls of the Corinth Canal. In spite of his disappointment about Chris'

* Real names: Jemal Naafi and Osman Shugli.

and his party's unheralded arrival instead of the stores he anxiously awaited, he had generously agreed that the Cypriots, Yani and Panioti, enlisted by him to help keep his signal fires alight, should transfer their allegiance to us.

The next morning, 9th October, an aircraft with extra stores being due that night, we collected firewood for our signal bonfires. Towards midnight we heard an aircraft approaching. We lit our fires, and not long afterwards were able to see the four spurts of flame coming out of the exhausts of the engines of a Liberator high overhead. After the aircraft's second run over us we saw some parachutes drop from it. They floated away and disappeared over the far side of our plateau. On its next run we saw the remaining parachutes carried in the same direction. We flashed an O.K. with a torch; we got an acknowledging signal back from the aircraft; it soon disappeared and all was quiet again.

I felt another chill of loneliness as I realised that in a few hours' time, all being well, the crew of the aircraft would be back in comparative civilisation in Egypt. I remember remarking to Chris that they would have some nice comfortable beds to sleep in when they got back. Chris replied that he wouldn't be them for anything, doing that sort of thing night after night. Although I agreed with him, I must admit that I felt a hollow feeling, somewhat akin to homesickness. I had far from got used to this strangely isolated life.

Chris, tall, broad-shouldered, fair and then twenty-three years old, with a war-time commission in the Royal Artillery, had already spent the best part of a year in enemy-occupied Crete, assisting the escape of our prisoners of war and directing the brave Cretans in sabotage work against the enemy. His past experience, his intimate knowledge of the Greeks and his fluent mastery of their language were always of the greatest value to me. In fact, without his advice in those early days, I would probably have made some serious mistakes, due to sheer ignorance of this new form of warfare in which I suddenly found myself engaged. I could not have asked for a more capable and generous Second-in-Command, who willingly and often gave me invaluable advice and who afterwards accepted my decisions, whatever they were, without further question, loyally seeing them through to the end. His tremendous stamina, which enabled him to outmarch the strongest Greek, was a major factor in the success of several operations.

We had spent the previous night in pouring rain, huddled inside our parachute-rigged tent. We had the greatest difficulty in keeping this improvised structure intact, and once it was blown down. The parachutes were poor protection against the rain, which soon seeped through and dripped on us wherever we were lying. We decided therefore to move into the cave and make it not only our store but our home as well. It was a funny home. I felt just like an animal wriggling my way in and out of it. But once inside, it was comparatively comfortable, even though it was poorly lit by the narrow beam of light which came through its tortuous entrance.

As dawn broke the following morning, 10th October, we all set out to collect the stores which had been dropped the previous night. We eventually found them, about a mile away, scattered over a wide area on an almost precipitous hillside. We had no mules immediately available to move the heavy containers, so we opened them where they lay, took the canisters out of each of them, and hid the empty containers. It was a laborious and tiring job, and by nightfall we had got only a small proportion of the total number of canisters on to the plateau, from which point they could be carried by mule to the mouth of our cave. Karalivanos had sent one of his men to a neighbouring village to fetch some mules. That evening they arrived with some rather frightened muleteers, who did not know what they were in for, whose morale was low, and who would obviously have been much hap-

pier to have been left to carry on a leisurely existence in their villages. They realised, however, that they had no alternative but to
obey Karalivanos' instructions, and they co-operated, for the most
part willingly, for the next few days.

As both the Cypriots, Yani and Panioti, spoke Greek fluently,
we sent one of them down each day to collect food from a village
about an hour away. On his return from such a journey on 11th
October, Yani told us that a party of Italian troops had just arrived
there. They had heard that an aeroplane had been over the area
and that it had dropped some stores somewhere near. The villagers expected that the Italians would begin scouring the countryside the following day, and they were most anxious that we should
clear out of the district, lest we should be discovered and bring
reprisals upon their heads.

I was determined not to leave our cave until we had gathered
all the stores, and if we could not take them with us to our next
resting-place, had safely hidden them. Karalivanos now began to
make difficulties. He said that he would have to leave us the following day, in order to collect his wife, who, he said, lived in a
village nearby, and whom he wished to take to a safer place. He
was obviously disappointed that no food had been dropped for us
in the last sortie. He said that it would be impossible to procure
food for us from the villages now that the Italians were in them.
Because Koukouvista had been raided, he said he was sure that it
would only be a matter of days at the most, if not hours, before the
Italians discovered our cave. He recommended that we should
travel with him two days south-east, to the mountains of Parnassus, where he thought it would be safe for us to hide for a while.

Chris and I argued with him. We explained to him that we
wanted to go in the opposite direction. At that moment Nikolaos
Beis, little Barba Niko, beckoned Chris and me aside: "Say, uz
guez uz can help," he said in his broken American English. "Uz
knoz ver fine cave on Giona, cloz village uz call Stromni. Uz

knoz all peoples round there. Uz zure thems helps you, and uz gez foods there."

After a short consultation, Chris and I agreed to put our faith in Barba Niko. It was a decision which we never regretted. As politely as I could, I thanked Karalivanos for his past services and told him that we needed him no longer. Two of his men, Yorgo and one Baphas, agreed to stay with us and help us plan our move to the Stromni cave as soon as possible.

From the neighbouring safe villages, Barba Niko, assisted by Yorgo and Baphas, mustered as many mules as he could, to transport our stores. Meanwhile we posted sentries to watch for any approach of Italians. I forget the exact order in which the various parties departed from Prophet Elias. We divided ourselves into independent groups of two or three, and for the next three days, daily growing more anxious about the Italians, a group of us left with a few heavily laden mules for Stromni. Chris and I remained to the last, because we were expecting a visit from a friend of the Greek whom he had met in Amphissa. On the fourth day after we had received warning of the approach of the Italians, Katsimbas turned up from Karoutes, merely to inform us that everything was quiet there and to report for any further instructions. By then only Yorgo, Baphas and two muleteers, with four mules for the rest of our stores, remained with us. We decided that it would be unwise to wait any longer for the Greek from Amphissa, and sent Baphas back to Karoutes with Katsimbas, to bring the stores which we had left hidden there to Stromni. We then departed with our remaining loads, leaving only the broken parts of one wireless set well hidden inside the cave at Prophet Elias.

The climb on to the main Giona ridge was long and tedious. On reaching a dilapidated shepherd's hut close to the divide, some five to six thousand feet high, one of our muleteers refused to travel any further with us. Organised Resistance was in its early days and I did not yet know the true character of the Greek mountain folk. I was anxious not to arouse animosity, for fear of treachery at a later date. So we re-sorted our stores, took what we thought to be most important on the two remaining mules, and left a note with the remainder in a conspicuous place for Baphas, who was due to pass by there in a day or two on his way back to us from Stromni. The note instructed him to pick them up on his way through. In a bitingly cold wind we crossed the main range of Giona and descended for two hours or more to a hut on the out-skirts of a tiny village, whose name I forget.

There, in the pouring rain and, speaking for myself, extremely footsore after the long day's walk and tiring descent from Mount Giona, we gladly rested for the night. A goat was brought to us the following morning. We killed and skinned the smelly brute and, in the usual fashion, roasted it whole on our open fire. It tasted rather like its smell. In the afternoon, with fresh mules and in still pouring rain, we set out towards Stromni. We had hardly started when a frightened and breathless villager rushed up to us and told us to return quickly, as the Italians were in the village just ahead of us. This we did, but in due course we found out that it was a false alarm, like so many rumours in the mountains. The reported Italians were only two Greek policemen, who had de-serted and were returning to their native village. They were far more frightened at the prospect of meeting Italians than we were.

We made a fresh start. The only track took us through the centre of the village, on the far side of which we stopped at a cottage door for a few moments to have a mouthful of bread and honey. On up the steep valley we clambered all the afternoon, in pouring rain. Towards dusk we halted for the night in a little dell, surrounded by fir trees, not two hours away from the cave for which we were aiming. I was again exhausted by the hard day's journey. How I wished I had not been sitting in an office in Cairo for the last two months, and that I had been properly hardened up for this work. We were relieved to discover some firwood wigwams which, unmistakably, one of our previous parties had used only a night or two before.

The next morning, after a bathe in a nearby stream and a light meal of bread and olives, washed down by mountain water, we set off on the final stage of our journey to Barba Niko's cave near Stromni.

CHAPTER III

We Gather Strength

OUR NEW cave had a wide entrance which let in plenty of daylight. It was far more congenial than the dark cavern-like one on the high stony plateau of Prophet Elias. Nearly an hour's climb from Stromni, it was situated on a wooded mountain-side at the foot of a rocky escarpment about fifty feet high. It opened on to a small patch of ground, around which closely packed fir trees obscured it from the opposite side of the valley.

On my arrival with Chris I found that our strength had already increased by yet one more person. This was Michael Khuri, a Palestinian Arab soldier. He, like the Cypriots, Yani and Panioti, had been unable to get away in April, 1941. He had been taken prisoner and had escaped from the Germans by jumping from the train which was taking him away from Greece. A robust young Arab with a pale olive skin and jet-black hair, when he first greeted me he was immaculately dressed as a British officer, with the badges of rank of a second-lieutenant. Draped around him were bandoliers containing several hundred rounds of ammunition for a well-oiled and beautifully polished German light automatic rifle, from which he was never parted. I asked him what his proper Army rank was. He said that he was really only a private, but that he found it easier to obtain food when dressed as a British officer. I soon discovered that the grandeur of his self-obtained commission had facilitated the successful wooing of a Greek girl in Stromni. I told him that, as a British soldier, he must put himself under my orders and, discarding his high rank together with its social benefits, he must revert to his proper rank of private. However, I immediately promoted him to acting unpaid lance-corporal. All honour was satisfied, and by the very next day he had already conjured from the mountains some lance-corporal's stripes and was again faultlessly dressed in his new rank. In fact Michael soon became a stalwart and valuable addition to our party. Before he finally returned to the bosom of his family in Haifa two years later, he had been promoted to sergeant and awarded a Military Medal and Bar for his outstanding gallantry and devotion to duty.

On the afternoon of my arrival, a villager brought up to our cave a Greek who wanted to see us. I interrogated him through Chris. It turned out that our agent in Athens, Prometheus, had received a signal from Cairo, saying that we had been dropped. As SOE was without further news of us, he had been asked to try and contact us, and so had sent a runner to see if we were safe and in need of anything. After a long conversation I asked this brave Greek to return to Athens and find out how we could get in touch with Zervas or any other andartes who happened to be in southern Greece. I told him that our chief material needs were boots and socks, of which we had no spares, and I gave him some gold sovereigns with which to buy them on the black market. I asked him to get Prometheus to signal Cairo that the eight of us were all well, also to find out whether John Cook and his party had been dropped, and if so where. Reports kept on coming in of their whereabouts. But each time I sent a local Greek to inquire, he invariably returned without proof that the information had been anything more than rumour. Even so, I was still mystified, because I was almost convinced that the stores which we had collected before departing from Karoutes had come from Cook's aircraft. I still feared, therefore, that his party were lying hidden somewhere, some, possibly all of them, badly hurt. Prometheus' runner from Athens left us the next day. He said he would be back in about ten days.

From Prophet Elias we had brought on to our new cave about four hundred pounds of explosives and accessories, which together would be just enough for one major demolition; also sixteen Stens with quite a lot of ammunition, and fifty hand-grenades. A similar amount was expected to be brought on by Baphas from what we had hidden near Karoutes and left in the shepherd's hut on top of Mount Giona.

The day after our arrival, 20th October, an excited villager came up to our hide-out to warn us that a strong force of Italians was moving into a temporary camp on the opposite side of the valley, not two miles from where we were. He was followed later in the evening by the President of the village of Stromni, who reported with great anxiety the arrival of another Italian force some three miles further down the valley. Towards nightfall a shepherd, who had come down from Giona, told us that he had heard that yet another force of Italians was marching towards Stromni from the direction of Karoutes. The situation did not look at all bright for us. It appeared that not only had the Italians learned of our existence but of our location, and that they were surrounding us. To avoid this encirclement it looked as though we would have to move away from our target, the railway, which now lay conveniently near—only a ten-hour trek away. After a long consultation, Barba Niko came to the rescue once again.

He said that he knew of a place, only an hour away, where the Italians wouldn't find us, even if they swept right through the mountains. He was prepared to take us there the following morning.

Chris and I willingly agreed to go there. At first light the next morning we hid our explosives and spare weapons by burying them in the forest nearby. We then packed up the remainder of our possessions. Towards midday we set off along the side of the valley under cover of the forest, each carrying a heavy bundle which included the pots and pans Barba Niko had previously obtained for us from the village. At one halt we peered through the trees across the valley on to a mountain pathway directly opposite and, not more than a few hundred yards away, watched a column of Italians leading heavily laden mules in the opposite direction. Silently we walked on through the endless forest, over a spur of a hill, and eventually up a subsidiary valley which took us away from the Italians. After half an hour we suddenly descended into a dell some fifty yards in diameter, which was almost completely cut off from the outside world. There was no cave here, but we were so well sheltered from the wind that it hardly mattered. We soon rigged up a parachute each, to keep off the worst of the rain. We established our wireless station on a promontory on the rocky mountain-side, some three hundred feet above us. Now without petrol for our charging engine, we had sent the batteries to a mill, not many hours away, where there was a water-driven charging apparatus; and a few days later our operators began again their attempts to contact Cairo.

So as not to waste time whilst we were awaiting the return of Prometheus' runner from Athens, I decided to carry out a reconnaissance of the railway viaducts. Through Barba Niko, I enlisted the support of a faithful ex-sergeant of the Greek Army, one Yani Pistolis, a native of the village of Stromni, to act as my guide. On the afternoon of 25th October, no Italian sweep through the mountains having materialised, Yani came up to our hide-out to fetch me. Because of Denys Hamson's previous Commando experience and knowledge of Greek, I selected him to accompany me. About thirty years of age, small yet wiry, I reckoned that he wouldn't tire before I did and that, should we unavoidably encounter one or two of the enemy, he would know best how to deal with them.

With Yani we set off through the forest down to Stromni, after having passed by our cache of explosives and weapons to see that everything there was still safe. The Italians had not moved from their encampments and appeared to be completely inactive. At dusk we reached the outskirts of the village. Here Denys and I waited whilst Yani went off to collect mufti overcoats for us. Twenty minutes later he returned with them. We put on the coats over our uniforms, took off our military hats and put them in our pockets. We then walked with him to his home in the middle of the village.

This was the first time I had ever been inside a Greek cottage. Yani's family greeted us warmly and sat us down to an excellent meal. At about ten o'clock, when the moon rose, we left the cosy fireside and started on our journey towards the railway. Giving a wide berth to the Italian camps, we walked throughout the night, resting occasionally to munch large apples, with which our pockets had been filled. About an hour before dawn we reached a point overlooking the Papadia viaduct. On the high ground about eight hundred yards to the south-west of it we found an excellent hide-out in some shrubbery. Here Yani left us to contact a reliable friend of his at a nearby railway station who might be able to give us additional information about the location and strength of the Italians guarding the viaduct.

Denys and I rested until the sun had risen sufficiently for us to get a good view of the viaduct with our field-glasses. Cautiously moving about, we studied it carefully in relation to the guard-posts, most of which we could see from where we were. An attack upon it from this direction would have been a formidable task. The hills were rolling and not too well covered with trees. Guard-posts seemed to cover all other possible approaches; and there also appeared to be too many Italians for any reasonable prospect of success without several hundred andartes.

During the afternoon we slept. About an hour after dark Yani rejoined us with further information about the garrison of the viaduct. This confirmed my own conclusions. There were apparently some two to three hundred guarding it. The Italians had only completed its reconstruction in the spring of 1942, after its destruction in our retreat a year before. Small wonder that they were jealously guarding their so recently completed work!

Shortly after Yani had rejoined us, we set off north-west, heading for the Asopos viaduct. An hour later we reached a point about thirteen hundred yards above it. Here the river, which eventually flows under it, enters a narrow and precipitous gorge between mountains towering up a thousand feet almost vertically on both sides. We sat down and ate the small quantity of bread, goats'-milk cheese and olives which Yani had managed to collect ostensibly for himself from a village through which he had passed that day. I then went a short way down the gorge, but was soon stopped by a high waterfall. I quickly realised that this was no possible approach for a large force of andartes. From the map, and from Yani's description, I formed a fair idea of what the approaches were like from the other end of the gorge, where it opened out into a flat valley immediately below the viaduct. I intensely disliked the prospect of having to attack it. It would have been an extremely chancy operation, and I could think of no method of blowing it up other than by stealth, with only a handful of picked men. This was not the sort of operation which I had in mind at that time. Our primary object, granted, was to cut the railway line, anywhere and anyhow, for as long as possible and as soon as possible. Even so, at the moment I could think of no plan which would be almost certain of success—the most important factor to be considered during my reconnaissance. Failure would have had a most disastrous effect, not only on the morale of my own party, but also on any efforts Chris might subsequently have to ask of the andartes.

We moved on towards the Gorgopotamos viaduct. As dawn was breaking we reached a hide-out in a small thicket between two and three hundred yards away from it. I was very weary. Denys had stood the journey well. Yani, who had been travelling more or less continuously for the last twenty-four hours, had reason to be more tired than I. But, thoroughly game, he left us almost immediately to contact another friend at the nearby railway junction of Lianokladi.

The view of the bridge which Denys and I got from our hide-out was a limited one. It was essential to carry out a first-class reconnaissance. On the other hand it was equally essential that we should run no risk of being captured, or in any way of arousing the interest or fear of the Italian guards, thereby jeopardising surprise and the chances of the success of our subsequent attack. I considered that we could not afford to take any risk of being seen by anybody, and so I never ventured outside our hide. During the day several people passed close by us on a pathway which ran through the middle of the thicket. From different view-points we could see the Italian guards as they strolled about on, and around, the bridge. We could not, however, see their guard-houses, nor gauge their numbers accurately. Most of the piers were of masonry and therefore unsuitable for rapid demolition, but two of them were of steel. After examining them through my field-glasses and after a careful study of the photographs I had with me, I came to the conclusion that the four legs of each of these steel piers were 'L'-shaped in cross-section.

Just before dusk Yani returned to us. He was in a frantic state. He was afraid that he had aroused the suspicion of the Italian guards who had stopped and questioned him on his return journey. They had discovered that he was a stranger in the district. They had warned him that nobody was allowed to move within a mile of the railway after dusk, and had ordered him to get back to his village quickly. He was afraid that they were about to send out a party to follow him. He insisted that we should move at once.

In the failing light we scrambled out on to a narrow pathway and had only been travelling a few minutes when we met a couple of Greek peasants coming down from Mount Oiti with a donkey laden with firewood. They said "Good evening" to us. We took no notice of them and walked briskly on. Tired and hungry, we started to clamber up the mountain. Up and up some of its four thousand feet we trudged in the darkness. At last, about ten o'clock at night, we considered that we had reached a place where it would be safe to stop and where the light of a fire would not be seen from the railway. A fire was essential. Without it, in the bitter cold, we would have frozen where we lay. We ate the meagre meal which Yani had collected for us, and then went to sleep. It was an uncomfortable and cold sleep. As soon as my feet became warm, by keeping them almost on top of the fire, my head and the top part of my body almost froze; and when I turned round to warm the upper part of my body, my feet became like icicles. Before dawn we put out the fire, and stiff, but glad to be on the move again, we began clambering up the remaining height of Mount Oiti. We eventually reached its more or less level top at about seven in the morning, and found a pathway which led along its edge. After an hour or two, however, Yani thought that it would be too dangerous to keep to it. He was in an unnecessary state of panic; but he was greatly over-tired. He had had hardly any sleep the last two days and nights, during which time he had been more or less continuously on the move. We struck off across country through the forest on the mountain-side, and it was not long before Yani became obviously lost, except for his sense of general direction. Tired as we were, the endless subsidiary valleys which we had to cross proved tantalisingly annoying to Denys and myself; and, as was his usual wont, Denys expressed his opinion of Yani as a guide in no mild terms. Poor Yani! He was doing his best.

Late in the afternoon, at one of our hourly halts, I pulled out a gold sovereign from the leather belt which I wore next to my skin, and, using Denys as my interpreter, I offered it to Yani as a reward for his efforts on our behalf. Mortally offended, he refused it. I reassured him that this was not pay, but that I wanted him to keep it as a memento and as a token of our esteem of him. Only then did he hesitatingly accept it.

Towards nightfall we reached the outskirts of a village. Denys and I settled in a comfortable nook, while Yani went off to collect some food. Once more we were off the beaten track of the Italians and it was safe to disclose our presence when we knew that the coast was clear. Some villagers brought us a marvellous meal. Denys ate five eggs without stopping. I'm not sure I didn't devour the same number. After blowing ourselves out in a most disgusting way, and after a refreshing rest of some two hours, we set off on the last part of our journey to Stromni, which we reached in the small hours of the morning of 29th October. In case the Italians might still be about Yani led us to an empty barn on the outskirts of the village. We slept soundly on some hay until well into the following morning. Towards midday the faithful Yani brought us some breakfast and with it the encouraging news that the Italians had struck their camps and had moved out of the district. Shortly afterwards, therefore, we set off up the hill towards our cave. On arrival there we were pleased to find the rest of our party, who had returned to it earlier the same day.

I discussed the results of my reconnaissance with Chris. In my own mind I was convinced that the Gorgopotamos viaduct was the one to go for. But I wanted to get confirmation of certain details about the Italian garrison and its defence. For this Yani Pistolis volunteered to produce a cousin of his, a schoolmaster called Costa Pistolis, from the county town of Lamia. Apparently Costa, who occasionally came to stay with Yani in Stromni, had a friend who lived in a cottage within a few hundred yards of the viaduct. When I met Costa a few days later I realised that it was a great risk to tell him, an inhabitant of an Italian-occupied town about my interest in the Gorgopotamos. But he seemed reliable, and I decided to take him into our confidence. As a result, in a week's time he returned with most valuable information about the strength and location of the Italians, the type of their emplacements, and with details of a barbed-wire fence which surrounded the piers of the viaduct. What he told me fitted in with practically everything which I had previously discovered. My mind was made up. We would attack the Gorgopotamos as soon as I could get the support of between forty and fifty armed andartes who, I reckoned, if stouthearted, would be sufficient to overcome the forty to eighty Italians, lines-of-communication troops of poor calibre, who guarded it.

Meanwhile, two days after my return from reconnoitring the railway viaducts, Prometheus' runner had returned from Athens, not only with some boots and socks, but with a means of getting into contact with Zervas. He told us that Zervas was still in the Valtos area, to the north-east of Arta, some four to six days from us; in fact, where we had thought him to be all the time. There was barely sufficient time to get a message to him, and for him to reach us by the next full moon. Early the following day—2nd November—therefore, I sent off Chris with Barba Niko to find Zervas, and to do his utmost to get us a large force of andartes by 18th November, so that we could operate with the aid of the next full moon. Three days later a very tired Barba Niko, who had been unable to keep up with Chris, returned in a state of collapse to our fireside. Chris had sent him back. Henceforth he would rely upon local Greek guides, whom he would drop off and pick up afresh at each night halt.

By now we had managed to find some petrol to run the charging-engine for our wireless batteries. Not many days after Chris' departure, early one morning the wireless operators brought in the promising news that on their mountain-top station the previous night, at the scheduled hour when they regularly listened and tried to get wireless contact, they had faintly heard the Cairo station. But its signals had quickly faded and they had been unable to get any message through.

Without delay I concocted for the twentieth time an up-to-date signal, in order to ensure that the most important information would be got back to Cairo in our first message. On 4th November we got it through.

In it I said that our operation would cause widespread reprisals and that it was of the utmost importance that all available aircraft should stand by from 18th to the end of November, the period of full moon, to drop pamphlets over a wide area of Central Greece to warn Axis forces that if they carried out reprisals against innocent Greeks they would not escape severe punishment at the end of the war. I finished up the message by saying that the signal to drop these pamphlets would be 'Operation Paper' or, alternatively, the news of our success. I asked for immediate acknowledgment.

For the next five days we got no further contact with Cairo. But on 9th November our operators' efforts were again rewarded and we received an acknowledgment of our message. We were congratulated on making contact at last and were told that the authorities in Cairo were taking the necessary steps to carry out our request. We were warned, however, that meteorological conditions might delay its execution.

Meanwhile Baphas, whom we had sent to Karoutes to fetch the remainder of our stores, had returned empty-handed. We had long given him up, thinking that he had deserted us and rejoined Karalivanos. But we had misjudged him. With a train of mules carrying our stores from Karoutes, he had run into a force of Italians near Giona, and had had to cut the mules loose. He had scattered them with his whip, hoping that they would all go home. But that was not all. Our dump on Mount Giona had been found by the Italians and only by the greatest luck had Baphas himself avoided capture. It was a sad story. We were left with the bare minimum quantity of explosives for the demolition of the Gorgopotamos viaduct.

On our next successful wireless contact with Cairo a few nights later, I urgently asked for an additional drop of explosives, and gave a rendezvous not far away. But the following day, before an acknowledgment had been received, our wireless set went out of action again, and this time it appeared to our two operators to be beyond repair without spares from Cairo. I sent Denys and two others to the dropping ground which we had selected. In the cold they waited six consecutive nights. But no aircraft came.

Whilst they were away, the rest of us were not idle. Our life soon slipped into a daily routine. When we weren't chopping up wood for our fires, we occupied our spare time in warming our plastic explosives in our hands and pressing the separate sticks into a wooden mould, which we had made for our charges, to fit the believed cross-section of the legs of the steel piers of the Gorgopotamos viaduct. It was a slow but relaxing job. It took us many days to get through our four hundred pounds of explosives. But it kept us occupied whilst we awaited Chris' return with the andarte support so essential to us.

Whereas the villagers of Stromni were quite content to have us living in a cave a good hour from their village, and to feed us there, they were too afraid of a casual visit by Italian gendarmerie to allow us to live in the village itself. Our food, which was brought up to us from Stromni most days by Michael the Arab, sometimes by villagers, was comparatively luxurious. We had plenty of brown bread and potatoes, which abounded in that district. Occasionally we were given delicious apples, for the excellence of which Stromni has quite a name. We were often brought walnuts and other nuts. Our meat we obtained by slaughtering sheep from nearby flocks, recompensing the shepherds concerned with gold. Barba Niko acted as our chef and administrative officer as well. He was an able cook, and nothing was wasted. When our tea ran out, he collected a mountain herb which served as a passable substitute. Only a few hundred yards away there was a stream from which we drew our drinking-water, and in which, lower down, we washed. An old woman from Stromni came up to us weekly and washed our clothes in the stream. Once Barba Niko went to his home. He returned the next day with his ten-year-old daughter. She stayed with us all that day and helped in mending our clothes. She was a sweet little child, and her presence struck a strange note of unreality amongst our masculine and bearded group, far away from our own homes.

Between the trees in front of the mouth of our cave we rigged up some parachutes to protect us from the wind and to hide as much as possible of our sometimes large fire at night. The day-time smoke, however, didn't concern us overmuch, because it was the practice of all shepherds in the evening, and often during daylight, to use fires to keep themselves warm. Inside the cave there was sufficient room for each of us to make ourselves a brushwood and bracken-covered bed. With additional blankets lent to us by the villagers in Stromni, we now had two each. Some of us still had our warm parachute overalls. These we used in the evening as smoking-suits and, later at night, as pyjamas.

At the end of the day we would gather round the large log-fire at the mouth of our cave and eagerly eye the meal which Barba Niko was preparing for us. We were usually ravenous and there never seemed enough meat. Afterwards, as we lay around the glowing embers, Barba Niko would sometimes tell fantastic stories in Greek to Denys and Nat Barker, one of whom would afterwards relay them to the rest of us. At other times Barba Niko would grasp Arthur Edmonds by the arm. "Tonight, Mister Arthur," he would announce with a merry twinkle in his eye, "we will hold the examinations," and he would jokingly test me, Tom Barnes and Arthur Edmonds, his keenest and most serious pupil.

One day I heard of the existence in the neighbourhood of an andarte leader known in the mountains as 'Aris' Veloukhiotis, who we subsequently discovered was Athanasios Klaras, a Communist who had taken part in the Spanish Civil War. His name appeared to be on the lips of every villager, but each time I had previously tried to get into contact with him I had failed. He did not answer my messages. It seemed that he was deliberately avoiding us. One or two roaming and armed Greeks turned up at our cave. They gave me vague promises of support. But no one was able to produce the numbers which I required; and most of them were leaders of 'bands' of two or three at the most. Whilst we were waiting for Chris we did, however, increase our number by the addition of yet one more British escaped prisoner of war, Corporal Aaron Deo, another Palestinian Arab. But he was not much use to us as a fighter. He spent most of his time anointing himself with foul-smelling scent, of which he somehow always obtained a fresh supply each time someone succeeded in throwing away what was thought to be his only bottle of it.

It was about this time that news of Karalivanos' return to our vicinity reached me in the form of a complaint from the villagers of Stromni. Apparently he was going about the district with the remaining three of his band, demanding food and stealing sheep in our name. The situation was brought to a head by a most agitated villager reporting to me that the previous evening two Greek gendarmerie, in the pay of the Italians, had come to Stromni, under the instructions of the Commander of an Italian garrison a few hours away, to requisition a large quantity of potatoes for his troops. Karalivanos had heard about them. At nightfall he had come into Stromni, raided the house in which they were lodging, seized the two Greeks and taken them off into the countryside. There he had beaten them up, stripped their uniforms off them, threatened them with death if they returned to the area, and then let them go in their underclothes. If he had killed them outright and hidden their bodies it would have been almost better from our point of view. His action might lead to the very thing which I wanted to avoid: not only reprisals but another visit by Italian troops to the area in which we were hiding.

I immediately sent off a message to be delivered personally to Karalivanos. I ordered him to meet me that night in a certain cottage on the outskirts of Stromni. At the appointed hour we duly met. I told him exactly what I thought of him, of his stupid action in going about the countryside demanding food in our name, and of his dangerous action of the previous evening. I ordered him to leave the district forthwith, and explained to him the vital necessity of keeping the area quiet because of an important project which I had in mind. Although I didn't know whether Chris was going to be successful in bringing back any andartes with which to attack the Gorgopotamos viaduct, I pretended that I had received a message from him that very day, stating that he was on his way to me with a large force. I told Karalivanos that, if he did not obey my orders, I would have him arrested and shot as soon as this force of andartes arrived.

My bluff succeeded. He agreed to carry out my instructions. Having made arrangements for the two Greek policemen to be re-clothed and sent away as mollified as possible, with their demand for potatoes met, I returned up the hill to our cave, hoping that no irrevocable harm had been done.

From then onwards, luck began to turn in our favour. Late that same night the village priest of Stromni came up to our cave and woke me up to say that he had an important and highly confidential message for me. Some British officers, who had been discovered by Chris on his journey westwards, were on their way to us. They were expected to reach us the next day, together with a band of andartes belonging to Aris.

The following afternoon, John Cook and the remainder of the party from the third aircraft arrived at our cave. They were

escorted by a band of twenty-five andartes. The four of them—
John Cook, Themie Marinos, Inder Gill and Sergeant Phillips—
had only the clothes in which they stood up. They told me that
on the night of our own arrival—30th September—they had failed
to see any signals, and that their pilot had refused to let them drop
because of clouds. They had not seen any of our flares, so they
had dropped their containers of stores near to Mount Giona and
had returned to Cairo. They must have been over the area whilst
our aircraft was looking for signals further west, and they must
have left it before we had arrived back from Giona immediately
prior to our drop. This only could account for the fact that they
had actually dropped their stores on to almost the identical spot
to that on which we had landed.

After two further attempts, abortive because of bad weather,
they had finally been dropped about two weeks previously in the
Karpenisi valley. Why there, Heaven knows. For they had
floated down on to the outskirts of an Italian garrison town, and
had been greeted with considerable mortar and small-arms' fire.
They had all had miraculous escapes. Hiding in bushes from
searching Italians, they had been forced to scatter to avoid capture. The Italians, they thought, had picked up all their containers, including, I was horrified to learn, new plans of the railway viaducts, which had stupidly been packed in one of the containers. I could but hope that some idiot Italian had found them
and not realised their importance.

During the next few days John Cook and his party had individually sought refuge in nearby villages or with isolated cottage
families. Finally they were all put in touch with each other and
with a band of andartes, which at that time was not far away. This
band turned out to be one belonging to Aris, to whom they were
taken some days later. Having satisfied Aris that they were
British, they were all looked after reasonably well. John told me
that he had explained to Aris his orders to get in touch with

me immediately. Aris had apparently feigned ignorance of my whereabouts, as he must have known that I was only two or three days' journey away to the east. He had taken them on a sort of publicity tour towards Agrinion, in almost exactly the opposite direction. It was by pure chance that Chris, who had passed close to them on his journey to find Zervas, had heard of their existence from a villager, and had sent John a message giving my exact location and telling him to report to me forthwith. Unwilling to overrule these instructions, Aris had sent the four of them off to me with an escort of twenty-five of his andartes.

The leader of the Greek band was called Dimitriou, and was known by the pseudonym of Nikiphoros. He was a bright-eyed youth, little over twenty years of age. He carried a German automatic. His band was a motley crowd. But each carried a rifle of some sort, Greek, German or Italian, and amongst them there were two Italian Breda light automatics. They were all ill-shod; many of them only had goatskin shoes. Their clothes were of every variety, but some of them wore a little fore-and-aft cap, on the front of which were embroidered the four Greek letters, ELAS. I asked what these stood for and was told: 'The National Popular Liberation Army'. I asked what this army was, how strong it was, and who controlled it. I got only vague replies. Aris was apparently the military leader of two to three hundred armed andartes of ELAS who were organised in bands of about twenty-five each, scattered throughout the mountains of Roumeli. During the next two or three days I learned from Nikiphoros that some people in Athens, whom he had never met, and whose names he said he did not even know, were in overall control of ELAS, and that there were bands of this organisation in other parts of the Greek mountains. He divulged no more; in fact I think that he knew little more.

By now we had completed the preparation of our explosives and had organised ourselves on the assumption that we would get a force of about fifty andartes to fight our way on to the Gorgopotamos viaduct. Tom Barnes, a fair-headed, stockily built and immensely strong New Zealander, who was an experienced sapper and a natural leader, I put in charge of the main demolition party. We co-opted the assistance of Lance-Corporal Michael, Yani the Cypriot and two Greek andartes from Nikiphoros' band, who, together with Tom Barnes, Arthur Edmonds, Inder Gill and Denys Hamson, were to make up the demolition party. Themie Marinos, Nat Barker and John Cook I kept up my sleeve for two small subsidiary demolition parties, which I thought would be necessary to cut the railway line on both sides of, and some distance away from, the viaduct, in order to prevent enemy reinforcements reaching us during the three or four hours which I anticipated would be necessary to complete our main demolition. We made a wooden model of parts of one of the steel piers, and we practised the demolition party both by day and by night, until its members could fix the charges and fuse them blindfold. We obtained some sawn strips of timber from a wood-cutter nearby, and we tied our demolition charges to them so that they could be carried on the backs of mules, dismantled near to the bridge, and rapidly fixed. We prepared the subsidiary charges for cutting the railway line. Then we waited for Chris' return. He was due, at the latest, on 18th November. The moon was already past its first quarter, and as each day passed I became more anxious about his return.

On 17th November the faithful Stromni priest came up to us with excellent news. He had received a message by runner that Chris expected to reach me the following day; and not only Chris, but accompanying him a large force of over a hundred andartes, headed by Zervas and Aris themselves.

The next day we passed in excited anticipation of the arrival of this force, which exceeded my greatest hopes. Throughout the afternoon and the evening we hourly awaited further news. But late, when we went to bed, we had heard no more. However, not long after I had gone to sleep, I was woken up to find Chris lightly tapping my shoulder:

"I've got back. I have carried out your instructions. Half a day behind me is Zervas, with a force of fifty andartes, and following him on the same route is Aris with more than that number. By tomorrow night both bands expect to reach the village of Mavrolithari, only two hours away from here. I have come on ahead with only Zervas' adjutant, Captain Michalli, so as not to be late."

I got up and shook hands with Michalli, a tall dark Cretan, who stood rigidly at attention whilst I spoke to him through Chris. I looked at my watch. It was a quarter of an hour after midnight. Chris, who had been on the move for fourteen days, and had travelled over the mountains right across Greece and back again, was a quarter of an hour late. But by Greenwich time, as he rightly pointed out to me, he was not even late; he had three-quarters of an hour in hand!

The following morning Chris told me about his journey. On his way to Valtos he had by chance heard that Aris and John Cook were in a nearby village. He had sent messages to John, instructing him to join me, and to Aris, asking him to meet him on his return. At the rendezvous in Valtos which Prometheus' runner had given us, Chris had been met by Michalli. He had found Zervas in the middle of a most successful battle against several hundred Italians whose commander was in the process of negotiating terms for an unmolested withdrawal.

Zervas had greeted Chris most warmly. He had embraced him and, in Greek fashion, had kissed him on both cheeks. "Evangelos! Evangelos!" (Greek for The Angel of Good Tidings) he had cried out. "You are our saviour. Evangelos will be your name in the Greek mountains."

After Chris had explained his mission and the necessity for

hurry, Zervas had immediately called off the action against the Italians, and the very next day had set out eastwards with Chris and a hundred and fifty of his andartes to come to our assistance. On their journey they had halted for the night in a village called Viniani, where they learnt that Aris was in an adjoining village. After an exchange of letters, both Aris and Zervas, to no little extent prompted by Chris, decided that it would be opportune for them to meet each other, and to discuss assistance to the British officers now in their midst in the mountains. After a dance in the village square, where the men of both bands had mixed and made merry, Zervas had succeeded in persuading Aris to help us with a force of a hundred men. Whereupon Zervas had sensibly decided to leave in that area a hundred of the hundred and fifty andartes which he had with him, in order to cover the concentration of so large a number further eastwards, to act as a decoy to the enemy, and, if necessary, ultimately to assist in a fighting withdrawal to his mountain stronghold in Valtos. With the remaining fifty of his men, followed a day behind by Aris with a hundred, Zervas and Chris had come on by forced marches, to rally by my side.

Over much of the way by which Chris had travelled on his outward journey there was no andarte organisation and no system to warn him of enemy troops in the vicinity. During the hours of daylight he had therefore been forced to circumvent every village. More than once he had been about to enter a village at dusk only to find Italian troops already in occupation of it. He had had to make many wide and trackless detours in the rugged mountains. He reckoned, in fact, that he had travelled over two hundred miles since he had set out from Stromni. His achievement was truly magnificent.

Zervas and the author in early December 1942 on their journey to Valtos after the Gorgopotamos Operation.

Lieutenant-Colonel Agoras (*left*) and another EDES officer, 1943. Agoras was one of the most able officers serving under Zervas.

Mule-tracks in the mountains showing members of the Military Mission on the move.

A typical ELAS officer, Second-Lieutenant 'Nikiphoros' Dimitriou.

A typical EDES officer.

Tom Barnes, Royal New Zealand Engineers.

General Zervas in his 'Sunday best'.

CHAPTER IV

The Gorgopotamos Operation

THAT AFTERNOON, 19th November, Zervas, accompanied by a small bodyguard, called on me at our cave. He kissed me warmly on both my now bearded cheeks. Undaunted, I kissed him back. With his fifty andartes he had arrived at Mavrolithari at midday. When he had billeted his men in the village, he had come straight on to meet me.

Zervas had a short and rotund figure. When he laughed, as he so often did, his whole body vibrated, and the merry sparkle in his eyes belied the black, hairy fierceness of a heavily bearded face. The moment he stopped smiling, his large brown eyes immediately gave his round face and full, generous mouth a serious, yet understanding expression. When he removed his peculiar khaki-coloured, civilian-shaped cap, it revealed a heavy crop of black, greying hair indicating an age of a little over fifty. He wore an old army officer's khaki tunic devoid of all insignia, khaki riding-breeches and a pair of brown, rather over-large riding-boots. An unpolished 'Sam-Browne' belt around his ample waist supported a small automatic pistol and a jewelled dagger whose sheath was liable to stick out from his stomach at a jaunty angle when he sat down.

I was immediately struck by his outstanding personality, and, after a polite delay for pleasantries, I took him fully into my confidence. I explained my task to him. I gave him all the information which I had obtained about the three viaducts and about the enemy guards at, and in the vicinity of, each; and I described to him at length the plan which I had evolved for attacking the Gorgopotamos viaduct. I offered him the men and all the meagre resources which I had at my disposal and requested him to take command of the operation. I said that I would be happy to regard myself as his Chief of Staff.

Subject to a final reconnaissance by a specially selected party of his andartes, Zervas readily agreed with my plan. He thought, however, that it would be tactful to ask Aris to be in joint command of the operation with both of us, as the latter was contributing proportionally such a large number of andartes. I was at a loss to see how three people could command the same operation, but Zervas reassured me. "I will command it," he said, "but the three of us will agree on all major decisions and plans beforehand."

I soon discovered that Zervas was called Strategos—or General —by all his men. He had adopted this title because many of the Greek generals who had been evacuated from Greece and Crete, and were now serving in the Middle East, were junior in rank to him. He had not been allowed to fight for Greece in 1941 because of his past associations with a Republican, Venizelist, political party, of which General Plastiras, at that time in exile in the south of France, was the nominal head. Much to my surprise, I learnt from him that no senior Greek officer who had had Republican sympathies had been allowed by Metaxas to take up arms against the Axis, even when their country was in dire peril and in the greatest need of them.

Zervas had tea with us before he left. This meal consisted of a cup of our mountain herb tea and a piece of brown bread, expertly fried in olive oil. We arranged to join him the following day in Mavrolithari, where he said he would obtain billets for us. Billets! What a change, and what luxury after our cave life! With such a large force of andartes in their midst, the morale of the villagers had soared to great heights, and from that time onwards, whenever there was an andarte organisation in the district, no Greeks raised any objection to our presence in their villages.

That night we experienced the first heavy fall of snow. At daybreak the next day those rugged mountain-tops, their slopes thickly draped with firs, presented a splendid scene in their fresh and sparkling white winter cloak. In spite of the thought of the warm cottage which awaited me in Mavrolithari, I felt quite sorry to be leaving the cave which had been such a happy refuge to us for so long; where, under Barba Niko's faithful care, the villagers of Stromni had so loyally fed us, whilst we, like young birds in a nest waiting for their wings to grow, unable to move about in the open or to fend for ourselves, had anxiously awaited, and eventually gained, the necessary andarte strength to emerge acclimatised and ready to accomplish our task.

On our way to Mavrolithari with a train of twenty mules laden with our gear, rounding a corner on the narrow mountain track, ahead of us I suddenly saw Karalivanos, waiting to greet us as we passed. As we drew near he came up to the attention and saluted. I walked on, ignoring him, and all my officers did the same. A few yards further on Chris came up to me and said: "If you weren't an Englishman, Karalivanos would cut your throat for that!"

"Yes," I replied. "But when I meet Aris, Karalivanos may have a job to keep his own head on his shoulders."

In Mavrolithari we were all dispersed in different cottages. Chris and I were allotted the one in which Zervas was billeted. Our hosts were desperately poor, but they went out of their way to make us comfortable, and they gave up their beds for us. The hospitality and generosity of these mountain villagers were truly magnificent.

That afternoon Aris arrived with his andartes. He was a small man, of the same height as Zervas, but of a more wiry build. His long black beard, which balanced his Cossack cap of black fur, could make his face look benign and almost monk-like. But his eyes were deep-set and, except when he smiled, there was much hardness in his features. Only when mellowed by alcohol did he ever relax. Silent and inclined to be dour, he always gave me the impression of being on guard against someone or something. I gathered from my first conversation with him that, in agreeing to co-operate with us in the attack upon the Gorgopotamos viaduct, he was disobeying the standing instructions of his superiors in Athens not to attack formed bodies of the enemy, and that he was liable to a severe reprimand. Moreover, he said that at any time he might receive instructions which would forbid him to assist us. But should these instructions not arrive, he would be prepared to co-operate.

The next day, 21st November, I recapitulated to both Aris and Zervas my plan for the attack. Having readjusted it to suit the unexpected and happy increase of andarte support available, I carefully explained the advantages of an attack during one of the next few nights, when there would be practically a full moon. Because of the deep gorge which separated the two extremities of the viaduct, which was nearly two hundred yards long, it was necessary to make up two entirely independent groups, one each to attack the Italian guards in their entrenched positions at either end of the viaduct. At the southern end a stronger group would be required, not only to attack the defensive position, but to overcome the occupants of three barrack huts nearby in which the whole garrison lived when off duty. Two additional small parties were required to cut the railway line a mile north and south of the viaduct, to delay reinforcements from neighbouring garrisons after they had been alerted by the sound of the battle in progress. I intended to keep the demolition party entirely independent of any of the attacking groups. At least two demolitions, separated by an hour or more, would be necessary to complete the destruction of the three spans and two steel piers which supported them.

Allowing two hours for preparation for each explosion, I considered that we might need a total of four hours from the time the demolition party first reached the viaduct. I reckoned that the nearest enemy reinforcements would come up by road or by rail about two hours after the receipt of a warning to move. Even after we had successfully overwhelmed the garrison we had therefore to be prepared to delay enemy reinforcements in a separate and later action which might last anything up to a further two hours.

That evening Aris and Zervas sent off a small reconnaissance party to learn the lie of the land and to select routes for the final approach to the viaduct. With this party went the leaders of the different attacking groups. They were told to be back in forty-eight hours. Meanwhile Aris disappeared. I learned afterwards that he had gone to a neighbouring village, where a case of cattle-thieving had been reported to him. He had had the culprit stripped and publicly beaten in the village square by the newest recruit, a mere boy. It was in this way that he 'blooded' his new adherents. He had then pulled out his revolver and shot the guilty man. Thus was law maintained by Aris in the mountains of Roumeli at that time. Small wonder that his name was on the lips of every man in the district. It was a cruel discipline, but one which startled these country people out of the lethargy into which they had sunk under Axis occupation, and which was his effective way of putting life into the growing movement of resistance against the enemy.

Late on 23rd November the reconnaissance party returned safely. All was well; they were satisfied with what they had seen.

During the night we made our final plans for the approach march and we decided to fix the attack for the night of the 25th. Aris and Zervas were both keen to see everything for themselves before they committed their andartes to the attack. Early the following morning, therefore, Zervas, Aris, Chris and I set off with a small bodyguard to carry out a final reconnaissance. The main body was to follow the next day. It was a good day's march to the forward concentration point, for which we had selected a group of wood-cutters' huts in the middle of the dense forests on Mount Oiti, a distance of 'about six hours' walking from the railway—all distances in the Greek mountains were measured by time, and no two local estimates were ever the same. One had to add or subtract according to the age and physical condition of the always willing informants, and according to the effectiveness of their footwear; sometimes even according to their eagerness for one to leave the district!

We spent the night of 24th November in a tiny and primitive shepherd's hut high up on Mount Oiti. The ground was covered with a foot or more of snow. We had planned to carry out our final reconnaissance from the slopes of the mountain at dawn the next day. It was still dark when a sentry awoke us. There was a thick mist, and as dawn approached it seemed to thicken. We were enveloped in the clouds. A bird's-eye view of the approaches to the Gorgopotamos viaduct proved to be impossible. Later in the morning it began to rain. We decided to return to the hut and wait until the following morning, in the hope that the clouds would have lifted by then. It would be our last opportunity.

All that day it alternately rained and snowed. As we lay in the bleak and draughty hut, with our eyes sore from the smoke of the fire that we kept going in the middle of its earth floor, we seemed strangely isolated from the rest of the world by the low-lying clouds. But when we awoke on the morning of the 25th, we found that the weather had cleared a little and, in fact, suited our purpose almost exactly. We cautiously descended the mountain to within a thousand yards of the railway. There, crawling on our hands and knees from cover to cover, through gaps in the slowly moving clouds we got some excellent glimpses of the viaduct. Several hundred feet below us, it looked like a toy bridge. Through our glasses we carefully studied all the approaches and

74

the surrounding country. After an hour of this, Aris and Zervas were satisfied with all that they had seen and with what I was able to describe to them from my previous visit. We retraced our steps up Mount Oiti, to meet the main body at a pre-arranged rendezvous on the edge of the forest, two-thirds of the way up the mountain side.

At about four o'clock in the afternoon the main body started arriving, silently winding its way in single file out of the clouds which now clung again to the sides of the mountain. The men sat down in the misty dampness to eat a hurried meal of cold meat and a hunk of bread, washed down with icy water or, by those who had filled their flasks in Mavrolithari, with *ouzo*, the local spirit, given to them by the villagers.

Although we were about a mile from the Gorgopotamos, and three to four thousand feet above it in the clouds, no one was allowed to make any noise or to light a fire. As it grew dark, the mist completely closed in on us and the atmosphere became eerie. With Chris I went from party to party, seeing that everything was in order, and that the last adjustments had been correctly made to the explosives, which were distributed on eight mules. These mules were the only ones with us. After the attack had begun, when the braying of any mule no longer mattered, they were to transport the charges to within a few hundred yards of the viaduct. From there the charges were to be carried by hand. Chris was indefatigable in his assistance to me, checking up all the andarte parties, interpreting for me, and ensuring that all the orders were clearly understood.

At a last-minute conference with Aris and Zervas to decide upon zero hour for the simultaneous attack by the two main parties at the north and south end of the viaduct, we calculated that the earliest hour by which all groups leaving our forward rendezvous at nightfall could reach their appointed places was 10 p.m. Zervas was keen to make zero hour at that time. But, out-voted by Aris and myself, he agreed on eleven o'clock, thus allowing what I thought to be a necessary margin of safety for all parties to get into position. Even with this late zero hour, allowing a little over four hours for the whole operation, we should be able to get away from the viaduct soon after three o'clock in the morning at the latest, and be well shielded again by the fir forests on Mount Oiti before daylight.

At about six o'clock in the evening we got to our feet and began our final approach march. For the first half-mile we were all to traverse the same pathway. In the lead was the group who had to go the farthest, a band of fifteen ELAS andartes with John Cook and Nat Barker, carrying explosives to cut the railway, and wire-cutters to cut the telephone wires beside it, at a point about a mile south of the viaduct. Next came Themie Marinos and an andarte Engineer officer, with a similar-sized band of ELAS, to cut the railway to the north. Both these parties were instructed to cut the telephone wires and to prepare their charges at zero hour; but, in order to ensure the maximum ambush effect, they were not to blow up the railway unless either enemy forces, or a train, actually approached. If, however, no enemy reinforcements had arrived by the time the green Very light—the signal for the general with-drawal—was fired into the air, they were to cut the railway before finally withdrawing.

Next came a group of about forty men which was to attack the south end of the bridge. This was a composite party of ELAS and Zervas' men under Captain Michalli's command. Amongst this group were Karalivanos and all his reunited band, with the excep-tion of Baphas, who was with the demolition party. They were out to prove their mettle; Karalivanos himself had literally to fight for his life; for, after telling Aris about his desertion of us, I had agreed that, as he was anxious to help us in our operation, he should be given one more chance. Then came a band of about thirty of Zervas' men, earmarked to attack the north end of the viaduct. Following them came our Joint Headquarters, Zervas, Aris, Chris and myself; and immediately behind us, under our control, a reserve of thirty andartes belonging for the most part to Aris, but containing a few of Zervas' men. Lastly came the demolition party under Tom Barnes with eight additional andartes each leading a mule.

We had over four hours in which to make our final approach. The party going the farthest had a good three miles to travel; the Joint Headquarters only a mile. But we all had to move carefully and slowly in the darkness. We had many short halts in order to check our route, and it was already ten o'clock when, with the exception of the demolition party, the last group had quietly faded away from us into the darkness.

At our forward concentration point Chris and I had, I thought, made it quite clear that our Headquarters, with the reserve and the demolition party, were to concentrate together at a point about two hundred yards from the viaduct and, in relation to our final approach down the mountain, on the far side of the ravine. From there we could control the battle and be in the best position to despatch the demolition party, with which I wanted to go, the moment that white Very signals indicating the capture of each end of the bridge were fired into the air by the two main attacking groups. But when we reached the point where we had to cross to the other side of the valley, I was alarmed to discover that it was the intention of both Aris and Zervas to keep our Headquarters and the reserve on the near side of the valley. The demolition party had to cross to the other side, in order to get a clear approach to the steel spans. This alteration or misunderstanding of my plans therefore meant leaving this party without any local protection whatsoever, and ourselves with no reliable means of instructing it when to advance to the viaduct and begin its work of fixing the prepared charges to the legs of the piers.

I could not get either Aris or Zervas to change his mind; so I told Tom Barnes that he would have to use his own people for local protection, and that I would signal to him across the valley with my torch when he was to advance to the viaduct. I said that, as soon as possible after I had signalled to him, I would come and join him from the other side of the valley. I realised, however, that I might have great difficulty in crossing the river, because of its torrential nature. We parted, both with some misgivings. Our Headquarters, now left only with the reserve force, waited in complete silence for some twenty minutes, and then, a few moments before zero hour, as a train rumbled by, we crawled forward to within about a hundred and fifty yards of the viaduct. There we found a fold in the ground, reasonably protected from all small-arms fire. The mist was now thinner, and the full moon, trying to get through it, lit up the surrounding country sufficiently for our purpose. Conditions, in fact, were ideal.

A minute or two before eleven o'clock Zervas, Aris, Chris and I advanced to within a few feet of the crest of the gently sloping ridge behind which the reserve was sheltering, and we peered over the edge. Through the light mist we could clearly see the viaduct ahead of us. It looked huge and gaunt. All was silent. For fourteen anxious minutes we waited thus, lying on our stomachs on the ground. Then at last, when we had begun to think that something had gone seriously wrong, that all the parties were late, or that in the darkness they had gone astray, pandemonium was let loose right in front of us around the north end of the viaduct.

Rifle and automatic fire seemed to come from every direction at once, a tremendous volume of it. I could distinguish four or five light machine-guns cracking away in a deafening manner. The attacking party at this end of the viaduct had only two such guns. We were up against something fairly strong. Bullets were flying high over our heads in considerable numbers. After about twenty minutes of this intense small-arms fire Zervas became worried and said to me, through Chris, that, at that rate of fire, we would soon run out of our ammunition. Shortly afterwards heavy firing broke out from the south end, and we distinctly heard Captain Michalli's voice, loudly cheering his andartes on. Then the firing somewhat died down in front of us, and a few minutes later an excited andarte approached and told us that the group attacking the north end of the viaduct had been beaten back. They had tried to cut their way silently through the barbed wire round the Italian guard-post, and had succeeded in getting a few people through a narrow gap when they had been spotted by the enemy, who had trained some light automatics right on to the gap. The andartes, inexperienced in a deliberate operation such as this, had not been able to face the intense fire, and they had all withdrawn to a position of cover.

From the cheering still occasionally audible above the noise of the firing on the far end of the viaduct, we gathered that all was going well there. The situation at our end demanded drastic action. We decided to put in the whole of our reserve to re-establish the situation. Zervas' second-in-command, Komninos Pyromaglou, was in charge of this party. Once a teacher of Greek in Paris, he was not only an able person but also full of courage. He was therefore entrusted with supreme command of the fresh attack on the north end. Not long after he had gone forward with the reserve, brisk firing broke out again in front of us. But there were still too many light automatics to be heard for my liking. After another twenty minutes' continuous firing Zervas became even more anxious. He told me that he was almost convinced that we had been betrayed, that the Italians had been forewarned of our attack and had been reinforced. He said that he would fire the green Very light for the general withdrawal if the north end of the bridge was not captured in the next ten minutes, and he asked for the Very pistol. No one had it! Fortunately, although inadvertently, it had been taken forward by Komninos in his pocket. I sent Chris forward to get it, with instructions to keep it in his own hands and on no account to allow anybody to handle it except under my orders. Ten minutes later he returned with it, and with the news also that Komninos was in good heart and hoped, before long, to gain possession of his end of the bridge.

Nearly an hour after the battle had started exceptionally loud cheering went up from the south end of the viaduct. It was followed almost immediately by a white Very light. The far end was in our hands.

The steel piers, which the demolition party were going to destroy, were nearer that end than ours; so I decided to take the risk of ordering Tom Barnes and his party forward to their work. I ran down to a point where I could look straight across to the opposite side of the valley, where Tom and his men were lying up, waiting for my signal. I flashed my torch and shouted at the top of my voice: "Go in, Tom! The south end of the bridge is in our hands. Go in! I will join you as soon as possible."

"O.K.," Tom shouted back.

I returned to remain with Zervas and Aris, and with Chris, who was essential to me as interpreter.

On the battle went in front of us. Zervas was convinced that we had almost run out of ammunition. I told him that we could not consider a withdrawal now, because the demolition party already had their task partially completed.

After about another fifteen minutes, unable to wait inactive any longer, I told Chris that I would go forward and join Komninos, who spoke English moderately well, and that I would leave him as my sole representative with Zervas and Aris. I repeated to him my instructions that on no account was the withdrawal signal to be fired without my orders. With one andarte, who did not speak a word of English, as my personal bodyguard, I crept over the odd hundred yards between our rise in the ground and the place where I could see the flashes coming from the rifles of Komninos' men. I crawled up alongside the leader of one of his sections; but he spoke no English. I could not find Komninos. By gesticulation I urged the section leader to move his men forward; but he would not do so. The enemy fire was by now far from intense, and I realised that the resistance in front of us was crumbling. A few moments later, above the noise of battle, a shrill whistle was heard. It was Tom Barnes' signal for everybody to take cover, as he was about to light fuses. Our firing ceased as we put our heads down, and almost automatically the enemy firing also eased. Two minutes later there was a tremendous explosion, and I saw one of the seventy-foot steel spans lift into the air and—oh, what joy!—drop into the gorge below, in a rending crash of breaking and bending steel-work.

At last I succeeded in getting the andartes around me to charge, and in the darkness they overran the few Italians who had not by now escaped. Seconds later, from somewhere just behind me, a white Very signal was fired into the air. Simultaneously with the successful accomplishment of half our task the Italian garrison had been completely overcome.

Through the barbed wire and the tall grass at the foot of the viaduct I made my way down to the river, intending to cross it in order to join Tom Barnes. But I found a raging torrent and, with no rope, and unassisted except for the single bodyguard at my side, I realised, after one attempt, that I could never keep my feet in it. I shouted at the top of my voice to Tom, who could only have been about fifty yards away from me. But I failed to make myself heard. As quickly as I could, I retraced my steps to the end of the viaduct, where I got on to the top of it and walked along until I reached its jagged end. In front of me I clearly discerned two complete spans which had been dropped into the gorge below, as a result of the demolition of one of the steel piers. Forty feet above the river which, even where I then stood, roared loudly below me, I shouted again at the top of my voice, and at last got Denys Hamson to hear me. He told me that they needed another forty minutes to bring down the other steel pier and a further span, and to twist and cut the two spans already lying partially on the ground.

At that moment there was a loud explosion from the north. Heavy firing broke out from that direction. Enemy reinforcements were approaching by rail from Lamia. I could but hope that Themie's party was doing its job properly. I shouted to Denys that they must be as quick as they could, as we had now insufficient ammunition to hold off any fresh enemy force for many minutes.

A few moments later I heard Chris' voice behind me, shouting from somewhere up the hill: "Zervas says he can only give you another ten minutes, and then we must fire the withdrawal signal."

"On no account will you allow it to be fired," I shouted back, "until you hear the next explosion from the bridge. This cannot be less than twenty minutes from now."

"All right," Chris shouted, "I'll do my best; but for heaven's sake don't make it more than twenty minutes."

I went back to the overhanging edge of the viaduct and shouted across to Denys the gist of this conversation. I told him to be as quick as he possibly could.

Some fifteen minutes later Tom blew his whistle again. I heaved a sigh of relief. The enemy firing from the north was getting nearer, and I knew it was touch and go whether we could hold out any longer. I went back to the end of the viaduct and took cover. There was another tremendous explosion. I couldn't see exactly what happened. No further span fell down, as I expected; but I distinctly saw the two already fallen ones jump up into the air and subside again. A second later a green Very signal went up into the air. I realised that it was foolhardy to try to get a final view of the bridge. It would have taken me several minutes to get up to the overhanging edge of the viaduct and back again; and I might be trapped on it as the enemy approached.

Every man had been instructed, on the firing of the withdrawal signal, to take his shortest way back to the forward concentration point, a mile away up Mount Oiti. With only a handful of andartes I struck off across country in the right general direction. We soon separated, and my bodyguard and I found ourselves boring our way through almost impenetrable thickets. Inspired by the success of our operation, although desperately weary, having been on the move more or less continuously since four o'clock the previous morning, we battled our way together through them, up and up, and gradually we emerged on to open, rocky moorland above it. Here we immediately made faster going, and we soon picked up the pathway by which we had descended a few hours before. On it there was already a procession of weary andartes, climbing their way up. I overtook one of the demolition party. He had lost the sole of one of his boots and was limping on with the aid of a stick. He told me that the second explosion had successfully cut and distorted the two already fallen spans, but that the charges on the second pier, which, if effective, would have brought down yet another span, had only cut two of the four legs, and that the pier and the span had remained in position.

"Never mind," I said; "you have all done marvellously," and I left him to trudge on in his own time.

When dawn broke I was still travelling on open, snow-covered, stony ground, unprotected by trees; but eventually, at about seven o'clock in the morning, I reached the forward concentration point on the edge of the forest, where I found a large part of our total andarte force already assembled, and chattering excitedly in little groups. I hunted out Zervas and found him with Aris. They had arrived some three-quarters of an hour before me, and were already preparing to move off. Chris was with them. I shook both Zervas and Aris warmly by the hand and congratulated them on their magnificent achievement and that of their men, and thanked them sincerely. A few moments later, with only some thirty andartes still unaccounted for, we moved on, making for the forest huts some six hours' away to the west.

We trudged on up the remaining thousand feet of Mount Oiti and halted for the first time only after we had got well into the thick forest some three hours later. I lay on the snow and almost immediately went into a sort of coma. I remember Chris prodding me from behind and saying quite fiercely: "Don't go to sleep. You are not to go to sleep, sir."

"All right," I replied rather feebly. "Don't worry about me."

When we got on the move again I realised that, being probably the softest member of our party, because of the office job I had had in Cairo, I was almost at the end of my tether, and rather ignominiously I accepted the offer of a ride on one of the mules which had carried down our explosives. I suddenly recalled that I had eaten practically nothing since five o'clock the previous evening. It was then about ten o'clock in the morning. I had nothing left on me except my emergency ration, a cake of chocolate substance. I took it out of my pocket and hungrily munched some of it. It immediately revived me.

We were enveloped in a thick mist. It gave us a tremendous sense of security to realise that, apart from the protection of the forests, no Italian aeroplane had a chance of picking us up in this weather, even in open country. Later it began to snow. God was with us. Even our tracks would soon be obliterated.

About three o'clock in the afternoon we reached the forest huts, and there found the faithful Barba Niko with a hot meal awaiting us. We lit some fires and, crowding round their warmth, my brain began to work once again. During the last twenty-four hours, apart from the actual operation, we had been continuously on the move; we had made a four-thousand-feet descent and ascent of Mount Oiti, as well as trudging for many hours through deep snow. The majority of us had covered, in all, close on thirty miles since we had last slept. Small wonder that I felt tired. I experienced a glow of satisfaction from the realisation that we had achieved our mission. With this glow and a full stomach, after having congratulated all ranks, and in particular Tom Barnes, on their gallant achievement, I fell asleep.

Late that afternoon and throughout the night stragglers kept on coming in, and by the morning, when we moved on, we had accounted for every single man. No one of our party had been killed. We had only four wounded men, whom we put on mules. Our general impression was that the total enemy garrison had consisted of about eighty Italians. According to reports, between twenty and thirty of these at least had been killed. I myself, in wandering about the north end of the viaduct, had seen over half a dozen Italian bodies.

We re-entered Mavrolithari in triumph on 27th November. The following day we spent in resting our sore feet and weary limbs, and in going over the various incidents of the Gorgopotamos operation.

On reaching the foot of the viaduct, Tom Barnes had found, to his consternation, that the actual cross-section of the four legs of each of the two steel piers was 'U'-shaped, whereas we had expected them to be 'L'-shaped. Then and there, whilst a battle was still raging above them not many yards away, he had had to call his party together to dismantle completely all the prepared charges and to repack the explosives by hand into the vertical 'U'-shaped girders. In spite of this, he was ready for the first blow little over an hour after reaching the viaduct. I reckoned that his great work and that of his demolition party had effectively cut the railway to Athens for from six to twelve weeks, depending upon whether the gap was bridged by a temporary or a permanent structure.

Themie related that he had blown his charges on the railway line to the north of the viaduct just in front of the train which was bringing Italian reinforcements from Lamia. But the engine had passed over the break in the line without being derailed. It had pulled up, with the Greek engine-driver shouting: "The andartes have got us!"; and, to add insult to injury, the driver had put the train in reverse and successfully got the front half of it back over the break in the line without derailment. But heavy casualties had been inflicted by his group of andartes on the enemy in the railway coaches before they succeeded in withdrawing to cover.

John Cook's party, a mile to the south, had been completely undisturbed; and, when the signal for the general withdrawal had been fired, he had blown up the railway line in his own time before finally departing.

I received several reports of the personal gallantry displayed by Karalivanos and his small band. I therefore asked Aris to forget all that I had said about him. I hunted out Karalivanos and, speaking to him for the first time since I had reprimanded him in Stromni, I asked him to consider bygones as bygones and shook him by the hand, thanking him at the same time for his gallant contribution towards the success of the operation.

Zervas said that he would leave the next day on his five or six days' journey back to Valtos. Chris, in accordance with the instructions given to him in Cairo, was accompanying him. I and the rest of our party were due for evacuation by submarine from the west coast of Greece, so I decided to travel with them as far as Valtos. As our own wireless set was still not working, we sent off a runner to Athens, to ask Prometheus to send news of our success to Cairo, and to give them the exact rendezvous for our submarine, and the dates between which we would wait for it. Chris also asked for a supply drop of boots, clothing and arms, and the present of a case of whisky, for Zervas, to take place between 12th and 18th December, after he should have got back to Valtos.

I told both Zervas and Aris that I was recommending them and several others for decorations. When I told Aris this, he replied: "I don't want a decoration. I would much sooner have boots for my andartes." I told him that I would get them for him as soon as I could, but that I was in great difficulty, as my wireless was not yet working. When he heard that we were all intending to move westwards the next day, he said that he would have to remain in the Roumeli area to fix up certain matters, but that he might come and visit us at a later date. Chris and I had hoped that he would join forces with Zervas, in order to unify the andarte movement. But he would not agree to do so. He asked if a British officer could remain with him as liaison officer. Chris told him that he would arrange this at the earliest possible moment, but, for the time being, he had no one to give him. Apart from himself and Themie, everyone was due for evacuation. We gave him two hundred and fifty gold sovereigns for his gallant services.

Our saddest farewell was with Barba Niko. He said that he must now return to his home in order to fend for his family. I told him that I was recommending him for a special decoration. Without him we could never have left our nest.

The next day we parted. We went our way westwards; Aris went his southwards, probably to try some other cattle-thief and to punish him in his accustomed method; and Barba Niko, with tears in his eyes, went home to his family.

CHAPTER V

No Evacuation

ZERVAS HAD only begun his guerilla activity early in the summer of 1942. Through Prometheus, the Allies had persuaded him to leave Athens and take to the mountains. He had made straight for the mountains of Valtos, north-east of Arta, where he had spent his childhood and was therefore well known.

It took us eight days to reach his mountain stronghold. Only once did the Italians worry us seriously, when we had to make a detour and lie up for two days in a tiny village high up in the mountains to avoid an enemy column which had come north from Agrinion to look for us. Occasionally we had to take cover from single enemy aircraft. But they did not concern us overmuch, as there was usually plenty of cover at hand. We had only one main road to cross, that leading from Lamia to Karpenisi. This we planned to do stealthily one morning, in the half-light of dawn, in order to avoid any risk of being intercepted by Italian convoys which ran up and down the road during the hours of daylight, supplying the enemy garrison in Karpenisi.

We timed our daily journeys so as to spend each night in a village. Everywhere Greek hospitality was most generous, in spite of the fact that the villagers were invariably poorly off and Zervas was travelling through an area in which he was not well known. Most of the villages through which we passed in Western Roumeli were already being frequently visited by small bands of ELAS, under Aris' control. In some of the villages these bands were more or less permanently billeted. In practically all of them there was a political organisation called EAM, or National Liberation Front, which appeared to be the parent civilian organisation to which the armed bands of ELAS owed allegiance. In our encounters with ELAS bands, what impressed me most was the youthfulness of their andartes.

On our journey across Roumeli, Zervas was obviously at pains to be tactful and polite to the local inhabitants. On entering each village he would always wait sufficient time for a gathering of as many villagers as could be mustered. He would then make a short speech, announcing the success of the Gorgopotamos operation, and laying stress on how ELAS had co-operated with his own forces to bring about the successful destruction of the viaduct. In these speeches, so Chris informed me, Zervas often praised ELAS. Never did he in any way denounce them or even hint at competition with them.

Through Chris or Themie Marinos as interpreter, I had conversations with many Greeks of different standing on our journey westwards. The majority of those of middle class were reluctant to talk about EAM and ELAS. But, with Chris's assistance, I gradually gathered much background information, and pieced together many of the factors which had led up to the existence and platforms of the two resistance movements, EAM and that of Zervas. I will describe these in the following chapter.

In a village on the eastern outskirts of Valtos we were joined by the decoy force which Zervas had left behind on his way eastwards, ten days earlier. A day or two later, in another village, we picked up Zervas' brother, Alexis, his sister and young nephew, the only members of his family who had succeeded in escaping with him from Athens earlier in the year.

One particular incident, which I remember clearly, was the relish with which three of us devoured a pound pot of honey at one evening village halt. Within a minute we had wolfed the lot down. Our systems must have been yearning for sugar, because the immediate satisfaction which we got from the honey was extraordinary. The disgusting exhibition of animal greed passed almost unnoticed amongst us.

Eventually, on 8th December, we reached the small village of Megalohari, which was at that time Zervas' headquarters in Valtos. He, Chris and I were billeted in the house of a doctor called Papachristo, who was a close friend of Zervas. Nothing which could contribute to our welfare was too much trouble for him, but his resources were limited. The district in which we now found ourselves was noticeably poorer than those through which we had passed in Roumeli.

In the signal which I had sent by runner from Mavrolithari to our agent in Athens, to transmit to Cairo, I had asked for a submarine to evacuate us from a point on the west coast of Greece, about five miles south of Parga, on one of the four nights from 22nd to 25th December, inclusive. As our set was still not working, I had as yet received no confirmation from Cairo that they were able to evacuate us. But I considered that the risk that our request might not be met had to be accepted. We estimated that, to allow a sufficient margin of time for detours and unexpected delays, we should leave for the coast twelve days before the submarine was due. This meant that we would have only one clear day's rest before starting. To escort us, Zervas generously gave us a small band of twelve andartes, under the command of his adjutant, Captain Michalli.

On the same day that we left Megalohari, Zervas set out with us on a recruiting tour. Two hours later our ways parted. After the warmest farewells all round, thinking that we would not meet again until the end of the war, we went on our way towards the west coast.

Two of the wireless operators—Sergeants Wilmot and Phillips who were staying on with Chris—had been left in Megalohari to continue their attempts to repair their set. Chris and Themie were

travelling with Zervas on his tour. The rest of us, including all
the escaped Allied prisoners of war whom we had by then gathered
to our side, were coming with me to the coast. The party for
evacuation thus totalled twelve: Tom Barnes, Arthur Edmonds,
John Cook, Nat Barker, Inder Gill, Denys Hamson, Sergeant
Chittis, Yani and Panioti, the Cypriot escaped prisoners of war,
Lance-Corporal Michael Khuri and Corporal Aaron Deo, the
Palestinians, and myself.

After we had crossed the main road from Arta to Yannina, our
route took us into an area in which there was no andarte organisation whatsoever. Here the villages were often visited by formed
bodies of Italian troops on duty and by small parties of them
unofficially on the scrounge. We were now careful to avoid
being seen in the day-time and to keep down the number of
Greeks who knew of our whereabouts at night time to the abso-
lute minimum possible. This was not because we questioned the
actual loyalty of the majority of the local Greeks. But we realised,
as well as they did, how difficult it is for a Greek peasant to keep a
secret to himself, and the Greeks themselves were petrified lest,
the next time police or occupational troops entered their village,
one of their number might inadvertently disclose that they had
seen or helped us. Our cover story was that we were on our way
to Albania.

The further west we got, the more frightened were the villagers
becoming whenever they heard we were in their vicinity and the
more necessary did it become to make ourselves scarce. Each
afternoon we would lie up, usually on snow-covered ground,
often in a biting cold wind, well away from the village in which
we planned to spend the night. At dusk Captain Michalli would
enter the village as unobtrusively as possible, to arrange our ac-
commodation. Because it was less likely to be visited at night by
other Greeks, and subsequently by Greek gendarmerie or Italian
troops, he almost invariably selected one of the smallest and poorest

cottages in the village. Into this cottage the whole of our party would in due course be crowded, to share what little food the inhabitants could spare us from their meagre larder and to sleep in comparative warmth until the small hours of the morning. We were always on our way again well before daylight. Small wonder, therefore, that as our journey continued we steadily became more hungry and in poorer physical condition. But for the stimulation by the approaching prospect of our evacuation, we would have been in a poor way long before we reached our rendezvous with the submarine.

Three days before we were due to reach the coast we were already only ten miles from it. Michalli told me that the area in the vicinity of the rendezvous was an extremely difficult one in which to lie up and hide. We decided to stay where we were for two days, so as not to reach the coast until the night before our submarine was due. We spent those two days shivering in a group of primitive huts of brushwood belonging to practically destitute Greek gipsies, who had once lived in what is now Albanian territory. On the afternoon of 21st December we left them and clambered up on to a high and bare ridge. Below us to the north lay the enemy-occupied airfield of Paramithia; to the west, clearly visible beyond six miles of flat marshland, was the sea!

Unwilling to by-pass villages on the edge of the marsh until it was dark, we lay low on this windswept and bitterly cold ridge, crouching under some stone walls which had been put up to protect sheep, and waited for the sun to go down. We warmed ourselves, in turn, in a shepherd's tiny wigwam of brushwood, in which there was not room for more than a few of us at a time.

At dusk we descended the mountain into the marshland. We skirted its southern edge, by-passing every village that we could. Once or twice during the night the stillness was broken by the barking of dogs, which gave away our presence. But we passed on without halting. Many times, in order to avoid a cottage with a light in it, we made detours off our pathway into the boggy marshland. Each time we did so, we put up masses of wild fowl. There must have been thousands in that sanctuary. I remember hoping that one day I might return there to spend a shooting holiday. As we approached the coast we entered some woods thick with undergrowth and our pace slowed up. It was still dark when Captain Michalli announced that we were near enough to our rendezvous and that we had better lie up until dawn. We selected some good cover under the bushes, rolled ourselves up in the blanket or greatcoat which each of us carried in our pack and, worn out with our long night's journey, we were soon asleep.

The sun was well up when I awoke, stiff and hungry. Michalli had already gone off to try to find food for us. Except for a little dry bread, we now had nothing in hand. Towards midday Michalli returned. He told me, through Denys Hamson, that he had taken the priest of a nearby village into his confidence, and that the latter had agreed to give him a little food for us each evening. Michalli warned me, however, that the people in this district were desperately poor, and that we could not expect as much as we had been used to. What a thought! My wretched party were hungry enough already, in spite of Michalli's valiant efforts on our behalf.

We were about a mile and a half south of the rendezvous which we had selected for the submarine. As it grew dusk our spirits rose, and we set off towards it. It turned out to be a sheltered little cove with trees right down to the rocky edge of the sea. In it we found a small sailing-boat, which was probably used by smugglers to bring food to the mainland from the island of Paxos, only a few miles away. But it was far too small to take us across the Mediterranean. With us we had brought two accumulators to provide the current for flashing out to sea the letter of the alphabet which we had arranged to use before leaving Cairo. To the accumulators we connected one of our torches, whose batteries had long expired. We fixed it on a large rock at the southern edge of the entrance to the cove so that it pointed in a south-westerly direction, clear of the island of Paxos. We then started signalling out to sea. We arranged shifts, and throughout the night we went on signalling; but in vain. Two hours before dawn, realising that the submarine was not coming that night, we packed up all our paraphernalia and returned to our hide-out. Most of that day we slept beneath the shrubbery, and the only thing which broke the monotony was the little exercise we took to stretch our cold limbs, and the very little food which we eked out.

The next evening we repeated the procedure; but again no submarine came. Anxious, but by no means yet without hope, we returned to our hide-out once more.

However small the amount of food which Michalli managed to procure for us each day, most of us kept a little in hand, not knowing whether he would find any the following day. It was the first time that I had experienced continuous hunger, and the feelings of insecurity and depression which accompany it. That Christmas Eve of 1942 we were rather a dejected group. As it grew dark, however, our renewed activity and the hope that the submarine would come that night buoyed us up once more. Shortly after midnight I was woken up excitedly by one of the shift on duty. A boat had been seen approaching. Hurrah! But by the time I had hurried down to the edge of the beach, it had vanished. Alas, it was soon obvious that it was no boat from a submarine, but more likely a Greek smuggler's boat from Paxos, frightened away from its secluded cove by our presence. Dejectedly, we carried on signalling until shortly before dawn.

Only one more night now remained. We trudged back to our hide-out, this time really depressed. Christmas Day broke fine upon us, and the sun shone out. But we were in no spirits to enjoy its warmth. However, towards midday Michalli's kind priest turned up with a sack of small brown loaves, each no bigger than a bun, as a Christmas present for us. As we thankfully devoured them, I wondered if I had ever spent, or would spend again, such a bleak and unhappy Christmas.

That night, just as we were about to leave for our final night's signalling, the priest returned with a strange Greek. He was a runner from Chris. He handed me a small piece of dirty paper. I unfolded it and read in Chris' handwriting:

"Last night I was dropped a new wireless set. I have also received a message from Cairo saying that they will not be sending a submarine for you. Fresh instructions are being sent to you by safe hand of one, Captain Bill Jordan, who is due to be dropped within the next two days."

Prepared for our journey to the coast, our few personal possessions and kit were already packed in our rucksacks. Within twenty minutes of the runner's arrival we left dejectedly on our return journey to Valtos. I was by now too weak and tired to succeed in instilling a measure of humour into this group of bitterly disappointed volunteers, who had gallantly carried out their part of the bargain. Apart from the fact that their morale was by then so low, they were all feeling the effect of poor and inadequate food, the lack of proper rest on our outward journey and the hard days and nights, half starved, during our way on the coast.

The memory of our journey back from the coast is still like that of a nightmare. In order to avoid any Italians who might have been alerted by our journey westwards, Captain Michalli deliberately led us back by a more circuitous route to the north, to within a few miles of Yannina, before we turned eastwards to cross the Louros valley. Night after night as we struggled on, clambering up and down steep and stony goat tracks, often drenched to the skin, I felt as I imagine a hunted hare does when, towards the end of a long run, with hounds close on its heels, it is hardly able to move its tired and stiffening limbs. But, apart from one rest of forty-eight hours in an old monastery called

Romanon in the valley of the river Akheron, Michalli insisted that we should make all possible haste until we had recrossed the Arta–Yannina road and were once more in an area in which most of the villages possessed organisations of Zervas' Resistance Movement. From then onwards we could travel by day and rest by night. Even so, the only bright incidents on the remainder of that otherwise ghastly journey were a warm welcome and proper meal on New Year's Day in the large and prosperous village of Khosepsi and a comparatively luxurious night's rest the following night in the house of one of Zervas' friends, Colonel Lambrakis.

On the afternoon of 3rd January we eventually reached Zervas' base at Megalohari. We were all exhausted. But we were grateful for the cheerful greetings from young Themie Marinos, and Captain Bill Jordan, who had arrived only a few nights before. Chris was away on another tour with Zervas. He had left Themie and Bill behind with the wireless operators. I was relieved to hear that our wireless was now working quite well. One of the entries in my diary for this day read: "A tin of bully beef each, but no tobacco or boots"! Our interests in life were reduced to a fairly basic level.

A little while after my arrival Bill brought me a bulky envelope. It contained my new instructions from Cairo.

CHAPTER VI

Stormy Political Horizon

LATE INTO the night, by the wavering light of a candle, I read and re-read the lengthy instructions from SOE (Cairo). Bill had brought them in cipher. Unfortunately, when he had deciphered them, the part which dealt with the reasons why Cairo had failed to evacuate us was too corrupt to be decipherable. Bill told me that the C.-in-C. Mediterranean had lost a submarine only a few days previously, in sending it to just such a pre-arranged rendez-vous as ours. He was desperately short of submarines at the time, and, according to Bill, he could not run the risk of losing another.

In the long message we were all warmly congratulated on the success of the Gorgopotamos operation, and were asked to stay on in Greece. I was greatly upset by this request. Every one of my party was a volunteer. Moreover, with the exception of Chris, Themie and the wireless operators, they had volunteered on the distinct understanding that as soon as they had completed the operation of cutting the railway line every effort would be made to evacuate them. They were bitterly disappointed and depressed as a result of their long, hard and fruitless journey to the coast. In their present state, the majority of them would have little heart in any new mission which would prolong their time inside Greece. Before I went to sleep I made up my mind to keep in Greece only those who were genuinely keen to stay on, and to try to get the remainder evacuated.

As for myself, I was asked by SOE (Cairo) to take command in co-ordinating and developing further activities of the andartes. This was a complete reversal of the original policy expounded to me before I left Egypt, which had been to let the andartes return to quiescence after we had cut the railway. Cairo explained to me that, through Prometheus, they had heard of a group of six Greek colonels in Athens, who had recently formed themselves into a Committee for the reputed purpose of organising and directing the Resistance Movements in the mountains. They thought that it would be a good idea if these Greek officers in Athens and I, in the field, should work together. It was suggested that Chris might move to Athens and become my liaison officer. I would be regarded as the senior Allied representative in Greece; and, together with these Greek officers in Athens, we would work under the direction of a body in Cairo known as the Anglo-Greek Committee. This Committee, with Panayiotis Kanellopoulos,* the Greek Vice-Premier, as its senior Greek representative, had been set up in Egypt to co-ordinate British activities in Greece, in the absence of the rest of the Greek Government and the King, who were still in London. I was instructed to send Chris to visit Athens, to see if this scheme was possible.

The next day, 4th January, I gave my officers the gist of these new instructions. Most of them were greatly upset that there was no mention of an alternative effort being made by Cairo to get them evacuated. But I said that I did not want any of them to stay on in Greece against their will, and that I would assist, in every way that I could, the evacuation of all those who wished to leave. Nat Barker and John Cook alone volunteered to stay on. At the time I had no suitable job for John, as he didn't speak Greek. So I accepted Nat only, and immediately signalled to Cairo, asking SOE to arrange another method of evacuation for the remainder. I suggested a seaplane to the Gulf of Amvrakia.

* Kanellopoulos was later briefly Prime Minister (1945) and has served in various posts in other post-war governments.

Anxious to discuss my new instructions with Chris as soon as possible, I sent off a runner, requesting him to meet me at Skoli-karia, a village about midway between us.

Whatever happened, I realised that we were all to have many more days together in Greece. During the past weeks Tom Barnes' personality and ability had continuously stood out above those of the other officers. On the other hand, John Cook, through no fault of his own, had been of little assistance to me as an acting second-in-command on our ghastly journey to the coast and back. That afternoon, therefore, after explaining to John what he had the sense to realise, I ordered him to revert to his acting rank of Captain, and I promoted Tom into John's place. I asked Cairo to confirm what I had done.

The following day, with Nat Barker and Captain Michalli, I crossed a mountain pass deeply covered with snow and, after a five-hour journey, reached Skolikaria. Here Michalli left us to rejoin Zervas, only a few hours away. Nat and I stayed in a cottage, on the ground floor of which Zervas was at that time keeping some of his stocks of clothing, food and luxuries which he had collected from previous supply drops or from Athens. We had coffee and sugar for breakfast the next day. What a treat they seemed! All that day, while we waited for Chris, it alternately rained or snowed. Huddled up in front of the cottage fire, I gladly rested and regained some of my strength.

Chris arrived the next day. He was in excellent health and in high spirits. I asked him for his story before I told him mine.

A few days after our departure, Aris had crossed the river Acheloos into Zervas' territory with no less than four hundred andartes. Apparently he had heard that an aeroplane had dropped supplies to Zervas, and he had marched over from Roumeli to claim what he considered to be his share of them. Chris had gone to meet Aris to explain that he had already asked Cairo to send him a complete aircraft load of supplies for his own use, and that the stores which had arrived a few nights previously had already been distributed to Zervas' men. Aris was not convinced; or, alternatively, with another purpose in mind, he had pretended not to be. He had then written a series of threatening letters to Zervas, and had advanced progressively deeper into Zervas' territory. As he did so, Zervas had correspondingly withdrawn in front of him, so as to avoid any chance of conflict. After several days of this manœuvring, Chris had succeeded in bringing about a meeting between the two of them on 'neutral' ground, with only a handful of advisers and personal bodyguards in attendance. At this meeting, as Chris put it, "they agreed not to fight each other, but they disagreed on practically every other point". With the promise of a supply drop as soon as it could be arranged, Aris and his andartes had finally withdrawn across the river Acheloos into his own domains in Roumeli.

After bringing Chris up to date with the story of our fruitless and wearying journey to the coast, I read out my new instructions to him. We then reviewed the situation as we saw it early in that January of 1943.

From our briefing before we left Egypt and from what we had discovered since our arrival in Greece, it was apparent that the authorities in the Middle East knew little about the military strength and composition of the andartes. Moreover, although we had one or two agents in Athens who were in touch by runner with some of the andarte bands in the field and by wireless with the Middle East, SOE (Cairo) had obviously been told little about the political aspects of the Greek Resistance Movements. The Greek Government in London, which was forced to leave day-to-day matters in the hands of Kanellopoulos and the Anglo-Greek Committee in Cairo, probably knew little more than SOE and the Middle East Command.

Chris and I had so far gathered that EAM must have come into existence soon after the Germans had overrun Greece in the spring of 1941, and that its closely knitted armed forces, ELAS, had made their first appearance in the field in January 1942, in the area of Mount Olympus. Judging by the number of bands which we had recently seen in Roumeli, ELAS had made rapid strides since then.

According to the civilian EAM political advisers, who were perpetually in attendance on the military commanders of every ELAS band, however small, EAM consisted of an amalgamation of many, if not all, of the Greek political parties, and it represented a 'democratic people's movement', with the aim of bettering the lot of the working classes on the liberation of their country. There certainly was considerable room for improvement in the lot of the Greek people whom we had so far encountered. In general they were desperately poor, and were living at a standard lower than any I thought could have existed in Europe in the twentieth century.

Although in those early days Zervas was always at considerable pains to say nothing in public that might offend EAM, when we talked to him in private he was very sceptical about their claim to represent many political parties. According to him, their leaders in Athens were organised as a governing body, called the 'Central Committee'. This Committee consisted of eight members, seven of whom were representatives either of the Communist or Socialist Parties, or of Left-wing organisations somewhat equivalent to our trade unions. The eighth member, Elias Tsirimokos, was the leader of an insignificantly small Social-Democratic party of 'the centre', called ELD, or Union of Popular Democracy, which he had founded in the early days of the occupation. The Communists and the Socialists, he stressed, thus outnumbered any 'genuinely democratic' parties by seven to one, and the Communists dictated their wishes on all matters. Zervas' officers, when talking to us about the leaders of EAM, invariably referred to them in bated breath simply and collectively as 'the Communists'. They obviously hated them and mistrusted their political aims. It was already clear to Chris and myself that EAM had a close connection with the Greek Communist Party, KKE, even if it was not under its actual domination.

Zervas told us that before he had taken to the mountains from Athens he had been invited by EAM to become the Commander-in-Chief of ELAS, and that he had refused because he would have been dominated by EAM which in turn was controlled by Communists. For this reason, and with the promise of British support, he had decided to take to the mountains independently, and to form a 'truly democratic' Resistance Movement which, he confided in us, was the field force of a political organisation in Athens called EDES, which stood for the 'National Republican Greek League'. The Republican, Plastiras, then in exile in the south of France because of his complicity in a Republican *coup d'état* some years previously, was the nominal head of both the political movement in Athens and of his military forces in the mountains. Zervas was the senior member of EDES in Greece. But, now that he was so busy in the field he could do little more than keep in touch with the political organisation which he had left behind in Athens. He told us that, although at present he had bands only in Valtos, he had many friends in Thessaly, Macedonia and the Peloponnese and that he planned to recruit bands in those districts.

We had already learnt that EAM rejected the leadership of Plastiras, to whom the members of EDES were all sworn. Because of this and because Zervas as a regular soldier refused to consider the Bolshevik method of command by a committee of three which existed in all ELAS bands and on which Aris insisted for any combined force, the prospects of obtaining any permanent amalgamation of the two military movements, EDES and ELAS, did not appear good. Both Zervas and Aris, in fact, already appeared to be recruiting military and civil members fast and competitively with an eye to the post-war situation.

In Valtos Zervas then had five hundred andartes. His bands

were quite well officered, nearly all of them by regular soldiers or reservists. But, unless he overcame his apparent unwillingness to delegate authority, I did not see how he could effectively control bands in more than a relatively small area round Valtos.

In Roumeli Aris then had four hundred andartes. Although we didn't know the strength of ELAS in other parts of Greece, from what we had seen of the active EAM/ELAS organisation in the villages of Roumeli (the penalty for desertion from ELAS was death) it appeared to us that ELAS would soon considerably out-number EDES. But it seemed unlikely that its fighting ability would outstrip that of EDES to the same extent, for two reasons. Firstly, EAM regarded most army officers as 'Royalists' or 'Fascists'. They associated them with the Metaxas regime, which they did not hesitate to denounce in front of us : and in denouncing Metaxas they coupled the name of King George II of Greece with his. As a result, in the bands of ELAS experienced army or ex-army officers were conspicuous by their absence. There were only a few very young ones. Secondly, the system whereby an ELAS military commander always had to obtain the prior agreement of his attendant EAM political adviser with every military action must certainly cause inefficiency or delay which in battle might be disastrous.

Apart from EAM/ELAS and EDES there appeared to be no other Resistance Movements in the mountains. We had so far met practically no officers of Royalist affiliations. There were already indications that the majority of influential Royalist officers had been ordered by the Greek Government in exile to remain in Athens, to have nothing to do with the Republican Resistance Movements and to await the return of the Royalist Government. If this were true, it seemed unlikely that the Royalist Party would ever emerge as a fighting force comparable with either ELAS or EDES.

Chris helped me to trace the roots of the political problems which were complicating our military task. As a result of the elections in the spring of 1936, a handful of Communists had held the balance between the main Liberal (republican or Venizelist) and Popular (Royalist) parties. Having failed to create a coalition, the King of Greece had formed a non-party government, headed by Demertzes, at one time a Liberal, but then of no party. Within a few months of his appointment, however, Demertzes had died, and the King had appointed in his place the Vice-Premier Metaxas, a strong-minded soldier and leader of one of the smallest Right-wing parties in the Chamber at that time.

Metaxas had quickly announced that his work would be impossible by ordinary Parliamentary procedure. He had persuaded the Greek Government to agree to its own temporary suspension pending new elections, and to empower him to govern by decree, advised as necessary by a proportionally represented Parliamentary Committee. His appointment of Right-wing friends and supporters to key positions had caused the trade unions to call a general strike. This was planned to start on 5th August, 1936. But Metaxas had forestalled them by getting the King's consent to his assumption of dictatorial powers on the 4th. All the Parliamentary leaders who had protested to the King against Metaxas were either exiled or put under house arrest; a dictatorship had been set up, and elections were never held.

Metaxas' measures were so strong that little political opposition was possible until the regime ended with his death early in 1941. The Royalist Government, which was formed after his death, contained few if any with Republican sympathies. Shortly afterwards, the German occupation of Greece forced the King to flee from the mainland to Crete, and a little later to the Middle East. It was therefore not difficult to realise why there were few Republican politicians in the Government in exile in London early in 1943.

When Greece was invaded by the Italians, Metaxas had not permitted retired Venizelist officers above the rank of Captain to join in the national war. He had arrested all Communists on whom he could lay hands, and had imprisoned all he could find in any way connected with Left-wing political movements. He had thereby become the bitter enemy, not only of all Communists, but of many Republicans. From most Republican accounts his dictatorship appeared to me to have been founded on Nazi lines and, with its secret police, youth movements and government by decree, to have differed in character from Nazism only slightly, and to have been almost as ruthless.

Of the better-known Communists, only a few had managed to escape arrest by Metaxas. These, with some of their unsuspected followers, in their hatred of the regime had started subversive activities towards the restoration of the people's rights. Such were their energy and skill that by 1941 there was, though weak numerically, an extensive and efficient cell organisation of Communists in many of the large towns. By then they had had over four years of valuable experience in subversive work, in which they had become proficient by the very nature of their precarious existence under the Metaxas regime.

When Greece was overrun by the Axis in the spring of 1941, and her people had waved a brave farewell to the last soldiers of the British Commonwealth, the enemy had taken away to Germany a few of the better-known Communists whom they had found in Metaxas' prisons. Many, however, by feigning false colours and milder creeds, had been liberated and had joined their luckier friends who had escaped Metaxas' clutches. EAM seemed to have been originated by these Communists and to have been based upon the pre-war country-wide cell organisation of the KKE.

Whereas in the middle of the national struggle against the invader thousands had mourned at Metaxas' funeral, wherever we had so far travelled in the mountains we had found only a mere handful who did not then speak against him. To begin with, I did not attach much importance to this. It seemed natural that the people, in their suffering under the Axis yoke and in their dire distress, should seek a scapegoat. What more natural ones could be found than the apparently totalitarian authorities in power shortly before their country was overrun by the Nazis and subsequently occupied by the despised Fascists? And, as a corollary, what could be more natural than a swing of political opinion towards democratic Republicanism as advocated by EDES? But EAM/ELAS appeared to be considerably more to the Left than was justifiable by this argument.

As the six Colonels in Athens, whom SOE (Cairo) suggested might direct the Resistance in the mountains, were probably Royalists, it seemed most unlikely that EAM/ELAS would have anything to do with them. As for Cairo's suggestion that Chris should be my liaison officer with them, it was a difficult enough problem to arrange his visit to Athens, let alone for him to live in that city, infested with Germans and their Gestapo. Chris, incidentally, was over six feet tall and had red hair; whereas most Greeks are five feet nothing and have black hair!

But we were not in a position to reject SOE's suggestions without firm evidence of the character and intentions of these senior Greek officers, and without confirmation of what EAM and ELAS were and really stood for. One of us would have to get to Athens somehow, in order to meet these Greeks and, if possible, the Central Committee of EAM as well. We knew that Zervas had runners travelling periodically between his headquarters and Athens, and we thought that one of them might be able to act as a guide. Provided Zervas thought that it would be possible for him to be got into the Greek capital, Chris, as usual without considering the grave personal risks that he would be taking, readily volunteered for the journey. We decided to seek Zervas' advice and help without delay.

We had a three- to four-hour journey the next day to Zervas' headquarters. Although his welcome was outwardly warm and, I feel sure, genuine, he greeted me somewhat cynically. At the back of his mind I believe he thought that our recent and fruitless journey to the coast had been deliberately schemed by the authorities in Cairo to disguise their intention all along that I and my other officers should remain in Greece.

It did not take Zervas long to make up his mind. Stroking his thick, black beard, he said he thought that the journey was bound to be extremely hazardous, but that it was possible. Although he believed that our struggle should be directed from the mountains rather than from Athens, he generously volunteered to help us in every way he could. He asked Chris when he wanted to start.

"As soon as possible," Chris replied.

Zervas said that he was expecting a runner from Athens in a few days' time, and that Chris could accompany him on his return journey. He was one of his most reliable men; also he knew how to get in touch with Prometheus.

Having decided on Chris' immediate future, we next had to make our plans for the rest of the Mission. There was not much to be decided on here. It was clear that we should send Nat Barker to Aris as soon as possible, to act as liaison officer with him. We could spare him one wireless operator and a set. Apart from myself, Themie Marinos, and the remaining two wireless operators under Bill Jordan, there was no one else to send anywhere, because the rest of the officers might have to be evacuated any day. I decided to keep my headquarters at Zervas' mountain base until Chris returned from Athens.

That night, 9th January, I sent word to Nat to join me at a village called Embeso, to which Zervas was moving the following day for recruiting purposes. At Zervas' request, I also sent a polite but firm note to a local ELAS leader, called Hermes, who was forcibly recruiting members in what Zervas regarded as his territory. Hermes had also been rather stupidly pin-pricking the enemy by persistently attacking isolated parties travelling along the main road between Arta and Messolonghi without regard to the resultant heavy reprisals on the local inhabitants.

Chris and I then sat down and together concocted a long signal, which was sent off to SOE (Cairo) on 13th January. In this signal I acknowledged my new instructions and said that I was willing to agree to the new responsibility which they wanted me to accept, provided I was free to visit Cairo whenever I considered necessary, on such occasions Chris taking my place. I summarised all that I then knew about EDES and EAM/ELAS, and explained the political factors which were likely to make further military co-operation between the two Movements difficult to obtain. I went on to give Chris' and my views on the prospects of maintenance of law and order in Greece. Although Zervas had told me that he was in favour of a plebiscite at the end of the war to decide whether there should be a republic or a continuation of the monarchy, we feared a *coup d'état* by EAM through ELAS in the event of the collapse of Italy. But if our own Government would now give immediate and tangible proof of their determination to ensure a free plebiscite at the end of the war, we thought that not only was it more likely that we could bring together ELAS and EDES now, but that civil war, which would otherwise be certain later, could be avoided and security could be maintained.

As most of the sabotage targets which could have a long-term effect were in Eastern Greece, in EAM/ELAS-controlled areas, it seemed to me that in the interests of the war effort we must make use of ELAS, and I ended this signal by asking SOE to suggest any specific targets which they would like us to prepare plans to attack.

Before the end of January I received two important signals from Cairo which showed me that at least SOE was now aware of some of the political complications already afoot. On 21st January I was asked for my reactions to a recent speech by Kanellopoulos in which he had authoritatively declared that the moment Greece was liberated, the Greek Government would resign to make way for another representing all political and social trends. I replied that I did not think that this went far enough to knock the bottom out of EAM's anti-Royalist propaganda. On 29th January I was informed that preliminary discussions were shortly to be held with the Anglo-Greek Committee about guaranteeing a plebiscite in Greece at the end of the war and I was asked to elaborate a number of the political factors raised in my signal of 13th January.

A web of Greek politics was already irrevocably woven around our activities; and the political horizon already appeared stormy.

CHAPTER VII

Plans for Expansion

NAT LEFT for Aris' headquarters in Roumeli on 11th January. He carried with him a long letter from me to Aris, explaining the situation about supply drops. In it I told him that I had asked for an aircraft-load for his bands as soon as he could arrange a dropping area direct with Cairo over the wireless set Nat was bringing him. I also told him I hoped that he would visit me soon to discuss future sabotage operations and to co-ordinate his activities with the requirements of the Middle East Command.

One of the entries in my diary for that day reads: "Slight fever in the evening." During the night I tried to sweat it out with the aid of some quinine. The next day, 12th January, I bade farewell to Chris and started on my return journey to Skolikaria, to set up my headquarters there with Themie, Bill Jordan and our wireless set and the rest of the officers until they were evacuated. I was feverish all that day, and, when I rested for the night in a squalid mud hut in a poor village called Kleidi, I was in a pretty bad state. The kind cottagers did what they could for me, and the next morning they got me a mule to ride on for the rest of my journey. It poured with rain, and I shivered on the mule most of the way to Skolikaria, too ill to walk.

On my arrival, I found that Themie, Bill Jordan and those due for evacuation had already arrived there from Megalohari, on the other side of the mountain. I went to bed. The next day I was worse, and Tom Barnes sent for Zervas' doctor, Dr. Papachristo. When he arrived he cupped me. It was a curious sensation to be treated with this ancient remedy. Half delirious, I watched the egg-cups being heated. One after the other they were pressed on to my pricked skin where, as the air cooled off, the vacuum painlessly drew quantities of blood from me.

On 16th January we received a warning rumour that the Italians were approaching in strength. Like all mountain rumours, we at first ignored this one. But, as the day wore on, it was confirmed beyond doubt. A strong force, which had come up into the foothills from Arta, was advancing steadily with the assistance of mortars, obviously bound for Zervas' temporary base at Skolikaria. A message arrived by runner from Zervas saying that, because of his unfortunate dispositions, he would be unable to prevent the enemy from reaching us, and that we must move back to Megalohari at once.

Although I was conscious of very little at the time, I learnt afterwards that I had pneumonia and that the doctor had considered me too ill to be moved. Young Themie Marinos, however, knew that my chances of living in the hands of the Italians were small, and he insisted on taking me to a safe hiding-place. From that moment, until I had finally recuperated, he made himself personally responsible for my safety.

When a mountain village was about to be raided by the enemy, a fatalistic and relatively quiet terror spread through it. Within a few minutes of the warning being given, an ever-intensifying stream of men, women, children and mules, all heavily laden with blankets, pots and pans, would be seen wending their different ways towards previously selected secret hiding-places higher up in the mountains. There most of them had already hidden their more valuable possessions and stocks of food, as a precaution against just such an eventuality. At times like these, mules, essential for carrying our wireless sets, batteries and charging engines, were extremely difficult to procure; and this eventually forced us to buy our own mules, so as to be mobile at all times.

In addition to procuring sufficient mules to move our wireless equipment, somehow or other Themie got one for me. Smothered in blankets I was lifted on to it and moved out of the village shortly before it became deserted, except for the aged and infirm, who were considered safe from Italian molestation. An hour later the Italians entered the village. They found Zervas' stores and other incriminating evidence, which there had not been time to hide or remove. They burnt half of the village to the ground.

Late that night Themie, Dr. Papachristo and I arrived at an isolated cottage off every frequented track. Only a handful of people knew where we had gone. The chance of our discovery by the Italians was remote. It seemed to me that we had been travelling for the best part of the day and all the previous night. Actually we had been on the journey only some eight hours in all. I was packed off to a comfortable, even though boarded and spring-less, bed in a warm room. Oblivious of my narrow escape and of my debt to Themie and exhausted by the journey, I vaguely remember going off to sleep without a care in the world, conscious only of the warmth of the room and the luxurious relief of the bed to my weary body.

Among the primitive surroundings of those rugged Greek mountains one would not have expected to find modern medicine. But the day after my arrival at Xyrokombos some 'M. & B.' which Zervas had discovered in his own private medical chest was brought to us in our hiding-place. Papachristo administered it to me, and from that moment onwards I never looked back. Tom Barnes had signalled my condition to Cairo, and late on 23rd January some additional medicines and medical comforts reached our hideout, having been safely dropped the night before.

My recovery was so quick that within a week of our escape from Skolikaria I was out of bed, and Dr. Papachristo returned to his home in Megalohari. But I was too weak at first to walk more than a few yards. As I regained my strength, the days passed quickly, most of them without incident and without news from the outside world. But on 25th January I was visited by two of Zervas' officers on their way to Epirus to organise EDES bands. Until that date, as we knew to our cost on our recent journey to the coast, there had been no andarte organisation whatsoever in that region.

I was anxious to rejoin my officers as soon as possible, and on 29th January, when I was strong enough to travel on a mule, Themie and I left our hiding-place. Breaking our journey at Megalohari, where we spent the night with Dr. Papachristo, we reached Tom Barnes and the others, then at Mesopyrgo, the following day.

On 2nd February a signal came in from SOE telling me that the Chiefs of Staff had directed that sabotage was to be applied to targets in the following order of priority:

1. Oil and transport of oil.
2. Minerals and transport of minerals.
3. Industrial sabotage without bangs (i.e. 'go-slow' tactics, faulty manufacture, etc.).

I immediately sent Nat Barker instructions to get Aris to attack railway trains, and impressed upon him the importance of an interview with Aris at Mesopyrgo, as I was not yet fit enough to journey to his headquarters.

Whilst I was convalescent and slowly regaining my strength, I tried incessantly to get the remainder of my officers evacuated to Cairo. During this period they had as hard a task as any. As I did not know when, where or how I might eventually be called upon by Cairo to evacuate them, I could not send them on any long mission. To all intents and purposes, therefore, they had nothing to do. This was hard on high-spirited men, who had volunteered specifically for the Gorgopotamos operation, and who were restless to return to the Middle East to get on with the war. Every suggestion which I made to Cairo was turned down as impracticable. In desperation I signalled to Chris, through Cairo, asking him to try to make arrangements for them to be evacuated by caique from somewhere on the east coast of Greece. But in due course Chris replied that this was impracticable for such a large party.

On 4th February a Greek officer named Colonel Saraphis, the leader of some independent bands in the northern Pindus Mountains, arrived unheralded, to discuss co-operation with Zervas and to find out what chances there were of obtaining supplies of arms, ammunition and clothing from the Middle East Command. Although a Republican of some fame because of his part in the 1935 anti-royalist revolution, I had not heard of him before. I should have paid more attention to his rather weak chin and evasive, watery blue eyes than to his aquiline features, military moustache and straight, short-cropped, dark but slightly greying hair, which gave him superficially quite a determined appearance. Upright, of average build and height, between forty and fifty years of age and dressed in a dilapidated knickerbocker suit, my first impression of him was that he looked like a reliable soldier.

Saraphis told me he had recently left Athens to organise an independent andarte movement in the northern Pindus in conjunction with a Major Kostopoulos, of whom I had already heard as being the leader of an independent band in that area. Although I subsequently discovered that he had already been a member of ELAS, Saraphis led me to believe that he held the same views as those of Zervas about EAM and ELAS.

I said that I didn't like the idea of another Resistance Movement with yet another political motive starting up in Greece, and that I wanted all bands to be non-political, militarily unified and unreservedly under the command of the C.-in-C. Middle East.

Saraphis agreed and went further. He suggested that if General Plastiras could be got back to Greece, he would be an ideal leader to unify purely national bands.

I was immediately struck by the idea of forming 'National Bands'. After further discussion, both Saraphis and Zervas agreed to my suggestion that SOE be asked to give the maximum support to all completely non-political 'National Bands' throughout Greece, wherever we could find or form them, and that when they were sufficiently strong we would invite ELAS to join this National Movement. Zervas decided forthwith to make his own movement non-political.

The next day, with the promise that I would arrange for aircraft to drop supplies in the area where he was forming his bands, Saraphis left us on his return journey to the north. He said he would let me know in a few days the exact point where he wanted these supplies to be dropped.

There had recently been an exchange of signals between me and Cairo about a certain Colonel Psaros, who was the military leader elect of a Republican Resistance Movement of the Centre in Athens, called EKKA or 'National and Social Liberation Movement'. EKKA bands existed in nucleus in the Parnassus Mountains. At present Psaros, who had no strong political leanings, was in Athens. SOE wanted to know whether I would agree to his taking to the field, and, if so, what tasks he should be given. My talks with Saraphis fitted in with this project. We would get Psaros to join in the 'National Bands' scheme.

Meanwhile Nat Barker reported that the recent supply of stores to Aris, and Nat's presence alongside him, appeared to be having a salutary effect and that Aris appeared more willing to co-operate with us. In my signal of 8th February about the 'National Bands' scheme, I therefore asked Cairo to continue supplying him, so long as he carried out our instructions. I asked for a British officer and a wireless link for both Saraphis and Psaros. I put forward Saraphis' and Zervas' suggestion that Plastiras should be got out of France for this purpose. I also pointed out that Saraphis, like Zervas, was in favour of controlling the Resistance from the field, rather than from Athens. I added that I reserved my final opinion on this matter until Chris got back from Athens.

Three days later I received SOE's wholehearted approval of our 'National Bands' scheme. But they rejected the suggestion that Plastiras should become its head on the grounds that he was too politically tainted as a Republican. They thought that greater unification would best be obtained by insisting on the organisation having national aims and acting under military orders, in conjunction with other forces in the Middle East. With this I entirely agreed.

On the same day as I had sent off my original signal about the proposal to form National Bands, a signal had come in from Cairo, informing me that a Major Sheppard, with an interpreter and a wireless operator, had been dropped on to andarte bands in the area of Mount Olympus where, so far as I knew, the only bands which existed belonged to ELAS. Although there was no actual understanding between SOE (Cairo) and myself, because it was not the original intention that I should stay on in Greece, they had promised Chris that they would not send any other parties of British officers into Greece without his prior agreement. Anyhow, I myself had only recently told them that the political situation was still delicate and, pending an agreement with Zervas, Aris and myself about the allocation of supply sorties, I had asked for nothing to be sent to Greece in the remotest way connected with military purposes without my approval.

When I signalled to Cairo for further details I was told that Sheppard was with ELAS bands, but that he would neither be under my command nor have anything to do with me. At this I was rather at a loss, because I had already suggested to Cairo a definite, and necessarily progressive, line of approach towards incorporating ELAS with our projected 'National Bands' scheme. Moreover, the Resistance Movements would infer from the despatch of this fresh British party into an EAM area that ELAS

Greek women help to carry canisters of stores after a parachute drop.

This snow drift would not have stopped a laden Greek woman of the mountains.

The snow-capped Pindos Mountains.

A Greek mountain family of Vlach (nomadic) descent in north-west Greece, 1943.

had the full support and moral backing of the Allies. However, during the ensuing few days I became fully occupied in a quick succession of events of a more urgent nature.

The following day an alarming signal arrived. Prometheus, our chief agent in Athens, was reported to have been captured by the Germans. I was indeed thankful for the relief brought by this signal in its last three words: "Chris is safe."

The Italians now started to make a series of energetic attempts to drive Zervas out of his mountain fastness. Much to his delight, they circulated pamphlets offering a reward of three hundred and fifty million drachmae—equivalent at that time to about £15,000 —for his head.

Night after night thick clouds hung around and below the mountains. When the weather was not actually bad in the mountains, there was often a 'cold front' between Greece and the coast of North Africa, which prevented aeroplanes getting through. Only four sorties succeeded in dropping us supplies that month. Meanwhile Zervas' band were continuously in action against the enemy, and, although they managed to hold up the Italians in the now snow-covered mountain passes, they were running seriously short of ammunition. I sent several urgent signals to Cairo, but not a quarter of our requirements could be met. From time to time the situation was critical. We hid all our stores which we did not require daily. We had mules standing by, often for days on end, ready to move our wireless at short notice.

Early in February we had taken the precaution of moving our headquarters from Mesopyrgo to a little village called Avlaki, three hours further south. The now flooded river Acheloos ran a little to the west of both these villages. But, whereas there was no means of crossing it near Mesopyrgo, within forty minutes of Avlaki there was an old Turkish pack-bridge which would give us a way out to the west should the enemy succeed in getting over the mountains from the direction of Arta.

Only the day after our move an Italian force caught Zervas on the wrong leg; some Alpini troops succeeded in out-flanking his most northerly positions, and they reached Megalohari before he could stop them. In the short time during which they were in occupation of the village they burnt twenty-five houses to the ground, including that of Dr. Papachristo.

Within two hours their incendiarism was completed, and they fled before Zervas' andartes. But the damage, alas, was done. The only redeeming feature that day was the arrival of a runner from the east with the news that Chris was on his way back from Athens.

A few days later I heard that Karpenisi, a relatively important little town in Central Roumeli, had been evacuated by its garrison of two thousand Italians, and that ELAS had walked in and taken it over without a shot being fired. This was indeed an encouraging sign of the times, showing, as it did, that the Italians were short of troops, were reinforcing essential garrisons on the Axis lines of communication, but were prepared to leave the rest to the andartes.

On 20th February Chris, leg-weary but undaunted, reached Avlaki. The complete story of his journey to Athens, his meetings with both the EAM Central Committee and some of the six Greek Colonels, his miraculous escape when Prometheus was captured and his subsequent extrication from Athens by EAM would themselves take up half a book. By sheer courage and combination of both good management and good luck he had loyally and successfully accomplished a most difficult and dangerous mission.

Chris' first attempt to meet the six Greek Colonels had been unsuccessful. They had failed to keep their appointment with him. Subsequently he met two of them.* He found that they knew

* One of these was Colonel Spiliotopoulos who towards the end of 1944 became Military Governor of Athens and who subsequently held other high posts.

little about the Resistance Movements and that they had few practical ideas about directing them. They appeared to have little conception of guerilla life in the mountains. Chris not only confirmed my impression that it would be quite impossible to run the Resistance Movements from Athens, but added that neither of the two Greek officers he met was suitable to take charge in the mountains. Both of them, he said, had dismissed the danger of civil war, believing that, after the collapse of Italy, Greece would be too busy absorbing the andartes within the structure of the regular army in order to fight the Germans outside Greece. They considered that their role was to prepare the nucleus for this new national army, and they disliked what they called the 'pin-pricks' of Zervas and Aris, in spite of the fact that they themselves had contributed nothing to the andarte movements. Chris' opinion was that the six Colonels would be more useful when Greece was liberated.

Of the five members of the Central Committee of EAM whom he met, Chris established that at least two were Communists: Yioryios Siantos, the acting Secretary General * of the Greek Communist Party, and Andreas Tzimas, once KKE Deputy for Macedonia. They apparently interpreted the Atlantic Charter to give Greece the right first to a plebiscite on the Constitution, and secondly to elections for a Parliament. They said that they feared that the British Government, under pressure of Greek Royalists, would restore the King and not allow a plebiscite. As regards para-military activities, they appeared only too willing to co-operate with the Middle East Command, provided they could have sole control of the Resistance Movements. They expressed their desire to send representatives to the Middle East to discuss their mutual plans for the future.

Chris had sent to Cairo a full report of his meetings in Athens

* Nikos Zakhariadhis, the Secretary General of the Greek Communist Party, KKE, spent most of the war in a German concentration camp.

by hand of one of Prometheus' assistants. He had given the latter most of the gold sovereigns which he had on him at the time, so that he could hire a caique and escape from the Gestapo, who were close on his heels. Several months later we learnt that this long report had either been lost or destroyed; anyhow, it never reached Cairo. Fortunately we sent a précis of it by wireless the day after Chris' return. I added a postscript, strongly backing EAM's wish to send representatives to the Middle East and asking for details to be arranged direct between Cairo and the Central Committee in Athens, through their own wireless link, which had by then been established.

The days immediately following Chris' return to Avlaki were again full of incident. On the actual night of his arrival an aircraft dropped stores and an additional wireless operator for us. The next day Zervas left us in order personally to direct operations against the Italians, who, with the moon again approaching its first quarter, were making another attempt to drive him and his andartes out of the mountains.

Over half of Zervas' men were armed with Mannlicher rifles. These had been made under licence in Greece for the Greek Army. Although Italian rifles took the same sized ammunition, Cairo was apparently unable to find enough for us. This meant that, in order to provide sufficient ammunition to maintain his men in action, we had to rearm them with different rifles. Because of their awkward length, only about eighty rifles, with sufficient ammunition, could be packed into containers and dropped from one Liberator aircraft. Rearmament was therefore a slow business, and when this new threat occurred on 21st February, because of the previous actions against the enemy, Zervas' andartes had less than fifty rounds per rifle. Thirty-six hours later he sent me a desperate request for more ammunition. Not only more ammunition, but fresh rifles with ammunition to fit them, and automatics, were needed. With our wireless set on 'continuous watch', in case we had to move across the Acheloos river to avoid the enemy, I repeatedly sent urgent messages to Cairo. During the following few days the RAF managed to get three aircraft through the bad weather, and just saved the situation.

At that time the aircraft in the Middle East were still operating from bases in the Delta area. The only types available that could make the long journey to Greece and back were Liberators, of which there were, unknown to me at that time, still only a total of four for 'special operations'. These had to supply Michailovic in Yugoslavia, as well as ourselves. With one of these four aircraft nearly always being overhauled, there were usually only three available for operations. Small wonder, therefore, that Cairo could not fully meet our requirements.

By 20th February the Italians had had enough of it and withdrew. We breathed more freely once again. The following day what turned out to be a long new directive started coming over the air to me from SOE (Cairo). By the next day it was all in, and deciphered, in front of me. It started off by listing the various awards for those who took part in the Gorgopotamos operation. Tom Barnes, Arthur Edmonds, Denys Hamson and Captain Michalli, Zervas' lieutenant, were each to receive the M.C.; Zervas and Aris ★ the O.B.E.; Chris and I each the D.S.O.; and dear Barba Niko the M.B.E. We were all particularly delighted about this last award. I was sorry that Tom had not been given the D.S.O. for his magnificent and all important part in the operation. I had asked that he should be. Zervas was delighted with the news of his decoration.

The signal then went on to explain that it was the intention of the Allies to attempt to capture Sicily as soon as the enemy had

---

★ Aris' award was subsequently suppressed because of his anti-British behaviour. Zervas was presented with the ribbon of his award at a small ceremony in the mountains a few months later. He received the actual award from the British Ambassador to Greece in Athens in 1953.

been driven out of Tunisia. *Simultaneously with this* (my own italics), the Middle East Command would attack the Dodecanese in order to break the 'iron ring' which barred the approaches to Southern Greece and as a possible preliminary to attacking the mainland. The chief object of an attack on the Dodecanese would be to divert troops, aircraft and ships away from Southern Italy and Russia to the Balkans. Even if the attack in the first instance was limited to the Dodecanese, it might develop into an invasion of the mainland or precipitate a general withdrawal of Axis troops. It was estimated that the attack on the Dodecanese would not take place before August of that year. Whatever date was finally fixed, I was warned that the enemy would probably appreciate the imminence of an attack at least two months before it took place. German troops and aircraft could therefore be expected to move south into Greece about June to replace or reinforce Italians, particularly in the Aegean and the Dodecanese Islands.

I was instructed to prepare for three possible cases:

1. *In event of invasion of the mainland of Greece:* to harass enemy lines of communication and generally to support invasion plans.

2. *If Axis troops attempted a general withdrawal from Greece or became disaffected:* to attack, harass and pursue them.

3. *Should neither of the above occur:* to be ready at a later date, and at the right moment, to promote general organised and co-ordinated revolt.

To implement plans for any of these three eventualities I was told to organise, train and equip the andartes throughout Greece as soon as possible up to the full extent of the equipment which the Middle East could supply. I was ordered to pay particular attention to the Peloponnese, Attica and the Southern Pindus. I was asked to forward my views as to the maximum area which I could effectively control. SOE (Cairo) said that they could send Area

Commanders, directly controlled from the Middle East, to any area which I could not effectively cover.

The directive then went on to point out that my short-term task was to prepare the andartes so that they could be used at any given moment for sabotaging communications should it be necessary to do so in support of our Allied strategy. In particular we were to be prepared to interfere with Axis reinforcements and maintenance. Meanwhile, the andartes were to be used for sabotage of the production and transport of chrome and nickel. But I was warned that we were not to become involved in vigorous sabotage now, to the detriment of our longer-term preparations for the summer.

SOE said that they would equip and build us up with arms, ammunition and explosives to their utmost ability during the next three months, and that they would distribute this material in accordance with my plan. Lack of Liberators and of air engines, and unforeseen delays in sending Halifaxes from England to replace them, were likely, however, to retard any increase in available sorties. Their plan for supplying the whole of Greece was as follows: March, eight sorties; April, twelve; May, sixteen; June, and each successive month until winter interfered, twenty-four. This, however, was the number of sorties which would be attempted and not necessarily the number that would be successful.

As the target date changed according to other European events, I would be kept informed. I was asked for my comments and, in due course, my plan. Finally I was asked to try to link up with the Albanian and Serbian Resistance Movements.

Ahead of us we now had a task indeed. I realised that it would take several months to accumulate the necessary explosives and additional British personnel who, backed up by andartes, could achieve this widespread sabotage in from three to six months' time. I gathered together all my officers, including those who were awaiting evacuation. I told them about our new task; I explained that it was now almost essential, in the interest of the war effort, to retain them in Greece; I hoped, quite frankly, that they would volunteer to stay on until the job was completed. With something definite ahead of them to be done, they all volunteered to stay.

Poring over large-scale maps of Greece by candlelight, I divided the mountainous regions up into areas, so that they most suitably fitted the known whereabouts of both targets and andartes; and, after a full day's thought on the problem, I signalled back my plan to Cairo.

I decided to divide the mountains of Greece into four regions, each to be under a lieutenant-colonel; Tom Barnes in charge in Epirus, Arthur Edmonds in Roumeli, Sheppard, who would now come under my command, in Olympus, and a fourth, Nick Hammond,[*] who had just arrived, in Macedonia. Chris, who until then had been Zervas' own liaison officer, would be replaced by Themie, and would become fully occupied as my second-in-command. Each senior British Liaison Officer—BLO—would have a number of other BLOs with wireless sets under his command, the number varying according to the quantity and location of targets and bands in his region. John Cook would be sent to gain contact with the Albanian Resistance.

I asked SOE (Cairo) if they would take over the Peloponnese. As an immediate measure, however, I offered to send Denys Hamson there. But, even without the Peloponnese, I pointed out that I wanted a lot more officers with wireless sets, so that I could send them to the many different bands which still had no British element with them.

A few days later I heard that my plan was accepted, and we went straight ahead with it.

[*] N. G. L. Hammond, D.S.O., now Headmaster of Clifton College.

CHAPTER VIII

EAM/ELAS Bid for Power

I WAS BY now sufficiently strong to undertake long journeys on foot again. On 7th March, when I was about to set out on a visit to Aris in Eastern Roumeli and to Psaros in the Parnassus Mountains where he was daily expected from Athens, a runner arrived from the north with infuriating news. Saraphis, Kostopoulos and all their officers had been taken prisoner by some bands of ELAS. Some of Kostopoulos' men who had previously deserted from ELAS had been killed outright. Of the remainder, those who had refused to join ELAS had been forcibly disarmed and sent home to their villages.

At first I refused to believe this. But within twenty-four hours one of Kostopoulos' officers, named Vlakhos, arrived at Avlaki with a handful of survivors and its truth was established beyond doubt.

A few weeks earlier, before Sheppard in Olympus had been put under my command, I had heard that an ELAS force of two or three hundred, under command of a man called Kozakas, had marched over from Olympus to the Northern Pindus to organise bands there. As soon as I had received my new directive from Cairo I had signalled Sheppard, through Cairo, to stop further transfers to ELAS, as they would all be needed in the Olympus area for sabotage work in the near future. But I was too late to prevent the clash between ELAS and Saraphis' bands.

Shortly after reaching the Pindus, Kozakas had got in touch with Saraphis under the pretext of joining up forces with him.

On 4th March, Saraphis and all his andartes had paid a courtesy visit to the village in which Kozakas and his bands were billeted, to celebrate the signature of an agreement to co-operate. During the night, Kozakas' men, without warning, had simultaneously crept into every cottage in which Saraphis' men were billeted, and had disarmed them without a shot being fired. Only Vlakhos and the few with him had escaped to tell the tale

I immediately sent a strongly worded signal to Cairo, to be re-transmitted to the Central Committee of EAM, ordering them to release Saraphis and his officers and to hand back the arms to his andartes. Until they did so, I urged Cairo to send no stores whatsoever to any ELAS bands anywhere in Greece.

Zervas beseeched me to allow him to march northwards and attack Kozakas, but I instructed him in the name of the C.-in-C. not to allow any of his men to cross the Acheloos river. Meanwhile rumours kept on coming in that Kozakas was actually marching south, and skirmishes between outlying parties of EDES and ELAS bands, just within the perimeter of what Zervas regarded as his territory, became daily more frequent. If civil war in the mountains was to be prevented, I had to take immediate action; for, although Zervas, with his better officered andartes, should eventually be able to overcome any force that EAM/ELAS could at that time have pitted against him, such a conflict would not only result in a severe setback to the Resistance Movements; it might even frustrate the execution of our plans for widespread sabotage in the early summer.

On 8th March, the day I received confirmation of the ELAS outrage, I signalled Cairo that EAM appeared to have decided that now was the time to clear all obstacles for the establishment of a Communist regime at the end of the war. I pointed out that until now Zervas had acted with the greatest patience towards EAM. If EAM refused to come to heel Zervas, I said, was prepared, with the full backing and the publicity of the Middle East, to take over all military forces. I considered half-measures now might eventually lead to civil war and the loss of any further assistance from Greece towards the Allied war effort.

During the ensuing few days there was an intense exchange of telegrams between myself and Cairo. SOE insisted that I should not irrevocably break off relations with EAM. They kept on sending me repeats of telegrams which Sheppard was sending them about the character of EAM in the area of Mount Olympus. These descriptions were couched in the most glowing terms. ELAS, he reported, had "no political aims whatsoever", and was "purely a military Resistance Movement". The andartes did not discuss politics. The leaders had no wish to compete or come into conflict with any other organisations in the mountains. EAM was a genuine body formed to free Greece, and for this purpose uniting all political parties from Communist to Royalist.

Sheppard, Cairo went on, reported that Saraphis was suspected of Italian associations. It was therefore conceivable that the ELAS bands, which had recently disarmed Saraphis' andartes and were now threatening Zervas, were fighting not for the Communists but under the illusion that they were attacking traitors. Alternatively, if the leaders of ELAS were fighting for Communism, this was concealed from their rank and file.

In another signal Cairo almost insinuated that I had got hold of the wrong end of the stick, that the ELAS bands on the frontiers of Zervas' domains were possibly incited by Zervas to action against him. I replied in firm language that I thought that Sheppard was having dust thrown in his eyes; that I was as good as convinced that EAM was controlled by Communists; and that its leaders had ulterior motives in that they wished, with the aid of their ELAS forces, to overcome at once and for ever all possible competitive Resistance Movements in the mountains.

Cairo then submitted that the information at their disposal regarding EAM indicated that it originated as a result of the fusion of two blocs, Communists and Socialists, and that there was a strong indication that they had, or were about to, split. As it might be possible to get the Socialist element to join our 'National Bands', I was ordered to attempt to detach them from the Communists. SOE considered it essential that I should satisfy myself about the true issues of the present crisis, and whether it really was an attempt by the Communists to seek complete control of EAM.

On 9th March, as a result of a suggestion by Chris that it would help to clear the air in Cairo, Zervas sent over our wireless a message of greetings and loyalty to the Greek King and Government.

The next day I reiterated to Cairo that I was convinced that, both in relation to our short-term military interests, as well as to the long-term political interests of Greece, we should immediately take the firmest possible line. I had the greatest hopes, I added, that immediate and stern measures would not only prevent civil war, but that they would eventually bring ELAS into the fold to assist us militarily in the future. I reported that Zervas would not declare open conflict against EAM without full Allied backing. I impressed upon SOE the great importance I attached to obtaining an immediate reply to our ultimatum to the EAM Central Committee, which I assumed * had already been retransmitted by them to Athens. I considered that any delay in their final decision might lead to disaster.

Meanwhile, Vlakhos, with his dozen andartes, was still with us at Avlaki. They were a demoralised group of men, and I longed to give them something useful to do. Denys, who was earmarked for the Peloponnese to start developing 'National Bands' there, was also still with me, impatiently awaiting a guide. Sufficiently confident that the Central Committee of EAM would ultimately order the reinstatement of Saraphis' bands, I decided to send Denys

---

* I never discovered whether SOE (Cairo) did in fact transmit this ultimatum to the Central Committee of EAM.

back to the Northern Pindus with Vlakhos and his band, to defy ELAS's high-handed action and await the aircraft with stores due for Saraphis in a few days' time. I realised it was a gamble; but I considered it one worth taking.

The next day, 12th March, I took up the issue again with Cairo. I pointed out that the EAM leaders appeared to regard English weapons primarily as a means of strengthening their control of Greece and only secondarily as the means of contributing to the war effort. The fact that we were fighting their enemy, Fascism, happened to suit them. The great majority of ELAS andartes, I reported, differed in no way from those of EDES, but, being in ignorance of the Communistic aims of their leaders, they blindly enslaved themselves to obey them on an oath, the penalty for the breaking of which was death. After the liberation of Greece I believed it was the intention of the EAM leaders to appoint a Government from EAM. I stressed the fact that EAM would seek to gain time by specious excuses for their calculated recent behaviour. I believed that Zervas' recent message to the Greek King and Government was sincere. Greece, I pointed out, was now in two camps; one doubtfully and the other certainly loyal to Britain. As tactfully as I could, I pointed out that the policy which Cairo now indicated, of continuing support to EAM in an attempt to wean the more moderate elements from the Movement, might make the loyalty of both doubtful, as each would resent us supplying the other. I urgently requested confirmation of their policy before I left for Eastern Roumeli on 14th March.

I got an acknowledgement the following day. The authorities in Cairo were "most interested" in the contents of my signal. British and Greek authorities and recent escapees, they said, confirmed that our policy of 'National Bands' was not only preferable, but also feasible. But I was given no further instructions nor any authority to impose the necessary stern measures upon EAM. The same day I received a signal that an EAM mission might proceed to Cairo, and that if they wished to continue to London, they might do so.

The next day matters took a turn for the worse. Zervas came into my little room in a cottage at Avlaki trembling with rage. In his hand he held out a letter.

"Read this to the Brigadier," he said to Chris, who was standing beside me.

Chris read out a rude and menacing ultimatum from Kozakas accusing Zervas of giving refuge to some of Saraphis' men—presumably Vlakhos and his band, who had already left for the north again—and ordering Zervas to hand them over forthwith. If he failed to do so, Kozakas would attack him and "drive him and all his forces into the sea".

That evening, 14th March, having received no more positive instructions, and realising that I could not hold Zervas in check much longer, Chris and I decided that we would have to act on our own, observing as far as possible the wishes of the authorities in Cairo and their previous instructions to me. Late into the night we slowly evolved a document which came to be known as 'The First Military Agreement of the Greek Resistance Forces with the Middle East'. Although subsequently amended in minor respects, its full text was as follows:

> "1. All andarte bands are to be known for military purposes as 'NATIONAL BANDS', which title will be the only one used by the Allies.
>
> "2. Greece is to be divided into areas. A competent leader, recognised by mutual agreement of Brigadier Eddie★ as representative of GHQ, Middle East, and of the Greeks, will be appointed military commander of each area. Each commander will be solely responsible for all military deci-

★ In the mountains we were all generally known by our Christian names, even for formal purposes.

sions in his area. All 'National Bands' in the same area will co-operate fully under the military commander's orders.

"3. The 'National Bands' of one area will not enter another area except by mutual agreement of respective military commanders.

"4. The 'National Bands' of one area will give maximum assistance to those of another area on request by the other area commander concerned, or by GHQ, Middle East, through their liaison officers.

"5. No member of any 'National Band' is ever to mention politics in public. Every member is to be free to have his own political views.

"6. There must be no barbarism against anyone by any member of 'National Bands'. No one must be executed without fair trial and without the nearest British liaison officer being made fully aware of the facts.

"7. Any Greek andarte who, up to the date of the signature of this Agreement by his own previous recognised leaders, has transferred his allegiance to another 'National Band', will be given complete amnesty.

"8. All Greeks enlisted in the future will be free to choose which 'National Band' they will join.

"9. If, in the opinion of the British Liaison Staff, there is any failure to carry out the above Agreement, GHQ, Middle East will immediately order the cessation of supply of war material until the failure is rectified.

"10. These terms are to be given publication in the Press of the Resistance Movements, to be read to all andartes, and will be recognised by GHQ, Middle East."

In short, this was an agreement which I intended all bands in the mountains of Free Greece to sign, in order to qualify them for material support by the Allies. In itself it was simple; for its signatories merely bound themselves to allow all bands, to whatever organisation they belonged, to exist unmolested by them, and to be free to carry out operations against the enemy, in accordance with instructions received from the Middle East Command, through me or any of my officers. In return they would be supplied with arms, ammunition and other essentials by the Allies so far as was within their means. We made a few copies of this Agreement; Chris took one for Zervas; another we got ready for transmission to Cairo on our next contact the following morning.

I wrote out a short signal for Cairo, informing them of the threatening and insulting ultimatum which Kozakas had delivered to Zervas, and telling them that an ELAS force of several hundreds from all parts of Thessaly was reported to be approaching Zervas. Although I was convinced that EAM wished to establish complete Communist control now, I said that I was proposing to leave forthwith to present the threatening ELAS bands with an ultimatum based upon their instructions. I believed that the terms of this ultimatum would be acceptable to Zervas, and we were going to insist that he should sign the same document. I asked for their confirmation that we should from now on adopt the sole title of 'National Bands' for the andartes and their full backing in both material support and BBC propaganda for them and none else.

By the time this message had been despatched I had already set out with Themie. In my pocket I carried several copies of the 'Military Agreement'. I was intent upon finding Kozakas and getting both him and the leaders of all other bands I met to sign it. I had little enough time to spare in order to save the lives of Saraphis and his other officers. I might already be too late.

CHAPTER IX

Volte-face by Saraphis

ON THE second afternoon of our journey northwards, in a snow-covered pass a little to the south of a village called Mesounda, we suddenly came upon a group of five andartes. They were wearing the usual ELAS insignia on their hats. They seemed to have a rather guilty look about them, and Themie whispered in my ear: "They are guarding the pass, and watching for any more of Saraphis' andartes escaping southwards to Zervas."

Themie's supposition proved to be correct. After trudging a few yards farther through the deep snow, there, a little bit to one side of the track, was another ELAS andarte, this time lying on the ground and manning an LMG, facing the way we were going.

We spent the next night in Merophilo. The village doctor, in whose house we stayed, told me that the local schoolmaster was, like many others in the mountain villages, the senior local member of EAM, but that there was a considerable division of opinion in the village as regards the Resistance Movements, a few of the younger men supporting EAM, all the older ones being much against it. I formed the impression that a good many in this district were at heart Royalists, but that they didn't like to admit it to a stranger. I learnt that Denys and Vlakhos were at a place called Mesokhora. As I would be passing near there the following day, I sent Denys a message by 'phone, asking him to meet me on my route. We had been travelling fast all that day, and had covered a considerable distance towards the southern edge of the Thessaly

Plain, where I expected to find the main ELAS bands of Kozakas. I was anxious to meet Kozakas face to face as soon as possible because every hour's delay might mean that I would arrive too late, not only to save the lives of Saraphis, Kostopoulos and their officers, but also to prevent Kozakas embarking irrevocably upon an attack on Zervas.

We set off early the following morning. I was extremely stiff, as a result of my first serious walking since my illness. Up and up we climbed to a 6,000-feet-high, snow-covered pass, one of the highest in those rugged but beautiful Pindus Mountains, eventually crossing it and descending to a little village called Vathyremma, which nestled in a small hollow a few hundred feet below. Here Denys intercepted me. I handed him a copy of the Military Agreement and instructed him to get Vlakhos to sign it.

Themie and I made an early start again on the 17th, and late in the afternoon we reached Porta, a large village at the foot of the mountains on the south-west edge of the Plains of Thessaly.

My unheralded entry into the village created quite a stir. The inhabitants had apparently not seen a British officer since we withdrew from Greece in 1941, and I was given a most enthusiastic welcome. Within five minutes of my arrival everybody seemed to be in the streets, and they were only finally dispersed by an officer of ELAS, who approached and asked me what I was doing there. I explained to him briefly who I was, and that I wanted to get into touch with Kozakas immediately—that night, in fact. He asked me if I was expected, and I replied that I was not. He told me that Kozakas was on the move, but not far away in the Plains, and that he would get a horse and ride off to find out where exactly he was. As soon as he had discovered in which village he was spending the night, he would come back and guide me to him.

Two to three hours later another mounted ELAS officer galloped back into the village, and within a few minutes Themie and

I had been given horses and were following him in the gathering
darkness at a brisk canter across level, grass-covered tracks, in a
north-easterly direction. Shortly after nine o'clock we arrived at
Varibobi, which lay about five miles out in the open and unprotected plain. I was quickly escorted to the house in which
Kozakas was spending the night. I was led upstairs into a small
room, and introduced to him. He appeared to be extremely
surprised to see me.

Straight away I got down to the object of my visit. I asked him
where Saraphis and his other officers were. In the name of the
C.-in-C., who had authorised me to arm his bands, I demanded
their immediate release. Kozakas replied that only the day before
he had received instructions to send these officers under escort to
Roumeli, where they were going to be tried as collaborators with
the enemy. I asked him who had given him these instructions.
"Karayioryis, * the leader of EAM in Central Greece," he replied,
"I am expecting him here any day now."

I asked him what evidence he had against Saraphis and the
others. "Plenty," he said. I demanded to see or hear it. He said
that he could provide me with irrefutable documentary evidence
that Saraphis had been in touch with the Italians in Trikkala. I
refused to believe this until I saw it. He promised to produce it;
but neither he, nor anyone else ever did so. Long afterwards,
however, I learnt that this accusation was based upon the fact that
an organisation in Athens which had sponsored Saraphis' original
activities in the mountains used to communicate to him through
the Greek Mayor of Trikkala, called Sarandis, who, not unnaturally, had dealings with the enemy.

I then went on to explain to Kozakas the ill effects his threats
against Zervas were having on the andarte war against the com-

---

* Karayioryis, whose real name was Yiphtodimopoulos, played a leading
part in the civil war of 1947–9 but was later disgraced and court-martialled by
the KKE.

mon enemy. Kozakas replied by asking what else could he do if
Zervas was hiding andartes who had been collaborators under
Saraphis. I told him that Zervas was not hiding any of Saraphis'
men, and that Vlakhos and those few who had sought shelter with
him had already returned to re-form their bands in the Northern
Pindus. I also stressed the fact that the Middle East Command was
allotting a steadily increasing number of aircraft for supplying
arms to the andartes, and that not only he, but no ELAS bands
would get any of these supplies if they attacked Zervas or the
bands of any other organisation in the mountains. I pulled out of
my pocket a copy of the 'Military Agreement', saying that I would
be only too happy to ask the Middle East to supply him with arms
if he would first of all give back the arms to Saraphis' men and
then sign this Agreement and abide by it.

He replied that he was very sorry that it was too late to hand
back the arms. Quite a number of Saraphis' andartes had already
willingly joined the ranks of ELAS. Those who were unwilling to
do so had been disarmed and sent back to their villages. Their
arms had already been distributed to his own men, and he could
not possibly take them away from them. To do so would be a
personal insult to those who now bore them.

Kozakas then read the 'Military Agreement' carefully. Chris
had translated copies into Greek before I left Avlaki. When he had
finished, he remarked: "Well, there is nothing unreasonable in
this." I asked him to sign it. He immediately replied that he was
unable to do so without Karayioryis' authority.

"But I am prepared to abide by it in principle," he added, "and
if what you say about Zervas not sheltering any of Saraphis' men
is true, I will issue orders tomorrow morning to withdraw my
bands from the areas adjoining Zervas."

Kozakas then accused me of giving an unfair preponderance of
material support to Zervas in comparison with what we were
giving ELAS. "Look," he said, "your headquarters is with Zervas.

Moreover, all of your officers are with him. Why haven't we seen you before?"

Late into the night I recounted to him the sequence of events since the Gorgopotamos operation; that it had been intended that only Chris and Themie should remain in Greece, and the rest should be evacuated. I told him about our journey to the coast, and my recent illness; that we had sent a liaison officer and supplies to Aris as soon as this could be arranged; and I pointed out that Sheppard had already been some weeks with ELAS in the Olympus area. After a lot of talking I think I eventually convinced Kozakas that I was speaking the truth. Anyhow, he seemed more satisfied. It was well past midnight when we parted, and I had the feeling that our long conversation had been worth while. Themie and I were given a room to ourselves. Tired out by my three days' hard travelling, I was soon asleep.

The next day I moved westwards with Kozakas and the band of about a hundred men with him to a place called Prodhromos, on the edge of the Plain. I was glad to have the mountains close to me again. In the village where we had spent the previous night there was little to stop the unheralded arrival across the plains of mobile columns of the enemy from large garrison towns like Trikkala, and I had felt extremely conscious of our nakedness. Late in the afternoon, when Karayioryis had not arrived, I got Themie to enquire into the cause of his delay. Kozakas could not say why he had not yet arrived, but he assured us that news had been received that he was on his way. I was told, moreover, that the trial of Saraphis and his officers would not, in fact could not, take place until some days after Karayioryis' arrival, because he would be going through the evidence against them before sending it on to Roumeli. It was possible, even, that representatives of the Central Committee might come up to the mountains to preside at the trial. Reassured somewhat that Saraphis and the others were in no immediate danger of death, and wanting to get Karayioryis to sign the 'Military Agreement', I decided to await his arrival.

I waited three days. During that time I met a good many ELAS leaders. I had long talks with each of them, explaining our policy and our preparedness to arm all bands who would fight against the common enemy and not against each other. Several of them asked me to get Zervas to publish his political aims. They said that they did not trust him. I assured them that Zervas had agreed with me to drop all politics in favour of joining up with the National Bands. I managed to get in one or two private talks with different local Greeks, who were not members of any andarte organisation. A few of these Greeks told me that the people wished that Zervas would come to Thessaly; that they were afraid of EAM; and that there would be a very different political opinion in these EAM controlled mountain villages when Greece was freed.

By 24th March, Karayioryis had still not arrived. I decided to wait no longer and to set out for Roumeli, thinking that, if Kozakas was not deliberately delaying my departure, at any rate he had inadequate information about Karayioryis' movements.

Themie and I travelled by mule as far as Mouzaki, a few miles east of Porta. From Mouzaki we continued our journey in a little combination motor-cycle: my first experience of motor travel since I had left Egypt, six months before. After a bitterly cold drive we reached Karditsa, some twenty miles to the east, well into the Thessaly Plain. This was the first town I had been in since I had arrived in Greece. It had several thousand inhabitants, and was at that time only occasionally visited by enemy armoured car or cavalry patrols from the larger garrison towns in the Plain. There were only a few ELAS andartes billeted in the town itself, but there was a strong EAM organisation there, including an active printing press. The few andartes there would disappear as soon as they received warning of any visit by the enemy. To avoid reprisals no sabotage whatsoever was carried out in the district.

Karditsa, therefore, had so far been unmolested by the enemy. In fact, driving through its streets it was difficult to believe that I was in a town in enemy-occupied country. The shops were open; the streets and the cafés were full. The air of unreality was completed by Themie asking me if I would permit him to look up an old aunt of his. Her home was only a few yards off our route. Watching the dear old lady's joyful but otherwise quite unaffected greeting of her nephew in her pleasantly furnished sitting-room, I had almost to pinch myself to make sure that the scene was real and I was not dreaming about a peace-time holiday abroad.

In due course I was directed to the local headquarters of EAM. Here I was given an old Austin car to take me on the next stage of my journey to a little place called Smokovo, some fifteen miles to the south-east of Karditsa, on the edge of the Plain.

In peace-time Smokovo had many visitors, because of its natural hot sulphur baths. We drove up to a large, deserted hotel. On its ground floor there were thirty or forty cubicles, in each of which there was a large marble bath. Themie managed to find the caretaker, and not long after our arrival both of us had the exhilarating experience of a real hot bath, foaming with sulphur. Although the smell was unpleasant, the bath itself was most refreshing and warming after our cold and bumpy journey.

In the middle of the night we were woken up by the noisy return of the car in which we had arrived the previous evening. The driver brought a message from the EAM leader in Karditsa, informing me that Karayioryis had at last turned up and that he was waiting to see me. Unwillingly I decided to retrace my steps to meet him. We got back to Karditsa at about ten o'clock in the morning, and were then driven on to the south-east into the countryside. At a level crossing, where the narrow-gauge railway to Kalambaka crossed our road, we pulled up and a man dressed in dusty civilian clothes, with badly worn shoes, got into the car beside me and introduced himself as Karayioryis. At his request we drove on to a roadside café, where we could talk in reasonable comfort.

He told me that he had only reached Karditsa the previous evening, having come on foot all the way from Olympus, and that he had been with Sheppard when he learnt of my arrival at Kozakas' headquarters. Small wonder that he had not arrived sooner! He spoke quite good French in which language we conversed throughout, without the need, therefore, of Themie as interpreter. He was obviously a cultured and much-travelled man. I learnt later that he was by profession a lawyer. He confirmed that Saraphis, Kostopoulos and four other officers had been sent down to Aris' headquarters in Roumeli to await their trial by representatives of EAM from Athens. He admitted that he had not yet seen documentary evidence against them, but he assured me that this would be forthcoming at the trial.

I did not mince my words in explaining to him the serious view which I took of the situation in general, as a result of EAM/ELAS excesses. He appeared surprised when I told him that I knew that the Central Committee of EAM was dominated by Communists, and he denied it flatly. When I named two of them he remarked: "Well, maybe it is true, but that has nothing to do with me."

I recounted once more the whole story of how it came about that the British Mission was in the mountains of Greece, and what it was doing there. I told him that it was my firm intention to stand no further nonsense, and that he must make up his mind there and then to call off his andartes from threatening Zervas and get down to more serious work against the real enemy. I explained what ELAS should do in Thessaly in order to qualify for material support by the British. I also told him that Sheppard was now under my orders, and that I was requesting Cairo to send no more stores to any ELAS bands until they had signed the 'Military Agreement', which I then showed to him.

Karayioryis read through the document, and then, much as

Kozakas had done, remarked: "I agree in principle with every-thing that is in this paper. But I am afraid I am not empowered to sign it. It will have to go to Athens."

By that time, knowing a little about the character and organisa-tion of EAM, I managed to stifle the sense of frustration which I was continually feeling. Realising the importance of gaining Karayioryis' confidence, in order to make use of the widespread organisation of EAM and ELAS in Thessaly to assist us in our sabotage action against the enemy in a few months' time, I did my best to achieve what little I could from this chance interview. Before we parted, as in my talk with Kozakas, I felt that I had con-vinced Karayioryis that I was sincere and that my viewpoint was an impartial one. For his part, he assured me that I need no longer worry about Zervas. He would issue orders forthwith to his men not to attack. But, when I demanded their withdrawal from the Pindus Mountains back to the area of Mount Olympus, he told me that he was afraid he could not do this, because he had been instructed by Athens to carry out their transfer. He assured me, however, that, pending the signature of the 'Military Agreement' by the Central Committee of EAM, I could tell Zervas that he, or anyone else, was free to organise any bands they wanted in the Pindus, and that they would be unmolested by ELAS. After a talk which had lasted for two or three hours without a break we parted and I motored back to Smokovo with Themie.

Early next morning, 26th March, we set out on foot southwards across the low, rolling, fir-covered hills which separate the Thes-saly Plain from the valley of the River Sperkhios. At midday we halted in quite a large and prosperous-looking village named Ren-dina. The occupants had been forewarned of our arrival by tele-phone that morning from Smokovo, and they had laid on a most lavish reception. A guard of honour of some andartes all in pic-turesque Evzone uniform with spotless white kilts, was paraded in our honour, and, after attending a short service in the village church, we were given a sumptuous meal before we could make good our escape. The andartes were more like village guards than active guerillas. They owed allegiance to no particular Resistance Movement. A high proportion of the villagers, however, were ardent supporters of Plastiras. Several of them told me that they wished to form independent bands, if only they could be given arms and ammunition by the Allies, and they expressed their fear of being forced to join EAM and ELAS against their will.

It was nearly midnight when, shortly after crossing the road from Lamia to Karpenisi, we reached the farmhouse of a retired army captain, a friend of Nat Barker's. Here we rested comfortably for the remainder of the night. Our host telephoned to Nat, warning him that we expected to arrive towards midday the following day.

A four hours' journey next morning brought us uneventfully to the prosperous village of Gardiki, in which we had spent a night on our journey westwards with Zervas after the Gorgopotamos operation. Here I found not only Nat Barker and Arthur Edmonds, whom I had sent over from Valtos to help plan further sabotage operations in Roumeli, but also two New Zealanders, Captain Donald Stott and Sergeant Morton, who had been dropped a few nights before, for liaison with Colonel Psaros in the Parnassus Mountains.

I discovered, much to my relief, that Saraphis and his other officers were only two hours' away, and in no immediate danger, awaiting prosecution witnesses for their trial by EAM.

That afternoon a party of ELAS andartes brought a so-called Australian in to us for interrogation. They had picked him up two days' journey to the east of Gardiki. He had told them in faltering Greek that his name was 'Captain Benson', that he was an Australian escaped prisoner of war, and that he wished to be put in touch with the British. Apparently, when the andartes had told him that they would bring him to Arthur's headquarters, he had said that he did not wish to be taken to the headquarters of the British, but would be quite satisfied to meet any English officer, however humble. The andartes, however, had not been deterred, and had brought him to Gardiki for Arthur Edmonds to interrogate.

When this wretched man was shown in to me he presented an almost incredible appearance. On his head he wore a badgeless British army hat. On one of the shoulders of his khaki greatcoat there was a solitary pip, and on the other an Australian hat-badge. When I started interrogating him in English he replied in Greek that he did not speak English, and that he only spoke 'Australian'. I immediately called in Arthur Edmonds, telling him that the New Zealanders and Australians spoke the same language. When he found that he could not converse with Arthur, he asked to speak to me alone in confidence. I turned everyone out of the room, except for one armed guard, the Palestinian Arab, Michael, who had come over from Valtos with Arthur Edmonds, and was then a sergeant.

'Benson' unfolded his story, which Michael translated to me. He said that he was really a Greek, and that he had been sent into the mountains by some people in Athens to warn me that EAM were planning a civil war against all other andarte movements. When I asked him who had sent him, he gave me the name of somebody of whom I had never heard. I told him that I would check the truth of his story, which I doubted. Meanwhile, he would be put into the custody of ELAS. At this last remark his face became ashen grey, and he pleaded with me to do anything with him rather than hand him back to ELAS. I said that I would only grant this request if he told me why he had at first pretended to be an Australian. He could not explain this; for both he and I knew that, if his sole reason was to gain contact with me, he had a far greater chance of doing so dressed as an ordinary Greek. A few weeks later it was confirmed beyond doubt that

'Benson' was a dupe of the Gestapo, and a pretty low-grade one at that. He had been sent up into the mountains by the Germans in Athens to pick up information about us. It was an incredibly poor piece of work. He paid the penalty of all spies.

By means of Arthur Edmonds' wireless set at Gardiki I was at last able to get on the air again with Cairo, and, through Cairo, with Chris. I sent a full report of my recent activities to both, and from Chris I received news that Zervas had signed the National Bands agreement.

The next day I sent off Themie, with Donald Stott, to the Parnassus Mountains to reconnoitre and report what ELAS and EKKA bands were already in that area. Having learnt that Saraphis' trial would not take place for several days, I decided to await the arrival of Aris, and his political adviser Tassos Eleftherias, who, journeying from the south-west, were shortly due to pass through Gardiki.

The following day, 30th March, Tassos, a young Cretan, arrived. I had some lengthy talks with him about the misbehaviour of EAM and ELAS. But the force of my argument was somewhat diminished by the news, received late that night, that ELAS andartes, in accordance with my recently issued instructions, had successfully attacked some chromium mines near Domokos and had put them out of action for many weeks. At the same time I learnt that another band of ELAS had captured a mixed bag of German and Italian troops in the plains west of Lamia.

Learning from Tassos that Aris did not intend to pass through Gardiki, the next day I left with him for Kolokythia, where Saraphis and his officers were held prisoners.

In a village through which we passed that day I was accosted by a shabbily dressed but obviously educated Greek. He turned out to be Professor Alexis Seferiades, whose name had been given to me in Cairo shortly before our departure the previous autumn.

He told me a long story about how he had been briefed by Prometheus to arrange for our reception near the village of Koukouvista; that he and his band of helpers had been fully prepared to receive us on the night of 28th September; but that they had been betrayed, and the Italians had raided Koukouvista the day before. He and all the menfolk of the village had—as we already knew—been taken away as prisoners, and he had been sent to Athens. He had only recently been released, after the Italians had failed to prove anything against him. Small wonder that we had seen no signals when we flew over Greece that night and again two nights later.

On my arrival at Kolokythia that evening, I found Aris already there. A representative of the Central Committee of EAM had just arrived from Athens: in connection, I presumed, with the trial of Saraphis. This was more than welcome news. At last it looked as though I was going to be able to talk to a member of EAM who was empowered to make decisions.

The next day I had two lengthy sessions with this Greek, an intelligent middle-aged man whose real name was Andreas Tzimas, but who had adopted the andarte pseudonym of 'Evmaios'. Before the war, when Communist Deputy for Macedonia, he had been imprisoned by Metaxas; and, although less than forty years of age, the greater part of his hair had already turned white, apparently due to the trials he had undergone in prison. Some months later, when the Germans had occupied Athens, he had managed to obtain his release from prison by feigning to be a Yugoslav Macedonian. It was he who had been largely responsible for Chris' safe evacuation from Athens, after he had just missed being captured with Prometheus by the Germans.

I explained to Evmaios my indignation at the recent misbehaviour of ELAS in the Northern Pindus, and the insult to GHQ, Middle East which they had caused by their outrageous disarmament of National Bands which owed allegiance to the Allies. I asked him on what authority they had acted; and also on what authority Saraphis and his officers were still held prisoner. I told him that I would report his answers to Cairo and that, unless they were entirely satisfactory, I would recommend that the full facts be published by all the Allies; furthermore, that I would recommend to Cairo that we should cease to supply and to have anything more to do with EAM and ELAS until just retribution had been made.

Evmaios began by excusing EAM and ELAS by means of false arguments, with which he had obviously been primed by Aris, or by other ELAS officers he had recently met in the mountains. He claimed that the British were giving preferential treatment to Zervas, who, he said, had been bribed by British gold to take to the mountains, and who was out to become a military dictator of Greece, like Metaxas. I refuted most of his accusations with facts which he was unable to deny. Evmaios then referred to the unrepresentative Greek Government, which, with the King, had recently arrived back in the Middle East from London. He blamed Great Britain for supporting the King, who, by setting up the Metaxas dictatorship in 1936, had proved himself to be a traitor to Greece. I told him that this was nothing to do with me, and that I was only here in Greece for military reasons. Lastly I presented him with a copy of the 'Military Agreement', and told him that our final condition of support to ELAS was the signature by ELAS of this document, and their strict observance of it. He took it away, telling me he would come back the following morning to talk about it after he had read it through.

In the morning Evmaios came back to my cottage and told me that he personally had no objection to the Agreement in principle, but that he objected to British Liaison Officers having a controlling influence over what should be an entirely Greek matter, namely Greek Resistance. He also objected to the name 'National Bands', because ELAS had had their name long before any other bands existed, and he did not see why they should have to change it.

I asked him to sign the Agreement unaltered, according to the wishes of the Middle East Command. He replied in the way to which I was getting accustomed, that he would have to take it back to Athens for discussion with the Central Committee, without whose authority he was not empowered to act. Once again I was frustrated.

I asked him what his intentions were as regards Saraphis and his officers. He replied that this matter was under consideration, and that he would give me the reply later in the day.

That afternoon Denys Hamson unexpectedly arrived with yet another infuriating story. Not more than a day after I had left Kozakas in the Thessaly Plains some of his bands had surrounded Vlakhos' andartes and had disarmed them. Both Vlakhos and Denys had been warned about their approach. Vlakhos, with a few of his officers, had deserted his men and had fled into hiding. Denys had gone to meet ELAS. He had been rudely received by them and then allowed to return unmolested to my headquarters at Avlaki. Chris had sent him on post haste to me to tell me the story in his own words. He was still bubbling with indignation.

I immediately summoned Evmaios and told him briefly that this was the last straw. Evmaios was unmoved. He took some of the wind out of my sails by coolly announcing that he planned to set Saraphis and all his officers free the following morning, and that from then onwards they could do as they wanted. The whole matter, like this new incident, had been "a great mistake". He would see that Kozakas was severely admonished.

Whether ELAS in the mountains were under the strict control of EAM in Athens; whether they were acting in accordance with EAM orders; or whether they were out of control and acting according to the whims of their local commanders, their recent behaviour all over the mainland of Greece was sufficient to convince me more than ever before that whatever and however just their reasons, they were primarily in arms against any competition by other Greek movements, and only secondarily in arms against the common enemy. I had been instructed, however, not to break off relations with them, and I had continually to bear in mind that, within the next two or three months, I had to have a widespread plan for sabotage ready for execution. EAM already had a virile, even though totalitarian, organisation in over four-fifths of the areas from which such a plan could be effectively carried out, while Zervas controlled the remaining one fifth only. Although SOE had armed only a total of five to six hundred andartes of ELAS since we had started supplying them earlier in the year, they then had, to my knowledge, a total of between four and five thousand armed and embodied andartes, whereas Zervas then only had a total of about a thousand. If I cut off all relations with ELAS I knew I would be faced with an impossible task in trying to get National Bands to fill the gap by the summer; for wherever they extended their activities they would come into unavoidable contact with ELAS, who were already in existence there. I had only two alternatives: either to induce SOE to accept a reduction of our sabotage by four-fifths when the big day came, or to try and keep ELAS under some sort of control, with a measure of allegiance by them to the Middle East Command. Rightly or wrongly, I considered that our maximum contribution towards the war effort was of primary importance; moreover, SOE had already made it clear that we ought not to break off relations with ELAS until all other measures had failed.

The next day Saraphis came to see me. He confirmed that he was now free to do exactly what he wanted. I congratulated him upon his release and escape. In return he just thanked me for my congratulations. To this day I do not believe he realises that my presence at Kolokythia had probably saved his life. Sometimes I even wondered whether he was not originally sent out from Athens into the mountains in order to trap Zervas and the other 'opposition' Movements in the Pindus, the only area in which rival movements of any importance then existed. I told him that I considered it his duty to go back to the Northern Pindus hot foot, and to set about re-forming his bands. I was astonished when he replied that he had already carefully considered the matter, and that he did not wish to do so. The Allies, he said, were advancing fast along the north coast of Africa. Greece would soon be invaded. He had not time to get a new Resistance Movement of National Bands going before Greece was liberated. He considered it his duty to throw in his lot with ELAS, who were already effectively organised.

What an insight into Saraphis' character! To join the Resistance Movement which, up to a few hours before, had threatened him with death, and from which, for many days previously, he had suffered insults! Had he not, in fact, walked from the Northern Pindus to Roumeli, not only under ELAS guard, but with his hands in chains, a mark of fallen authority and mockery to all whom he had passed by the wayside? And now he was going to join ELAS! I was dumbfounded.

I asked him what his actual job was going to be in ELAS. I was even further taken aback when he said that he had been offered the post of C. in C. of all ELAS forces in the field.

Saraphis had once been the Greek Military Attaché in Paris. He was an educated man, and, although he may not have been blessed with many of the qualities of a leader, I believe that, in his own mind, he thought that what he was doing was, under the circumstances, the best thing for his country. Although I argued with him for some considerable time, I failed to make him change his mind, and later that day he left with Evmaios for Athens, to go before the Central Committee to be approved by them for his new post.

Before his departure Evmaios promised to return to the mountains to meet me in Roumeli in approximately three weeks' time, and he said that he would bring with him the decision of the

Central Committee regarding the 'Military Agreement'. I told him that I would meanwhile be returning to Avlaki, and we agreed that he would inform me by wireless, through Cairo, as soon as he was leaving for the mountains.

That evening I sent a long signal to SOE (Cairo), reporting my recent conversations with Evmaios. I told them how important I thought it was for an early public announcement to be made stating that there would be free and constitutional elections under the ægis of the Allies as soon as possible after the liberation of Greece, and that it was not our intention to enforce the return of the King. If we did not do something on these lines, I felt that EAM would continue to distrust the intentions of the Allies, and that my chances of maintaining even sufficient control over them to get any useful para-military activity out of them were extremely small.

On 6th April, having despatched Nat and Denys to Southern Thessaly, to work under Sheppard, and having put Arthur Edmonds in Nat's place, as Senior Liaison Officer in Roumeli, I left Kolokythia to rejoin Chris. Before I did so, I had the satisfaction of learning that ELAS and EKKA bands, in accordance with our instructions, had put out of action two more chromium mines in Eastern Roumeli.

Four days later I arrived back at Avlaki.

CHAPTER X

Progress in Spite of EAM/ELAS

ON MY arrival at Avlaki I found a signal from Cairo awaiting me, in which I was told that I had their full support in the organisation of 'National Bands'; that the Foreign Office also had agreed with our policy and that they were supporting it by broadcasts. This gave me some welcome and timely reassurance.

During the four weeks I had been away from my headquarters much had happened. A staff officer from SOE (Cairo), Lieut.-Colonel John Stevens,* had been parachuted into us, to see with his own eyes the situation inside Greece, and, in due course, to report back to Cairo. Chris had already despatched him on a tour of Eastern Roumeli, via the district north of Agrinion called Evrytania, where Zervas now had some bands under an officer named Papaiannou, and the Mission had an excellent English-speaking Greek officer called 'Kitso' with them. John Stevens was due to return to my headquarters in the Pindus to discuss matters with me before continuing northwards to Thessaly, and later to the east coast, whence it was intended that he should be taken by caique to Turkey, on his way back to the Middle East.

There was another recent arrival, a Captain Ross Bower. He had been dropped in answer to my request for a personal assistant on my staff, to cope not only with local administrative matters, but with the increasing amount of wireless traffic and paper work with which I now found myself too much occupied.

---

* Colonel J. M. Stevens, D.S.O., O.B.E., now with the International Monetary Fund in Washington.

Awaiting my arrival I also found full reports from Tom Barnes about his sabotage plans for Epirus, and from John Cook, who, a week earlier, had returned after the successful accomplishment of his mission to gain contact with the guerillas in Albania. Chris had sent on to Cairo the information about Albania, and, as a result, it had already been decided to drop a party of three officers and a wireless operator for the Albanian guerillas to Tom Barnes in Epirus. Two days before my return Chris had sent John Cook over to Epirus to await the arrival of this party and to guide them northwards to their destination.

Several matters wanted tidying up in Epirus, where Tom was in charge of sabotage planning, working with a Major Micklethwait. He needed more British officers, and I wanted to discuss with him his other requirements. Micklethwait, at that time the senior liaison officer with EDES andartes there, was experiencing a certain amount of trouble, not only with competitive bands of ELAS, but with the so-called Turco-Albanians residing in Northern Greece, whom the Italians were attempting to enlist on their side to develop guerilla warfare against us. As I had about fourteen days to spare before I need trudge eastwards again to meet Evmaios on his return from Athens, and as I wanted not only to greet the Albanian party, but also to co-ordinate certain details with them before their departure northwards, I decided to visit Tom and Micklethwait in Western Epirus as soon as I could get my work done in Avlaki.

The day after my return to headquarters Zervas arrived there. He was full of complaints against EAM. The Chief Constable of Arta, when on his way to visit Zervas to arrange the wide scale desertion of his gendarmes to the mountains, had been arrested by an EAM leader and sent off under escort to Thessaly. Since then nothing had been heard of him. Zervas then showed me a copy of an EAM paper, produced in Karditsa, stating that "anyone not joining EAM would be regarded as a traitor to Greece". There were other similar complaints. I sent the more important of them on by wireless through Cairo to Evmaios in Athens, to show him the way his subordinates were apparently flouting his instructions. At the same time I told Cairo I thought that these actions by irresponsible EAM leaders should not be allowed to cause the breakdown of the present negotiations; moreover that I believed the Central Committee would do their utmost to co-operate with us, in order to justify EAM in the eyes of all Greeks, whose support they wanted.

I discussed with Zervas the desirability of moving our headquarters further north into a less accessible area in the Pindus Mountains; for, with the approach of summer and the consequent melting of the snow, it was becoming increasingly easy for the Italians to get over the mountains to the west of Avlaki and to approach our headquarters by many different routes. Soon they would be no longer confined to the mountain passes, in which it had been comparatively easy to stop them during the winter months. With this in view, Chris had already made a reconnaissance and, two days' journey to the north-west, had found what he reported to be a most suitable and, incidentally, charming village, called Theodhoriana. We decided to move there within the next few days.

Before I left Avlaki on 12th April, I got Zervas to give me a written declaration, for which several EAM leaders had asked me, to the effect that he had no political ambitions whatsoever and certainly no intention of becoming a dictator. I sent this verbatim to Cairo for re-transmission to Evmaios.

Since Themie had not rejoined me from Parnassus before my departure from Roumeli, I was without an interpreter. Zervas offered me an educated Greek boy about twenty years of age, called Tommy Athanassiades, who had recently arrived from Athens. He came of a rich Greek family, well known to Zervas, and appeared to me to be keen and to have quite a fluent knowledge of English. But, as I was to learn to my cost later, he had a far from adequate knowledge of how to talk to and deal with the proud though poor Greek people in the mountains. Moreover, in the difficult translation work which he had sometimes to do for me, I found him on occasions seriously inaccurate.

Tommy and I spent the night of the 13th at Khosepsi, the little village in which, on our miserable journey back from the west coast earlier in the year, we had received such a generous welcome. Now, only four months later, it had quite a different atmosphere. The people seemed restrained in their welcome. EAM were now in control and had their local headquarters there.

The ELAS commander at that time was a Colonel Pisperis. I had a talk with him about the usual local grievances between ELAS and EDES, and I patched them up as far as I could. I spent a most comfortable night in the house of a retired general named Nasis. He told me that he had been offered a high position in ELAS and that he was considering accepting it, largely in order to try to keep EAM and ELAS to a path of moderation.

The following night I stayed in Platanousa, another village through which I had passed on our way back from the coast. Here I met Alexis Zervas, General Zervas' brother, again. He was at that time nominally in charge of Epirus. But he was not cut out for guerilla warfare in the mountains. He was not half pugnacious enough. Moreover he lacked the necessary personality to be in any real sense a commander. Zervas presumably gave him this position out of brotherly kindness.

Tommy and I stayed in Platanousa until just before dark on 15th April, when we moved off in order to cross the main road from Messolonghi to Yannina in the darkness. On the 18th we arrived at Tom Barnes' headquarters, the lovely old monastery of Romanon where we had rested on our way back from the coast.

Tom Barnes told me that, two days before my arrival, the high perimeter walls around the monastery had been completely surrounded by several hundred ELAS, whose military and political leaders, Yioryiades and Anagnostakis respectively, had demanded the unconditional surrender of all the EDES andartes in it. Tom had naturally refused to consider such an ultimatum and had warned Yioryiades that, should his forces attack, he would have no hesitation in advising Major Konstantinides, Zervas' local commander, to open fire. The ELAS andartes surrounding the monastery were a pretty nondescript crowd, who had been gathered together from their villages and fields obviously for this sole purpose. After twenty-four hours mock siege, their bluff had been called, and they had dispersed of their own accord without a shot being fired.

Tom and I went over his plans for sabotage, evolved from his recent reconnaissances. We discussed the Turco-Albanian problem and decided to try to get in touch with their leaders and to offer better terms than the Italians, in order to win them over to our side. I briefed John Cook for his next trip to Albania, instructing him to return after he had safely deposited the British party, which was expected the following night. I was just about to consider how I could get hold of Yioryiades to tell him what I thought about him, when I received a message from him, inviting me to attend an ELAS gathering the following afternoon. Not knowing what I was in for, I unhesitatingly accepted. It would be a good opportunity to make a public speech to ELAS in Epirus; for although most ELAS leaders knew by now that the British Mission was ready to support andarte bands of all organisations who were prepared to fight against the common enemy, this fact was sometimes misconstrued behind our backs by EAM political advisers, to suit their propaganda to the rank and file of ELAS.

That night, the 17th, the party for Albania was safely dropped on to Tom's local ground, about three hours' walk from the monastery. It consisted of two cavalrymen, Major Billy Maclean *

* Now Conservative Member of Parliament for Inverness.

and Captain David Smiley,★ a young Sapper officer named Duffy and a wireless operator. They stayed overnight on the dropping ground to supervise the collection of their kit. By midday the following day, when I left for the ELAS gathering, they had still not arrived at the monastery.

When Tommy and I got to the village of Romanon we were directed to the school yard. Here I found about two hundred and fifty ELAS assembled. I noticed that only about a quarter of them were armed; all of these were in the front ranks. After a mock inspection during which I was not taken round the rear ranks, the party was stood at ease and I was led a short distance away to talk to some of the leaders of the different bands privately.

Anagnostakis, the senior 'Political Adviser', started off with the usual complaint that the British Mission was giving preferential support to Zervas' andartes. He asked me what authority I had to act in this way, and why ELAS, which had been organised in Epirus long before Zervas had started EDES activities there—this was true—had received no supplies of arms, ammunition and clothes. Then another Greek from the circle sitting round me told me that there was grave discontent amongst the andartes gathered there that day, and that they could not prevent their men from attacking the monastery unless Zervas' officer, Konstantinides, and all his andartes, promised to clear out of the area within the next two days.

I explained to this little group that we were in Greece to support all bands of andartes who were prepared to fight against the enemy under the orders of GHQ, Middle East. I told them all they need do was to sign the 'Military Agreement' and abide by it. As I expected, they were unable to do this because of orders from above. I asked them when their bands had fought against the Italians, and which of them had approached Tom Barnes to offer

★ Colonel D. de C. Smiley, M.V.O., O.B.E., M.C., now Military Attaché, Stockholm.

their services to the Allies and carry out sabotage under the instructions of the Middle East Command. I was immediately able to refute a number of false claims with facts, with which Tom Barnes had previously primed me. They still insisted that it was beyond their power to control their men, that, even if what I said was true, these men would attack Konstantinides' andartes and there would be frightful bloodshed to the detriment of the fight against the common enemy, unless Konstantinides cleared out. After similar talk lasting for some two hours, I told the leaders that I would address their men myself. They welcomed this. I soon regretted my mistake!

To these Greeks, who had been gathered together from widely scattered villages in the Epirus Mountains just to make a show of force for the purposes of their political leaders, I gave my, by now, more or less stock speech. I explained my orders from the Middle East Command, the object of the British Mission, the instructions I had given to all my officers and the terms on which the Middle East Command was prepared to supply arms and equipment to ELAS. I told them that at this moment their Central Committee in Athens was deciding whether or not to sign the 'Military Agreement' with the Middle East Command and that, until I heard the result of their decision, I was unable to supply arms to any bands unless they independently signed the Agreement. Their leaders had this afternoon refused to sign it; and that, so far as I was concerned, was that. It was up to them to choose fresh leaders, or to await the decision of their Central Committee.

Then the party began.

After a short while it became obvious to me that several 'Political Advisers' had been placed in the ranks to shoot awkward questions at me. I had taken the precaution of asking the ELAS leaders I had been talking to privately to stand behind me so that they would not mix with their men. But, one after the other, orators in the ranks threw arguments at me and made political speeches, every one of which, had I possessed a fluent mastery of their language, I would have easily been able to turn to my advantage. Unfortunately, however, I had to speak through Tommy, my interpreter, and the delay in translation took all the sting and punch out of my counter-arguments. After nearly an hour, in which I can with all modesty say that I stood my ground by British standards of argument and did not lose a point, I realised that we were getting nowhere. I stopped all further questions and told the men that, so far as I was concerned, the situation was quite clear. In the eyes of the Middle East Command they had no right whatever either to order Konstantinides' men out of the area or to attack them. If they did so, either with or without the instructions of their leaders, Greek blood would be on their heads; and, if they did attack, then from that time onwards, even after EAM had signed the 'Military Agreement', I would see to it that, in this area of Epirus, ELAS got no military supplies whatsoever and that their action and my decision would be reported in full to the Middle East Command.

As I was finishing my speech, Tom Barnes, by now anxious about my safety, appeared on the scene. We left together. The andartes, at the instigation of their leaders, raised a half-hearted cheer for me. As I walked away past Yioryiades I told him that I would be leaving Romanon within an hour for Khosepsi, their Epirus headquarters, and that, before my departure I required an assurance from him that his men were under control. Otherwise I said, I would report the matter in full to Colonel Pisperis, and see that he was relieved of his command immediately.

When Tom and I got back to the monastery I greeted Maclean and Smiley, and gave them what advice I could. I had a brief talk with Micklethwait, who, having taken a different route from mine, had just got back from a visit to Colonel Pisperis, to complain about the siege of Romanon a few days earlier. I then sat down with Tommy to a solid meal, determined to leave that night, in order to get back to Khosepsi as quickly as possible, to get Colonel Pisperis to straighten out this local ELAS trouble and to appoint new leaders.

Shortly before I was ready to leave, an ELAS messenger arrived at the doorway in the monastery wall and requested an interview with me. He told me that Yioryiades had sent him to report that he had "got his men under control again" and that they were dispersing to their villages. Half an hour later, as dusk was falling, I left on my journey back to my own headquarters, which by now I expected to find in Theodhoriana.

The route which we took was slightly different from the one on our outward journey. For the first five hours of darkness our path meandered through gently undulating country, thickly covered with low-growing trees and shrubbery. The night was fine, still and moonlit. The air soon became filled with songs from literally dozens of nightingales. Alternately shrill, deep and warbling their notes rang out all around us. Only the clank of our hob-nailed boots and of our mules' feet on the stony track, the shuffling of our poorly shod guide, or an occasional cough from one of us, disturbed mile after mile of that fairyland of music.

Just before dawn we safely re-crossed the main road, and the following afternoon I reached Pisperis in his comfortable headquarters in Khosepsi. I told him about the insulting behaviour of ELAS at Romanon. He promised to send a new leader there immediately.

Late on 21st April I crossed a high pass, to see Theodhoriana below me. Half an hour later we entered the village. Chris and the advance party of our headquarters had arrived the day before. By now we had two independent wireless sets, operating on different wave-lengths. For the move of our headquarters, it had, therefore, been possible to leave one set behind, operating at Avlaki, until the other one had been established. Our forward wireless link was set up and Bill Jordan had already established contact with Cairo.

Since his arrival in January, Bill, a New Zealand press correspondent in peace time, had raised the standard of our communications from a state of almost continuous failure to obtain contact
with Cairo to one of the highest efficiency. He was now assisted
by an able staff-sergeant, Stan Smith, and two other operators
who had been dropped at different periods in the early spring.
The daily, and often twice daily, schedules with Cairo worked so
regularly that it was possible to maintain an extensive flow of
traffic both ways on each schedule. We were even able to let the
RAF have weather forecasts each afternoon a night sortie was due,
so as to prevent aircraft making useless journeys if the weather
our end was hopeless.

Theodhoriana is situated in the centre of a terraced and fertile
bowl more than two miles in diameter. It is almost totally en-
closed by mountains of the Pindus range, which rise steeply from
stony green foothills to rocky slopes and a sky-line of high, jagged
peaks. Nature's only outlet is in the east. Here, when I first saw
it, a narrow gorge bore a torrent of grey-green melting snow
down into the flooded Acheloos river four miles away. On a fine
clear morning, as the sun rose between distant peaks, it would
cast its golden beams first on to the snow draped peaks opposite,
then on to their rugged grey slopes and, spreading quickly down
to the kinder foothills, would light up the fertile terraces of the
bowl below, which, interspersed with tall dark green cypress and
rounded silvery olive trees, was already covered with a faint
spring-green carpet; finally the sun would set aglow the windows
of the simple white walled cottages of Theodhoriana. Such was
the panorama which I watched from my bedroom balcony that
first April morning I was there, yet clearly imprinted upon my
memory; peaceful and quiet except for the occasional distant
bleating of sheep and the faint jingle of the bells round their necks.

By the standard of most Greek mountain villages Theodhoriana
is quite a large one. As a result of the initiative of its progressive

doctor it even had electric light, generated by a water turbine and sufficiently powerful to light the tortuous little village alleyways and the market square, as well as most of the cottages. Naturally at that time there were no open lights at night, for fear of attracting the attention of enemy aircraft. But we enjoyed the luxury of electric light in our 'blacked-out' rooms in the evening. Ross soon got to work and organised messing on a comparatively lavish scale. We spent many comfortable days in Theodhoriana, until our presence brought tragedy to some of the villagers in these happy surroundings.

On 23rd April a somewhat disturbing signal was re-transmitted to me by Cairo from Sheppard in Olympus. According to him the Germans were about to start a determined drive against the ELAS forces in the Olympus area, which then numbered about two thousand; and it had been decided to move them all several days march across the plains of Thessaly to safety in the mountains of south-western Macedonia and the Northern Pindus range.

This was the very last thing I wanted to happen. I had already made plans to get all the National Bands I could re-organised in the Northern Pindus by Denys Hamson and Nat Barker, and I needed Sheppard and his andartes in the Olympus area to carry out sabotage against the main road and railway communications up the east side of Greece later in the summer.

I signalled Sheppard to keep his ELAS forces where they were. He replied that it was impossible, and a few days later these two thousand ELAS andartes marched right across the plains of Thessaly. I received a glowing report from Sheppard about the wonderful discipline of their long columns on night marches across the plain. I sent back a curt message saying that they had no reason to emulate regular troop movements and that their strength lay in their ability to carry out guerilla activity. I told him to discourage any future attempts by ELAS to ape purely military tactics. If this large force had bumped the enemy on its journey across the plain and had suffered heavy casualties, it would have been the fault of its own leaders for having adopted such an inappropriate method instead of coming across in small, independent parties.

In picturesque Theodhoriana many days of comparative luxury and contentment quickly passed. Dotted around the village the beautifully coloured almond blossom was bursting forth into bud and changing its tint each day as the flowers matured. Ross incessantly studied our welfare and comfort. One day he heard of a Greek pedlar who periodically visited the country town of Yannina for black market activities on behalf of the mountain villagers. He got into contact with this man and arranged for luxuries such as chocolate, raisins and 'halva'—a Greek sweet made from honey and almonds—to be brought out to us every week or ten days. When I was away from Theodhoriana, this pedlar returned from one of his trips to Yannina accompanied by three young and quite presentable women, whom, he informed Ross without a flutter of his eyelids, he had brought for the British officers for 'recreational purposes'. Ross was naturally rather taken aback; but he had the sense to order them out of the village immediately. Within an hour of their arrival a deputation of village elders, headed by the President, arrived on Chris' doorstep and asked if the rumour which they had heard was true. Chris had to admit that it was, but that the matter had been a complete mistake, an 'error of judgment' on the part of the Greek pedlar. Fortunately Chris had already ordered the three women to be locked up under guard. He promised the village elders that they would remain there until he had found out all about their past history. Andarte agents subsequently proved that all of the women had consorted with different Italians and that one of them was without doubt in the pay of the Italian Intelligence. This miserable woman was convicted as a spy and shot. The other two spent the rest of the war in 'temporary retirement' in the mountains.

For Easter Sunday, 25th April, I had accepted a long-standing invitation to renew my acquaintance with Colonel Lambrakis, with whom I had spent a night towards the end of our journey back from the coast nearly four months earlier. He lived in a delightful house in the mountains, only a few hours' journey from Theodhoriana. As Bill Jordan was badly in need of a rest I took him with me on that relatively peaceful Sunday morning. For two days and nights we enjoyed Lambrakis' generous hospitality. I slept those two nights on a spring bed and between white sheets. A little Greek servant girl waited on us at our meals, which were washed down with some of Colonel Lambrakis' excellent home-made wine. On the 27th I had to return to work. Bill Jordan stayed on for a few more days' well-earned rest.

On 29th April I learnt from Cairo that they planned to send us no less than forty sorties of supplies and equipment during the following month of May. This sounded almost too good to be true. Hitherto I had been led to expect no more than twenty. On the assumption that the 'Military Agreement' with EAM would soon be signed, I signalled back where all these sorties were to go and informed my stations throughout the mountains accordingly.

We worked out the distribution in the following way. First of all we considered what essential explosives and sabotage equipment were required by my different liaison officers to carry out their sabotage tasks for our concerted plan later in the summer. We then took into consideration the direct and indirect guerilla support that each of them would require in order to carry out this sabotage. To those who had not yet got sufficient andartes, or a sufficiently widespread organisation to ensure freedom of movement for sabotage parties, I allocated additional arms and equipment. Whatever sorties were left over I divided in proportion to the known strength of the bands in the different area, regardless of their organisation.

It was about this time that the enemy began to pay us special attention. High-flying aircraft dropped leaflets signed by Rallis, the acting Prime Minister in enemy-occupied Greece, urging the people in the mountains to go down into the Italian-occupied towns in the plains and surrender their arms. Fourteen days' grace were given. If, after that time, they continued to hide arms or to harbour what were called "Communist rebels", they would be arrested by the Italians and shot. They did not say how they proposed to do this!

Three weeks later reconnaissance 'planes started flying about at safe heights over the mountains, and one day, early in May, Voulgareli was heavily bombed without warning. Twenty people were killed, many of them innocent women and children. More than a dozen families were rendered homeless. This was the first time that the enemy had got close to our headquarters, and I felt guilty at having brought misfortune to this village, whose occupants were always so helpful to us. It was, however, ridiculous psychology on the part of the Germans to order the bombing or burning of villages. It merely resulted in the menfolk, who were thus rendered homeless, being forced to take to the mountains and swell the ranks of the andartes.

By now I was daily expecting a message from Evmaios informing me of his impending departure from Athens. On 4th May I sent Chris off on a visit to Sheppard, whose headquarters were then reasonably close to us on the western edges of the Thessaly Plain. I was anxious to do this so that Chris could enlighten him as to the true character of EAM and our opinion of them; for Sheppard, by his signals, was obviously still under the impression that EAM had no ulterior political motives, and was a completely straightforward Resistance Movement, whose sole object was to fight against the enemy. I told Chris to be back, if possible, within four days, by which time I had decided to leave for Roumeli, whether or not I had news from Evmaios, because I wanted to satisfy myself that Arthur Edmonds' arrangements were all in order for another important attack we were preparing upon the railway to Piræus.

On 6th May, John Stevens, the liaison officer from SOE (Cairo), turned up at Theodhoriana. We had a long talk together about the impressions which he had so far formed. I found him somewhat reserved in his views. He appeared worried by the fact that we were authorised to support ELAS, which inevitably meant supporting revolutionary EAM as well. John now planned to move on northwards, calling at both Sheppard's and Hammond's headquarters on his way to the east coast of Greece.

Two days later I signalled to Evmaios that I was leaving for Roumeli. The same day Chris arrived back from his visit to Sheppard, with an interesting account of how he had tried to convince him of the true character of EAM.* I gave John Stevens several personal messages for the Middle East, and, wishing him good luck, set off, with Tommy still as my interpreter, on yet another tiring march across Greece to Arthur Edmonds' headquarters in Eastern Roumeli.

In 1941, when the British had been forced to evacuate Greece, a considerable number of Cypriots, mostly belonging to Pioneer Units, had been left behind. Through their knowledge of the Greek language many of them had avoided capture by posing as Greeks. Most of these had eventually found safe refuge in Greek families in the mountains. In due course some had joined up with local andarte bands. As our Mission extended its activities, and as our presence became more widely known, our ranks were progressively swollen with these Cypriots. We now had about thirty of them with us, and I made them into a 'Cypriot Runner Service', for carrying messages on regular circuits between my different officers.

---

* Sheppard, who was never convinced that our view of EAM was correct, was killed by a mine laid by ELAS in a street in Athens during the civil war in 1944.

In spite of this runner service, the time was fast approaching when I could ill afford to be out of wireless contact for more than a day. Before my departure from Theodhoriana I instructed my P.A., Ross Bower, to ask Cairo for an additional wireless set with batteries and charging engine in order to form a self-contained mobile unit, on pack-mules, to travel with me wherever I went in future.

In a small village called Siklista, through which I passed on my way eastwards, I had to iron out some friction caused by ELAS refusing to allow the poor mountain-folk in Valtos to buy wheat from the rich Thessaly Plains, where it was invariably surplus to local requirements. On their meagre plots of levelled land, the villagers in those rugged mountains were always unable to grow sufficient wheat or maize to last them throughout the winter. It was, in fact, the normal custom, as soon as the snows had melted sufficiently, for a regular pilgrimage of hungry buyers, mostly womenfolk, to travel over the Pindus mountain passes to the comparatively rich market towns, such as Mouzaki, in the Thessaly Plain. EAM were 'in power' in all of the villages on the fringe of the plain and they held a trump card in their ability to refuse to allow hungry Greeks from Valtos, in which area EDES was in a strong preponderance, to buy wheat unless they were, or became, members of EAM. I investigated the particular case which was brought to my notice in Siklista; I promised to report to EAM headquarters in Roumeli and to do my utmost to have this restriction removed as soon as I saw the Central Committee representative, which I hoped would be within the next few days.

Before the war the Greeks had planned to drive a road through the mountains of Roumeli from Lamia to Agrinion. They had started work at both ends; but, when the war came, these ends had fortunately not yet been linked, and were still separated by some twenty-five miles of wooded and mountainous country.

This allowed the andarte bands in Roumeli considerable security and freedom of movement, since the enemy by that time seldom wandered far from the roads.

I spent the night of 10th May in the charming village of Frangista. The next morning I set off at 5.30 for the southern extremity of the incompleted section of road from Lamia. Having arranged by telephone to be met there by an ELAS car, I was driven on to the local EAM headquarters at Karpenisi. Later the same day I continued my journey by car to Sperkhiadha, a large village in the broad valley of the Sperkhios River, not more than fifteen miles from the enemy garrison town of Lamia. Here I enjoyed a delightfully warm spring evening in the garden of a private house. Vines, growing up the pillars of its veranda, were in bloom, and the garden was full of sweet-smelling spring flowers. After dark, lolling comfortably in garden chairs, Tommy, my hosts and I were sipping our ouzo when we heard an aircraft approaching. I recognised the note as that of one of our own Halifaxes, a type of aircraft which had at last arrived in the Middle East for our 'Special Operations' squadrons, and which, as a result of our advance from El Alamein along the coast of North Africa, the RAF were now able to use to bring us supplies from airfields in the vicinity of Derna, several hundred miles closer to Greece than the old ones in the Nile Delta. Two sorties were due for Arthur Edmonds, one of them including in its load three Sapper officers, who were being specially sent for our next attack on the railway. The aircraft overhead must be one of them.

The memory of the arrival of our original party in Greece passed through my mind as I pictured the arrival of these three young officers. What changes and developments had occurred since, eight months ago, the first of us had been dropped as good as 'blind' into the mountains of Greece, to live for many weeks a virtual cave life. Within an hour of their arrival, these officers, who would at this moment be actually dropping, would, without bad luck,* be warmly and comfortably established in a cottage in comparative luxury.

In Sperkhiadha my hosts informed me that the village had recently been raided by a party of Germans from Lamia, as an act of reprisal for the ambushing by ELAS of a party of Germans in that area. Although, on their arrival in the village, there had naturally been no sign of ELAS andartes, the enemy had wantonly burned to the ground about a dozen cottages, both in Sperkhiadha and in the adjoining village of Macracomi, with all the private possessions of the unfortunate occupants, who, as a result, were left penniless and destitute. The following morning, before leaving, I gave the headman of the village a few sovereigns out of my belt for the destitute families of each village. A gold sovereign at that time was worth several thousand drachmae, and on the black market bought sufficient for a family to exist for many weeks.

Setting off early that day, 12th May, I completed the remainder of my journey on a mule, arriving shortly before dark at Arthur Edmonds' headquarters, then at Anatoli, a tiny village high up in the mountains between Gardiki and Mavrolithari.

---

* Up to the time of Greece's liberation, among the two hundred officers and men dropped into Greece, I know for certain of only two fatal casualties directly attributable to the parachute jump itself.

CHAPTER XI

The Asopos Operation

Towards the end of January we had learnt that trains were again passing over the Gorgopotamos viaduct. By means of hastily constructed wooden 'crib' piers, the Italians had succeeded in re-opening the railway for slow traffic six weeks after we had cut it.

We were distressed to hear that the enemy had seized thirteen innocent Greeks from Lamia and taken them to the viaduct, where they had shot them only a few days after our attack on the night of 25th November. But that was not all. The Italians had arrested Costa Pistolis, the schoolmaster from Lamia who had obtained such valuable information for us about the enemy defences around the viaduct. I never discovered whether he was betrayed, whether his movements gave him away or whether he gave himself up to save the lives of other innocent Greeks. But at some time whilst in the hands of the Gestapo in Athens he probably confessed his complicity because, in spite of the personal intervention of the Archbishop of Athens on his behalf, many weeks later he was put to death. He left a widow and two children, of whom I heard shortly after the end of the war and for whom, I am glad to say, some assistance was arranged.

Thus died many a gallant Greek in the service of his country and the Allied cause; a tragic consequence of Resistance. But before condemning guerilla warfare because of resultant enemy reprisals, one should take into account its material and morale-raising contribution towards victory, and also remember that total war inevitably lacks discrimination in its impact upon the civilian population. The extent of the cruel carnage from enemy bombing initiated by Goering, and wrought on the women and children of this country, bore some comparison with the cold-blooded reprisals on the innocent in overrun countries where Resistance was gallantly carried out against the Axis. Both were horrible, but both were parts of the price of ultimate victory.

In the middle of February I had heard that the Germans were slowly but systematically taking over guard duties on the railway from the Italians. I wished to destroy another of the big viaducts in Eastern Roumeli whilst they were still guarded by low category Italians; for I knew that our chances of success once the Germans had taken over were much more slender. Cairo had approved of the idea, and even before the receipt of my new directive to prepare for widespread sabotage in the summer, Arthur Edmonds had volunteered for the job with the assistance of Aris' andartes. The target we chose was the Asopos viaduct.

This viaduct was about two hundred yards long and of unique construction. From the mouth of one tunnel in an almost vertical mountain face it carried the single main-line railway to Athens on an incline and a curve across a gorge over a drop of two hundred feet, almost immediately into another tunnel in an equally steep mountain face. At about seventy-feet intervals from the southern tunnel mouth stone piers supported three straight steel spans. Two further spans were cantilevered inwards, one from each direction, on to the main central span of a hundred yards, which consisted of a huge archway of steel lattice work. This was what is technically known as a 'three-pin arch', in that it comprised two main sections, joined together by three large steel pins; one joining the two sections at the crown of the arch, one fixing each of the other two ends to the face of the gorge.

It was almost impossible, as I already knew, to approach the bridge down the gorge from the west. There were only three

The Asopos Viaduct.

Chris Woodhouse, Themie Marinos and Donald Stott.

Captain Ehrgott, first U.S. officer to join the Allied Military Mission
in Greece.

Arthur Edmonds, Royal New Zealand Engineers.

Rufus Sheppard.

Bill Jordan, a New Zealander, in charge of W.T. communications at Brigadier Myers' H.Q. in the mountains.

practicable approaches, two of them being through the tunnels. The third was from below the bridge, from the east, where the gorge opened out into a wide valley. From all other directions the faces of the gorge were too steep for any man or beast.

The plan which Arthur and I evolved was that andartes should seize a train by night as, invariably headed by two engines, it climbed slowly up hill from the direction of Lamia to the south. The train would be boarded and driven on by us to the viaduct, where the guard would be overwhelmed and the bridge destroyed by British sappers.

With all the spare explosives then in hand, and a small party of Aris' andartes who had come over from Roumeli to escort him back, and with the promise of three specially selected Royal Engineer officers from the Middle East to assist him, Arthur had left Avlaki for Roumeli on 7th March, to supervise preparations for the destruction of the viaduct.

After several reconnaissances, Arthur decided that the original plan to seize a train was too chancy and that the surest way of success was by mass attack with an overwhelming force of andartes from the east, simultaneously with the seizure of both tunnels. He had come to this conclusion mainly because, although the guards on the viaduct numbered less than fifty, there was a battalion of the enemy in a camp only half an hour away and he didn't think that a train could be seized noiselessly and without arousing this battalion in time for it to reach the viaduct before we could complete its destruction. Aris had agreed to co-operate and to provide a thousand andartes.

It had taken several weeks for Cairo to select three suitable Sapper officer volunteers, Major Wingate and Captains Scott and McIntyre,* and to complete their parachute and commando train-

---

* Lieut.-Colonel P. J. F. Wingate, M.C., RE, and Major H. N. McIntyre, M.C., RE, both regular officers, got through the war safely and are still serving in the Royal Engineers. Captain Scott is now a civil engineer.

ing. My arrival at Arthur Edmonds' headquarters on 12th May had almost coincided with theirs the previous night.

I found that Arthur had made considerable progress with his plans for the attack on the Asopos viaduct. As he and Aris had already planned to depart on a final reconnaissance of the approaches within the next few days I decided to accompany them.

Early the following morning, however, Arthur woke me up with the gloomy news that one of my officers, Major Geoffrey Gordon-Creed, who had been dropped a week earlier to become the first British Liaison Officer with Psaros, at his newly established headquarters in the mountains near Stromni, had rung Arthur up on the EAM-operated telephone and informed him that, a few hours earlier, Aris had delivered an ultimatum to Psaros. He had ordered Psaros to disarm his bands and to disperse them to their villages, or else Aris would disarm them by force. I told Arthur to get on to Geoffrey again and tell him to come and meet me at Mavrolithari, which was midway between Anatoli and Stromni, as soon as he could get there.

I arrived at the rendezvous at about midday, and shortly afterwards I met Geoffrey Gordon-Creed for the first time. He brought with him the news that, to save pointless bloodshed, Psaros had already given in to Aris' demands; his bands had scattered, and at that very moment Psaros was held prisoner by Aris in Stromni. Accompanied by Geoffrey, I immediately travelled on to Stromni. On the way we passed a long stream of ELAS andartes, returning to Mavrolithari. They were heavily laden with arms and equipment obtained from Psaros' bands.

On reaching Stromni, of which I had hitherto such pleasant memories, I demanded to be taken to where Psaros was held captive. I found Aris in occupation of his house. I immediately asked him upon what authority he had disarmed Psaros' bands and now held the latter prisoner. He replied that he had received verbal orders from the Central Committee of EAM that "none other than ELAS bands were to exist in Roumeli". I asked him who had given him these orders. To this he replied that he did not know exactly; they had come from the Central Committee. I demanded Psaros' release; but Aris refused to accede to my request, saying that he was not empowered to do so. I then told him that, so long as he and his men held the arms supplied by the Allies for EKKA, I would have to advise GHQ, Middle East to send no further supplies to ELAS in Roumeli.

"That is your business," he replied. "I am carrying out my orders. You must carry out your own."

I asked him what he intended to do with Psaros. I was told that he would be taken back to his headquarters in Mavrolithari, where he would be held pending further instructions.

Psaros, grey-haired, clean-shaven, square-faced, of average height, and dressed in an army officer's khaki uniform, appeared to me to be rather shy and incredibly philosophical about his arrest. I spoke a few encouraging words to him, and then, greatly disheartened, I returned to Mavrolithari to await Evmaios' arrival from Athens. Aris had indeed not been idle that day; for later came the news that Kranias, the leader of another National Band in his area, based on a village in the plains called Kastelli, had also been taken prisoner by ELAS, and that he was being brought up to Aris at Mavrolithari. The following day came the additional news of the disarming by ELAS in Evrytania of the large band of EDES, under Papaiannou. In the evening I told Aris that all these actions, for which I held him entirely responsible, would probably mean the end of British support to ELAS in Central Greece. In my eyes they were inexcusable.

"But these bands which you call 'National Bands' are double-crossing you," Aris replied. "They are intriguing with the enemy. My bands are prepared to do exactly what the Middle East Command wish. Moreover, what I promised Arthur Edmonds a few days ago in connection with the Asopos operation still holds good.

I propose that we leave on our final reconnaissance tomorrow, and, so long as I am satisfied with its results, I am prepared to provide what andartes are required to assist you and your British Engineer officers to destroy the viaduct."

Maybe, after Aris' high-handed action throughout Roumeli, I ought to have refused to have any further dealings with him until he had made amends by restoring the arms to the National Bands which he had disarmed, or ordered to be disarmed, and until he had reinstated Psaros, Kranias and Papaiannou. But I put the contribution towards the war effort uppermost amongst all other things, and I told him that if he was prepared to assist us to destroy the Asopos viaduct, that factor would undoubtedly be taken into due consideration in mitigation of the offence which he had committed in disarming these National Bands. But I could accept no responsibility for the Middle East Command's decision on this matter. I warned him that there would undoubtedly be sanctions imposed upon him for his recent high-handed action. I strongly recommended him, therefore, to go through with his intention to assist us to destroy the viaduct. I concluded by telling him that I would accompany him the following day. Before we left I again saw Psaros in the cottage in which he was held captive, and was able to assure both him and myself that he was in no immediate danger. I told him that I would continue to do all in my power to obtain his release as soon as possible.

To obtain a comprehensive view of the Asopos viaduct it was necessary for us to cross the railway and main road to Athens and examine it from the foothills to the east, across the valley which opened out beneath it. Our route took us through the village of Koukouvista, near where we had been destined to drop in September of the previous year. We reached Kastelli that night. We intended to cross the railway and main road before dawn the following morning. In the middle of the night, however, I was woken up by one of Aris' andartes, who told me, through

Tommy, that Evmaios had just arrived in the mountains from Athens and that a message had been received from him ordering Aris to retrace his steps. I immediately went to see Aris; but no amount of argument would persuade him to continue. He said that he must obey orders and that he must return to Koukouvista, where he was to meet Evmaios. We could discuss the Asopos operation with him, he said, when we met him.

We got back to Koukouvista about midday, to find not only Evmaios, but also Saraphis waiting for us. Evmaios told me that he, Saraphis and Aris had been selected by the Central Committee of EAM to be the 'chief committee of leadership' and General Headquarters of all ELAS in Greece, and that from now onwards the three of them must agree on any future operations before they were carried out by ELAS. He himself, he added, was to be the EAM representative on GHQ, ELAS.

He told me that he could not permit ELAS andartes to attack the Asopos viaduct. It was an extremely hazardous operation, he said, and it would undoubtedly bring about widespread reprisals by the enemy on innocent villagers. He saw no reason whatsoever why the Middle East Command should insist that this specific viaduct be attacked, when there were many other simpler operations possible, which would be as effective, if not more so, in cutting railway communication with Athens.

I was by then towards the end of my patience. I explained as coolly as I could that this bridge was a unique one, that it had taken years to build, that its destruction would cut the railway to Athens for many months, and that it was for this reason that it had been specially selected by the Middle East Command. There was no other target whose destruction would have the same effect.

Evmaios replied that, although this might be true, he could not accept the responsibility for the casualties to andartes which might result if the operation were undertaken and, in view of the element of risk regarding its ultimate success, he could not agree to attack it.

"In that case," I said, "I have no further use for ELAS and I will take on the task with my own officers." At that time, I must admit, although I had a few ideas at the back of my mind, I had no definite plan. I then accused Evmaios of deceiving me, and told him all about Aris' recent action in disarming the National Bands throughout Roumeli.

He replied that all this had obviously been the result of a "gross misunderstanding" by Aris. Psaros, Kranias, Papaiannou and any others held prisoner would be set free as soon as he had satisfied himself that there was no justification for their arrest.

I demanded that the arms which had been taken by Aris from these different bands should immediately be handed back. He quietly assured me that even this would be done. We then began discussing the 'Military Agreement', which he had taken back to Athens for approval and signature by the rest of the Central Committee. I will deal with this matter in the subsequent chapter.

Later that night Evmaios informed me that he had just heard from a reliable source that the Germans intended to embark upon widespread anti-guerilla sweeps through the mountains of Roumeli, and that he had no alternative but to order the withdrawal of ELAS into the Pindus Mountains. This was a more severe blow to me than any other, because I realised that, should ELAS withdraw from this part of the mountains, it would become denuded of andarte support and cause a severe restriction of movement to British saboteurs for the widespread sabotage operations shortly to be undertaken in conjunction with the Allied assaults across the Mediterranean.

I considered it necessary to tell Evmaios that the Middle East Command had a number of war-time intelligence agents in Greece, acting independently of the British Mission—he himself knew of one or two already—who were in wireless communication with the authorities in Cairo. If such a widespread plan for sweeping through the mountains had been envisaged by the enemy, I said that I would undoubtedly have been told about it. But I did not tell him that, in point of fact I had actually been warned by Cairo of the possibility of such a sweep. It was not until some weeks later that I learnt with relief from SOE (Cairo) that this sweep had at the last minute been called off by the Germans because they had been led to believe that there was an immediate threat of invasion of Crete by the Allies. Many months later I discovered that, for reasons not concerned with us the Middle East Command had deliberately prepared a special cover plan to lead the enemy to believe that an assault on Crete was imminent.

I eventually succeeded in persuading both Evmaios and Saraphis that they would be foolish to evacuate all their forces to the Pindus on the strength of the scanty information available. I got them to agree to make all the necessary plans for such an evacuation, but not to carry them out until they had specific evidence that such a sweep through the mountains was obviously about to begin.

Reverting to the Asopos operation, I asked Evmaios what hope he had of the 'Military Agreement' being accepted by our own GHQ if he still refused to carry out this operation. Saraphis interrupted and said that he regarded it militarily as quite impracticable. He had, however, learnt that a tunnel about a mile long, at a place called Turnavo, could be demolished. It had already been prepared for demolition, and all that was wanted was the necessary explosives to collapse several hundred yards of it at both ends. If this could be done whilst a train was passing through the tunnel it would block the railway for just as long as would the successful accomplishment of the Asopos viaduct operation.

I replied that, with mechanical earth-moving equipment, which the Germans had, such an operation would only block the railway for as many days as the destruction of the Asopos viaduct would block it for months. But when I saw that this was all they were prepared to do, I agreed to ask Cairo for the necessary explosives; incidentally, for half the quantity that ELAS had requested, and which I knew to be more than sufficient for the purpose. It is not unreasonable to assume that ELAS would have used the surplus explosives for such operations as that in 1944, when they attempted to blow up British officers in the Grande Bretagne Hotel in Athens.

The following morning, 19th May, Evmaios, Saraphis and Aris departed on a tour of Thessaly and Macedonia, flying the flag of their newly formed ELAS General Headquarters. Before breakfast on the morning of their departure I had had all three of them into my little cottage office in Mavrolithari. I wanted to go with them on this tour, not only to meet for the first time my senior liaison officers in Thessaly and Macedonia, Sheppard and Hammond, but to check their plans for widespread sabotage, and to see that ELAS played their all-important part in assisting them. I said that I would catch them up as soon as I had received instructions from Cairo as to my future action. I warned them solemnly that the day had come when they must decide whether EAM and ELAS were to turn over a completely new leaf, or, from then onwards, to cease having any further support from the British. Any more acts such as the disbanding of other National Bands, or any more refusals to carry out the wishes of the Middle East Command, would be looked upon with the gravest displeasure. In the interests of the war effort, we would reserve the right to take such counter-action as we thought fit. The patience of the Middle East Command and of the Mission in the mountains was nearing its end.

After the departure of GHQ, ELAS, I told Geoffrey Gordon-Creed all I knew about the gorge leading down to the Asopos viaduct, and we discussed the possibility of an attack on it with a small party of British officers. We came to the conclusion that the only possible way of destroying it was for a few men somehow to get down the gorge and to clamber up from it on to the viaduct. All other possible approaches were now too heavily guarded, and our only chance of success was with a very small party from this direction, which the enemy probably did not even consider worth covering. Donald Stott had arrived from the Parnassus mountains. Geoffrey and he volunteered to go and have a look at the gorge. They set off at dawn the following day.

They returned the next night. Although the guards were now Germans, Geoffrey was optimistic. They had got about forty yards down the gorge before they had been held up by a deep water-fall. But neither of them saw any reason why, with sufficient rope, and previously prepared explosive charges wrapped up in waterproof covering, and with food for several days, they should not be able to get right down the gorge to the viaduct.

Two days later Geoffrey, Donald, the three Sapper officers, Wingate, Scott and McIntyre, and a Greek interpreter George Karadjo-poulos, with Lance-Corporal Chester Lockwood, a British es-caped prisoner-of-war, left to attempt the task. The whole party were volunteers. They carried with them gym shoes to wear on entering the gorge, from which point onwards they would travel unarmed except for rubber 'coshes'. Their chances of success depended upon their ability to remain unobserved by the enemy. If they were spotted, at the best they would be taken prisoner; they would have no chance of escape.

Meanwhile we had asked Cairo for some additional explosives for ELAS for their doubtful 'tunnel' operation. On the night of 24th May, as a result of a most enterprising and courageous piece of work, the explosives arrived. It was already one o'clock in the morning when we heard overhead the aircraft carrying them. But there was thick cloud at the time, and the pilot could not see our bonfires. Undaunted, he flew away and came back half an hour later. The cloud-base was still too low for him to venture through it in that mountainous area. Back again at half-hourly intervals the pilot came, until, when he must have had little spare petrol for his return journey to the Middle East, at four o'clock in the morning he dived through a break in the clouds to drop the whole of his load close to our fires. On their return journey, in the fast-approaching daylight, the crew ran considerable risk of being attacked by enemy fighters before they were clear of the Peloponnese and the outlying Greek islands.

Although the chance of our being able to blow up the Asopos viaduct was a slender one now that the Germans had taken over guard duties, the task could not have been placed in better hands. I waited to see Geoffrey and his party complete their preparations and depart; I then set out to catch up ELAS headquarters. When I overtook them on 27th May at a pretty little village called Aya Trias which nestled in foothills below the steep Timfrestos mountain ridge, I found Psaros and Zervas' officer Papaiannou there, still held captives by ELAS. But before dealing further with the intransigence of EAM and ELAS, let me return to Geoffrey Gordon-Creed's progress in the Asopos gorge.

On 28th May a runner reached me from Arthur Edmonds. He brought a full report from Gordon-Creed.

The charges for the Asopos operation had been made up early in May. On the 21st, after Gordon-Creed and Stott's favourable reconnaissance, the explosives and accessories had been transported on mules to a place near the top of the gorge. On the morning of the 23rd the explosives were wrapped in pieces of waterproof cape into five separate bundles. With the exception of Lance-Corporal Chester, who remained at the head of the gorge to look after the clothes and equipment they had discarded, the party then took the bundles and began their slow and dangerous journey down the narrow gorge, never more than ten feet wide, sometimes only two or three. Great difficulty was experienced in keeping the explosives dry owing to high waterfalls, sometimes as high as forty feet, and owing to the considerable volume of torrential water and the many deep pools. These obstacles were overcome either by lowering the bundles to one side of the waterfall, or by making an aerial ropeway and attaching them in turn to the rope and allowing them to slide down it. Sometimes Gordon-Creed and his small party walked through the icy-cold water with the charges held above their heads. At the end of the first day they had got only a short way down the gorge. They found a dry spot and rested there for the night.

The following day they carried on to a point approximately two-thirds of the way down the gorge. They could get no further because of a particularly tricky waterfall, approximately twenty feet high, which required either rope ladders or a tree to negotiate it. By then they had run out of rope, and the moon was getting too low for them to have a chance of attacking by night even if they could have got any further. They left their charges in a dry place in the gorge and returned to Anatoli.

In a covering message Arthur Edmonds wrote that he had already signalled to Cairo for more rope to be dropped, and that it was planned to try again in the following moon period. Arthur added that several of Geoffrey's party had torn their hands and knees badly and that two of them were completely exhausted on their return. He was making minor alterations to the composition of the party. He was optimistic about the outcome of their next attempt.

Those who took part in the final attempt in June were Major Geoffrey Gordon-Creed and Captain Donald Stott, both Commando-trained officers; Major Scott and Captain McIntyre of the Royal Engineers—all four having taken part in the first attempt; Lance-Corporal Charlie Mutch, a British escaped prisoner-of-war, and Sergeant Michael Khuri, the Palestinian Arab who had joined us at Stromni in the previous autumn, and whose gallantry in the Gorgopotamos operation had already earned him a Military Medal.

A preliminary reconnaissance was made on 16th June by Captain Stott, Lance-Corporal Mutch and Sergeant Khuri. For the first time, using the extra rope, they succeeded in passing right down the gorge in daylight to a point immediately above the last bend above the viaduct. Stott now worked his way on alone to within a hundred yards of the viaduct. It was swarming with workmen. They were busy riveting and concreting on the bridge. There was scaffolding all round its ends.

On 19th June the remainder of the party, consisting of Gordon-Creed, Scott and McIntyre, arrived at the head of the gorge, and the following day they proceeded down it. Whilst the explosive charges were being repaired and altered at the point where they had left them the previous month, Gordon-Creed carried out another reconnaissance at dusk with Stott. This time a point almost underneath the viaduct was reached. They noticed a steep path which appeared to lead up to the scaffolding on the left—north—bank. It was decided to attack that night.

The party set off at six-thirty in the evening of 20th June to cover the remaining distance of about three hundred and fifty yards to the viaduct. At approximately eight o'clock they all reached the foot of the path. A final reconnaissance was then made of the bridge and scaffolding by Gordon-Creed and Stott. By great good fortune it was found that neat gaps had been cut through the barbed wire surrounding the foot of the big central span; also that the enemy had been kind enough to leave a ladder leading up through the scaffolding on to a platform about thirty feet up, from which point it would be possible to reach the main girders. Lance-Corporal Mutch and Sergeant Khuri were now sent back up the gorge to prepare something hot, to strike camp and to be ready for a hasty exit.

The four remaining members then hauled up the explosives and, in the moonlight, the two Sapper officers began placing them in position. Gordon-Creed and Stott stayed on the ground at the foot of the bridge.

Shortly after they had got all the explosives up on to the platform a German guard, on his round, approached them. They all remained motionless and, as he passed, Gordon-Creed, who was crouching behind a bush, jumped out and hit him on the head with his 'cosh'. The German silently toppled over the cliff, the noise of his fall drowned by the raging torrent below.

After a pause Stott and McIntyre went on connecting up the charges. They had not been working very long when one of them hit his foot against a loose bolt, which the workmen repairing the bridge must have left on the wooden platform. It fell on to the metal girders below with a resounding clang. The four officers froze where they were; but nothing stirred, except the German guards passing up and down on the bridge above them, who had apparently heard nothing. Scott and McIntyre then looked around the platform for more bolts. They saw a lot of dark circles; but these all turned out to be knots in the wooden platform. They continued fixing the charges.

There were times when no work could be done for minutes on end, owing to the brightness of the moon, or because of a searchlight with which the Germans periodically illuminated the bridge. After about an hour most of the charges had been placed in position and Stott left to find a suitable position from which to observe results. Half an hour later everything was ready. Fuses, each with one and a half-hour's delayed action, were fixed to the charges. It was already past midnight before they were ignited. The three remaining members of the party then left.

At that moment a searchlight turned right on them, apparently as a routine performance by the guard; but, quoting from Gordon Creed's report, "the enemy was apparently unsuspicious, in spite of the appalling noise all three of us made falling over and dropping things, and the guards' curiosity was not aroused".

Grave anxiety was felt as to whether the explosives were still serviceable since, owing to the depth of water, they had had to be dragged through it in some places on their way down to the viaduct. When the party was still only half way up the gorge, however, at 2.15 in the morning, a deafening roar reverberated up it. With one complete cut across the curved steel sections of the main arch, Donald Stott saw the whole central span collapse and drag with it both the cantilevered spans which projected on to it from either end. All three fell into the deep gorge below, where they settled, a twisted mass of steelwork. Twenty-four hours later the entire party was back at Anatoli. The operation had been a complete success.

We learnt later that the viaduct had been guarded by about forty Germans, with six heavy machine guns and more light automatics. The whole defence had been laid out in every direction except up the gorge. The Germans were so convinced that the viaduct had been blown up as a result of treachery that they shot the entire garrison guarding it. The RAF flew over the area a few days later to photograph the damage done, and a coloured stereoscopic pair of photographs was duly prepared. Some months later I was asked to show them to Mr. Churchill. I still remember his gleeful chuckle.

The Germans soon began to have the bridge repaired. Polish labour, mixed with Greek, was employed night and day to get the line reopened. A number of tall, concrete piers were put up, and at the end of two months the work was completed. But it had been too quickly done, or else deliberately sabotaged by some of the men employed on the work; for, when the Germans drove their first engine across it, one of the piers collapsed, and part of the bridge and the engine fell into the gorge. It was not until another two months later that the viaduct was finally reopened. The operation had thus caused the main line to Athens to be cut for over four months.

There were many magnificent exploits during the war behind the enemy lines in the Balkans; but, for sheer endurance, determination to succeed and pluck there was probably no more gallant achievement of its type. Not only did General Sir Henry Maitland Wilson,★ the C.-in-C. Middle East, send his congratulations by wireless to those who took part, but Mr. Churchill himself, when he learnt of the operation, also sent his personal congratulations. With little chance of escape should they have been discovered by the enemy whilst in the gorge, and living for days and nights hemmed in on both sides by vertical and overhanging rock-faces, with claustrophobia continually threatening them, these six men under Geoffrey Gordon-Creed's leadership successfully achieved a most gallant venture. Every one of them received an award: Gordon-Creed and Stott each the D.S.O.; the two Sapper officers each the M.C.; and the two other ranks the Military Medal. The absolutely fearless Donald Stott, whose enthusiasm dominated the party throughout, I put up for a V.C. But, because not a shot had been fired throughout the operation, I was told he was not qualified for this decoration. He thoroughly deserved it.

A week or two after the destruction of the Asopos viaduct, Donald Stott, who was then very run down, developed a bad and extremely painful abscess in his ear. A village doctor on Parnassus advised him that only an operation would relieve him of the incessant pain. On 16th July I received a signal that he was proceeding to Athens without delay, in order to get a specialist to operate on him. Three days later I heard that he had returned. He had been successfully operated on in a maternity clinic. He had entered Athens by night in uniform, completely

★ Now Field Marshal Lord Wilson of Libya, G.C.B., G.B.E., D.S.O.

undisguised—just a simple, everyday occurrence to a man of Stott's calibre.*

* When Greece was liberated, Donald Stott was transferred to the Far Eastern theatre of war. In 1945, whilst on his way to undertake a similar type of operation behind the Japanese lines, the submarine carrying him was lost. In due course he was reported missing, presumed killed. I hope that one day someone will write the full story of the many daring exploits of this outstandingly gallant officer.

CHAPTER XII

'National Bands' Agreement

ON EVMAIOS' return from Athens on 16th May he had told me that the 'Military Agreement' had been discussed by his leaders in Athens, and that they could not agree to allow British Liaison Officers to give instructions to ELAS in the field. All mention of their names must be deleted from the Agreement. EAM and their inseparable army, ELAS, would be pleased to accept general instructions from the Middle East Command; but the method of their execution and the selection of targets for attack must be left to the discretion and decision of the new ELAS GHQ. Otherwise, he said, they were prepared to sign the Agreement, and he handed me a redraft which he claimed, apart from the fact that it omitted any mention of British Liaison Officers, and instituted an andarte GHQ, was, to all intents and purposes, identical with the one which I required to be signed. He told me that, if I agreed to these amendments, he was empowered by the Central Committee to sign, both on their behalf and on behalf of ELAS.

After it was translated, I read carefully through his version and came to the conclusion that it would suffice; for although ELAS at that time possessed a large number of arms, the majority of which they had procured by their own means, the Movement was rapidly expanding and it would require a great number more. That being so the Middle East Command, through my Mission, held what I thought at the time was a trump card, in that, should ELAS not abide by the Agreement, or should they refuse to act operationally in accordance with our wishes we could stop the supply of arms to them.

On 18th May, when I got back to Mavrolithari, I sent to Cairo EAM's amended version of the Agreement, and recommended that we should accept it as soon as Psaros and all the other National Band leaders had been set free and their bands had been reinstated.

Recorded in my diary is a further long and frank talk with Evmaios on political matters. He told me—what I already knew —that the Central Committee in Athens gravely mistrusted the intentions of the British Government about the future of the King of Greece. He said they feared that it was our intention to re-impose the King with the aid of British bayonets when Greece was liberated. Until this matter was clarified, he stressed that there could be no wholehearted co-operation between EAM and the Middle East Command. "There must be a plebiscite of the people before the King returned," he added, "and he would only be permitted to return as a result of a free expression of the people's wish for him to do so. Until this had happened ELAS could not lay down their arms."

I asked him what this had to do with the war effort, and he replied that the people—meaning EAM, ELAS and the people in EAM controlled areas—would not obey the instructions of the Middle East Command unless they felt that their wishes would be carried out.

At that time more than half of the people in the mountains of Free Greece, perhaps a tenth of the total population of Greece, were under EAM control. If their political leaders could read into any public statements made by the King of Greece, or, alternatively, into any silence on his part, into official utterances of His Majesty's Government, or again, into silence on the latter's part, any indication that either the King of Greece or our own Government had ulterior motives, it would be comparatively easy for them to persuade the nucleus of their fervent supporters, and the conscripted masses in the areas under their control, that either the King of Greece did not intend to abide by the wishes of his people, or that our Government intended to meddle in what were purely Greek internal affairs.

In the last week of April, some ten days before leaving Theodhoriana for Roumeli, I had received my first political directive. Paraphrased notes which I made from it included the following:

"King George of Greece is and will continue to be regarded as the legal head of the Greek State until such time as the Greek Constitution might be altered as a result of the free expression of the will of the Greek people under conditions of tranquillity. His Majesty's Government obviously owe the King of Greece a considerable debt of gratitude for his steadfast loyalty to the Allies, particularly in 1941, when Greece, if she had capitulated, would have avoided having her small country overrun by the German hordes. Whereas, therefore, we in the mountains of Greece are authorised to give support to any and every Resistance Movement which is actively fighting, or prepared to fight, against the common enemy, we are not to allow vilification of the name of the King and the Government in exile to pass unnoticed; we are to point out that, not only according to International Law, but by their own Constitution, the Greek King is still the legal head of the State. This justifies our continued support to all ELAS bands which fight against the Axis. As, however, it appears impossible to separate ELAS from EAM, whose political aims run counter to those of the more moderate Movements in Greece, the authorities in Cairo consider that, after the liberation of Greece, civil war is almost inevitable."

I replied to Cairo that eventual civil war in Greece need not necessarily become inevitable. I laid great stress upon the inherent individuality of all Greeks and their abhorrence of dictatorship, be it of the Right or of the Left. I urged that, if only the British

Government could persuade the King of Greece publicly to announce that he would not set foot on Greek soil unless and until the people of Greece had, in a free plebiscite under conditions of tranquillity, expressed their wish for him to return as their constitutional King, the bottom could be knocked out of EAM's basket of propaganda.

When acknowledging my comments SOE (Cairo) said that they had been read with interest and that they were being forwarded to London.

As a result of this political directive I issued my own instructions to the officers under my command. I pointed out that, apart from the Atlantic Charter, until now we had had no policy laid down by our own Government to help us out of the many political entanglements in which we periodically found ourselves involved in connection with our military tasks. We now had a policy, which I wanted, and expected, to be loyally and tactfully followed. For the prosecution of the war, and the liberation of Greece, our Government wished to collaborate with as strong and as representative a Greek Government as possible. They were therefore supporting the Greek King and Government now in Cairo. They wished to see the Greek Government broadened and made fully representative. In the meantime, they strongly deprecated the raising of internal political issues which might not only prejudice the success of any invasion, but which would inevitably delay the day of liberation. The Greek King had already publicly declared that after the war he would abide by the freely expressed opinions of his people on all questions affecting them.

Whenever necessary or desirable, I instructed my officers to hand out the above assurance to EAM and to all other National Bands. I pointed out that we ourselves remained a purely military mission and that we were at all times to avoid becoming involved in political discussions. For their own personal information, I told them that it was our Government's wish that we should never hesitate to show our confidence in the Greek King and the present Greek Government, so that when Greece was liberated law and order could be maintained. All andarte leaders were to be told that everything now being sent to Greece should be accepted as a gesture of her Allies' appreciation of the great and gallant effort being made by the Greek people to resist and overthrow the Axis.

On 26th May, on my way from Arthur Edmonds' headquarters in Roumeli to catch up the newly formed GHQ of ELAS, I was overtaken by one of our runners with a message from Cairo. It instructed me on no account to sign the EAM version of the 'Military Agreement' as it now stood. To SOE it apparently seemed that its signature in the form suggested by EAM meant virtually handing over control of the Resistance Movements to that organisation. The C.-in-C., through the officers of the British Mission, Cairo insisted, must have a say in this matter, and all National Bands must have equal authority.

When I overtook ELAS headquarters at Aya Trias I found my new mobile wireless set and a temporary team awaiting me. But I also found that Psaros, Kranias and Zervas' officer, Papaiannou, were with them, still more or less prisoners. I carefully concocted a speech which I considered, in view of my instructions from Cairo, I was entitled to make to ELAS GHQ. Having previously informed them, through Tommy, that I had a most important announcement to make, I visited Evmaios, Saraphis and Aris by appointment, in the little, cluttered-up living-room of the cottage in which they were billeted. I remember the details so well. I stood to attention and Tommy stood similarly beside me. The three Greeks, impressed by the formality of the occasion, stood up also. I asked them to sit down and then made the following carefully prepared speech which I recorded verbatim in my diary.

"His Majesty's Government express the greatest displeasure at the persistence of the EAM policy of the past few months. They refer to the attempts made by EAM to seize power in the mountains by force, and to disband andartes loyal to the Allies. They do not regard this as an internal Greek affair, but as one affecting the Allies in the prosecution of the war.

"Although they regard the King of Greece as the legitimate authority in Greece until the country is freed, they have no intention of imposing the King against the will of the people.

"The Allies are pursuing a policy of freedom for all peoples and are opposed to any form of tyranny.

"The Military Agreement with GHQ, ME, as proposed by EAM, is unacceptable in its present form. The form of Agreement proposed by GHQ, ME is the only one which meets with their full approval.

"As a preliminary, before any Agreement can be signed, the National Bands dissolved are to be reformed, and those under arrest are to be freed. If this is not done, my Government reserve the right to take certain action in the interests of the Allies, and, in particular, in the interests of Greece, whose freedom they wish to secure as soon as possible."

Having delivered my speech, I immediately walked out and left them. A few hours later, Evmaios came to see me and politely asked me to transmit to the Central Committee of EAM the speech which I had read out to them. I agreed to transmit a shortened version.

Two weeks later I received, through Cairo, the Central Committee's reply. EAM categorically repudiated the intention attributed to them of seizing power by a *coup d'état*. The Central Committee insisted that, since it had been formed, its Movement had effectively struggled against the Axis alongside the Allies. It proclaimed that it was still struggling for the principles of the Atlantic Charter and against any attempt to oppose the free expression of the people's will in the solution of internal problems. It considered it a national obligation to facilitate the Andarte

Movement under a widespread direction, thus ensuring co-ordination of the struggle with the overall plans of the Middle East Command. It was ready to give proofs and guarantees of its sincerity.

With reference to the "deplorable events" in connection with the disarmament of other bands by ELAS forces, the EAM leaders stated that these actions did not express their policy and had been condemned from the first. They had already ordered the reinstatement of such disarmed bands and all prisoners to be set free, despite the fact that they claimed that these bands, from the moment of their formation, instead of turning against the Axis, had turned against EAM and ELAS to the great rejoicing of the Axis. They were pleased to learn that the British Government did not intend to impose the King against the will of the Greek people.

SOE informed me that, immediately upon the receipt of this message in Cairo, the Central Committee had been informed by signal that the Commander-in-Chief noted with satisfaction that EAM were fighting for the principles of liberty and freedom as laid down in the Atlantic Charter. The C.-in-C. paid tribute to ELAS's fine record of fighting and resistance to the invader. He said he was watching Greece with the closest attention; he considered the Greek guerillas a part of the forces under his command, and he expected from them the prompt execution of the tasks entrusted to them. He wished to form a combined Headquarters in Greece, in which I, as his Senior Liaison Officer, was to be responsible to him for the planning, timing and conduct of all military operations. The Central Committee was told that I would be kept fully briefed as to his requirements. Only by these means could the Greek guerillas be properly co-ordinated with the tasks of the invading armies of the United Nations. The signal ended up somewhat optimistically with words to the effect that the Commander-in-Chief was gratified to learn that there was no longer any difficulty in the realisation of his wishes.

The outcome of this exchange of telegrams was that the authorities in Cairo once more accepted on trial EAM's offer of goodwill. One immediate effect which my official outburst had was to obtain the release of Psaros, Kranias and Papaiannou, who ELAS now assured me were free to rejoin and reform their bands. As to the 'Military Agreement', Evmaios was very disheartened when I persisted that I was still not empowered to sign the EAM version of it. After a five hour conference, during which I failed to get EAM to modify their conditions for its signature, Evmaios informed me that, even if I were not empowered to sign it, for their part, ELAS GHQ would that day issue instructions to all their bands throughout Greece to obey their version of the Agreement, just as if it had been signed by both me and them. I was quite pleased with this, because, if it was carried out, it did at least mean that ELAS would no longer attack other National Bands, who would be able to form wherever they, or we, wished them to do so. But what was more important to me at that time, it meant that I had a greater chance of obtaining the agreement of ELAS GHQ to undertake operations I required of them, and consequently a far greater chance that they would be executed at a lower level.

On 28th May a runner from Arthur Edmonds had brought me a full report about the failure of Geoffrey Gordon-Creed's first attempt to reach the Asopos viaduct, and the necessity of delaying the next attempt until the following moon period. I received this news almost simultaneously with the announcement by ELAS GHQ that, the previous night, a band of theirs had succeeded in blowing up both ends of the Turnavo tunnel, just after a train had entered it. When I gave them the latest news about the Asopos, I could hardly blame them for treating my contribution rather coolly. The train in the Turnavo tunnel had crashed into the debris at the far end and had caught alight. Most of a train load of Germans had been burnt alive, but so had forty innocent Greeks, who were travelling in the front coach as preventive hostages against sabotage of the train. Saraphis told me that they had blocked the railway for at least six weeks. I replied that I thought the Germans, if they really set to it, could clear away the debris in as many days. A week later the railway was re-opened. Forty Greeks thus lost their lives for no effective purpose.

As my route to Western Thessaly with ELAS GHQ would take us close to the Acheloos River, on the far side of which was Zervas' area, and as the date for our widespread sabotage operations was drawing near, I thought that it would be worth while making a final attempt to reconcile EDES and ELAS, by bringing the respective leaders together at a meeting presided over by Chris and myself. ELAS GHQ, although sceptical, agreed to my proposals. Aris doubted if Zervas would either condescend or dare to meet them outside his own area. I accepted their challenge and sent a strongly worded signal to Chris, telling him to do all in his power to get Zervas to meet us at a little village called Liascovo, not more than a few miles east of the Acheloos River, for a conference to begin on 5th June.

Chris succeeded, and on the evening of 4th June we all duly gathered there. I explained to the assembled leaders the object of the conference. It was, I said, to establish a joint direction of the Resistance Movements. I recommended the establishment of a 'Joint General Headquarters', on the lines that EAM had suggested, but with ultimate control vested in the Middle East Command, and with all National Bands having equal representation. I pointed out that it was becoming increasingly important to co-ordinate the sabotage activities of the different Resistance Movements throughout Greece. The days of independent action were fast drawing to a close. I recommended that Saraphis, the military member of ELAS Headquarters, Zervas and I should form this joint headquarters, and I left Zervas, with his second-in-command and chief staff officer, Komninos Pyromaglou and Colonel

Gikopoulos, to argue out the matter with Evmaios, Saraphis and Aris. They talked for a good many hours, but eventually Chris and I were summoned back. They had failed to come to any agreement.

We re-assembled the next day, to go over the ground and see if, after a night's rest, there was any possible way of overcoming the obstacles to agreement. Zervas, knowing that I was not empowered to sign the ELAS version of the 'Military Agreement', and knowing that ELAS would not sign mine, was obstreperous. ELAS GHQ were obstinate, Saraphis childishly so. He made ridiculous speeches, apparently primed to do so by his confederates. Try as I did, I could not get ELAS to agree to join up with Zervas in a combined headquarters unless the whole of ELAS GHQ became members, and unless there was a procedure to vote on all future operations, in which voting EAM/ELAS, with their three members, "because of their larger forces in the field", were to be entitled to three votes to Zervas' one and my one. As this would have meant virtually handing over control of the Resistance Movements to ELAS—and EAM—I naturally could not agree; Zervas, knowing it, made play with the situation.

Eventually I was forced to admit failure, and we declared the conference closed. I sent back full details to Cairo and asked them for further instructions. I told them that it was essential to get some form of Agreement signed by ELAS because, unless I did so before the widespread sabotage, which I now knew was required in a few weeks' time, I could not guarantee adequate control over their activities in the all important sabotage areas of Roumeli, North-eastern Thessaly and Macedonia, where the main north–south communications ran through Greece. Rather crestfallen, I parted from ELAS headquarters next day, in order to return to Theodhoriana with Chris, and to change the composition of my mobile wireless team. I told Evmaios that I would rejoin him and Saraphis in Thessaly or Macedonia. Aris returned to Roumeli.

Chris, my interpreter, Tommy and I got back to Theodhoriana on 7th June. Ross by then had got such a comfortable head-quarters going that it was almost like returning home. Weary as the result of a hard day's travelling, Chris and I went to the cottage which we now regarded as almost our own, and were soon asleep.

It seemed no time afterwards when I was woken up by the scream of aircraft diving overhead and the falling of bombs all round. I was literally shaken out of bed. We had taken the precaution of digging slit trenches outside our houses in case we were one day bombed. As I slipped on my boots and made a dash for the trench, broken glass was flying from the window, and the house was shaking ominously from the burst of several bombs nearby. In ten minutes it was all over. A squadron of Stukas climbed up and, once beyond the mountain tops, disappeared from view.

In the relative stillness which followed I stood up in my trench and looked around. At the far end of the village several columns of smoke were rising vertically into the still, early morning air. Within a hundred yards of me two cottages had been completely destroyed.

All the members of our headquarters set to work to extricate the trapped and wounded. It was late in the evening before we had done all that we could and a doctor had arrived from the next village, Voulgareli. We felt terribly guilty in bringing tragedy to innocent and contented Theodhoriana. But when, towards evening, the villagers started to creep back from the mountains whither they had fled, they were extraordinarily kind in assuring us that we were not to blame. They blamed only the 'quislings' in Athens.

From that day onwards, whenever our headquarters was in the same area for more than a few days, I always had it set up some distance away from the village.

Not long afterwards the Germans made another attempt to bomb our base outside Theodhoriana. This time they sent over two squadrons of Stukas, one of which had obviously been briefed to attack a small, isolated mountain church, on a promontory about a mile from the village. The Stukas dived down out of the sun to attack the building. The first three or four raised such a cloud of dust that one of the aeroplanes, whilst hidden in the cloud, was inadvertently machine gunned by another diving close behind it. It caught alight; the pilot managed to get his machine up to a safe height before he and his gunner were forced to bale out. Not many hours later both were picked up by andartes and they were eventually brought in to our headquarters. Their interrogation was most refreshing. The German pilot had just been posted to Greece from Russia, where he had carried out over a hundred operational sorties without suffering a scratch. "And now," he complained bitterly, "here am I, on my first flight over our own territory, shot down by one of my own people! . . . This is not war. What right have you to hold me prisoner?"

After being fully interrogated, both Germans were entrusted to the care of Zervas' andartes. They subsequently escaped, but were recaptured within a day or two. This showed how difficult it was for a stranger to wander even in those wild mountains without detection by the Greek people, who were all morally in the Resistance Movement, whether they carried arms or not, and whatever their political views.

At the recent conference at Liascovo, in an attempt to achieve something constructive, I had asked both Zervas and ELAS to give me a senior representative to join my headquarters as liaison officers. ELAS had been unable to meet this request immediately, because, they said, they had no suitable officer available. But Zervas had straight away given me his chief staff officer, Colonel Gikopoulos.

I was anxious to catch up ELAS GHQ and to try to make sure

that, even at this late date, the maximum amount of sabotage would be carried out in Northern and Eastern Greece in little over a fortnight's time; so, on 11th June, Gikopoulos, Chris and I set off northwards with my mobile wireless set and two fresh operators. Knowing that a batch of new interpreters was expected from Athens any day now, I left Tommy behind, and gave orders for one of the new arrivals to be sent on to me.

On 13th June we reached Metzovo, a little village at the highest point on the mountain road between Kalambaka and Yannina. The next afternoon we arrived at Perivoli. Here, one of my officers, Captain Bliaux, of the Royal Corps of Signals, had a wireless school and was training Greek operators to use our sets. Late in the evening we reached Avdela, where Sheppard and Karayioryis had finally established their headquarters for the summer. It was here that we overtook ELAS GHQ.

The following day, anxious to get ELAS on the move towards their targets, I had an earnest conversation with Saraphis. It was immediately apparent to me that he had no authority to give way on any points regarding the 'Military Agreement'. I told him that, unless I could get some agreement signed by him, as C.-in-C., ELAS, it seemed to me very doubtful whether the Middle East Command would continue supplying them for many days more. I explained to him that very many sorties were due that month—Cairo had increased them from forty to seventy—and I told him that I intended allotting over two-thirds of them to ELAS areas if I could get an agreement signed. Eventually I got him to put his signature to a document which said that GHQ ELAS put itself at the disposal of the C.-in-C. Middle East, and that their bands would obey all orders of the Middle East Command, issued to them through their own GHQ. This was a considerable step forward. Saraphis asked me to request Cairo to have broadcast by the BBC the fact that ELAS had signed this document. I willingly agreed to do so. The same day, having previously discussed with

Sheppard his sabotage arrangements in Eastern Thessaly, I explained to Saraphis the operations for which the Middle East Command wanted him to authorise preparations without delay.

On 17th June I was at last given a free hand by Cairo to get the best possible terms out of ELAS, with a view to getting them to sign an agreement to co-operate with other andarte organisations under the orders of the Middle East Command. I was told that any decision I made would be backed up by the authorities in Cairo. That evening I handed a draft agreement to Evmaios. It was almost identical with EAM's version; but it included what I thought were sufficient references to my own liaison officers, and to my, and their, authority to avoid giving EAM and ELAS undue power. Evmaios appeared somewhat doubtful as to whether Zervas would sign such a document. I reassured him on this point, and told him that it was immaterial to ELAS whether or not Zervas did so. I would see about that, I said, and I asked him whether he would accept the draft as it stood. After a short discussion he replied that he agreed with it, but that he must just get confirmation by wireless, from the Central Committee in Athens. From his attitude I was confident that there would be no difficulties from Athens—particularly when he told me that he had no wish to send the Agreement by his own runner to Athens, but that I was at liberty to send it by my wireless link through Cairo. This I duly did, and at the same time I sent a copy to Zervas, with the request that he, in accordance with his promise to carry out the wishes of the Middle East Command, should also sign.

I immediately began discussions with Evmaios, Saraphis, Karayioryis, Chris and Sheppard about further targets for sabotage in Eastern Thessaly and Macedonia. I was soon satisfied that ELAS would make genuine attempts to help us with them all.

On 4th July I received news of the Central Committee's approval of the re-drafted 'Military Agreement', and the following day GHQ ELAS signed it, Evmaios doing so on behalf of the inseparable EAM as well. The next day I learnt that Zervas had refused to sign. His reasons were that the original Agreement which he had signed without hesitation the previous March was more suitable than this new one, and that he disagreed with the establishment of a Joint GHQ, on which, he said, he would always be in a one to three minority with the ELAS triumvirate. In the course of several signals I did my best to reassure him, at the same time telling him that it was the Middle East Command's wish that he should sign this new Agreement as it stood. He then did so, but not without once more voicing his misgivings about the functioning of the Andarte Joint GHQ. He promised that he would always have a representative at GHQ whenever he himself was unable personally to be present.

A few days later an official summary of the 'National Bands Agreement' was issued by GHQ Middle East. The announcement concluded: "It is therefore now an accomplished fact that all Greek andarte bands, irrespective of their political or other tendencies have been welded into a united and co-ordinated instrument for the furtherance of the Allied struggle."

CHAPTER XIII

Widespread Sabotage

On 29th May, while I was at Aya Trias, a historic signal came through from Cairo. It was addressed to me personally, and I was instructed to burn it immediately I had decoded and read it. In the second week of July, I was informed, Sicily would be invaded by the Allies. Commencing in the last week of June, we were therefore instructed to begin widespread sabotage throughout Greece, in order to lead the enemy to believe that this part of the Mediterranean was threatened with invasion. We were to continue our activities on all communications until news was received of the actual invasion of Sicily. There was no mention in the signal about any subsidiary assault on the Dodecanese.

At once I sent out by wireless or by runner a few pre-arranged code words to all the different stations throughout Greece. These gave them the necessary information to put our long-prepared plans for sabotage into execution.

On 22nd June, when I was in Macedonia, the great news about the successful destruction of the Asopos viaduct had reached me by wireless. Although this operation had been conceived four months earlier, its ultimate success could not have been more appropriately timed. The following day news started coming in about other successes in our widespread series of operations throughout Greece. Success signals followed hot-foot on one another for several days on end.

The railway line and roads between Larissa and Salonika were cut in many places by British Liaison Officers, assisted by small parties of ELAS andartes; and, in the Tempe valley beneath Olympus, the railway was kept cut for several weeks. A large band of ELAS ambushed an enemy motorised column on the main road through the Sarandoporon pass. Having blocked the road, the andartes took up defensive positions in the Pass, and beat off all enemy attempts, fortunately unconcerted, to break through and reopen the road. It was not until a force of more than two German battalions, supported by mortars and light artillery, made a co-ordinated attack some two weeks later that the pass was reopened.

Nat Barker, with a couple of assistants, rode across the plains of Thessaly by night and blew up two small bridges on the railway line right in the middle of the Plain on two separate occasions. East of Agrinion on the coastal road leading to Athens, not many days after his successful destruction of the Asopos viaduct, Gordon-Creed with a small band of andartes succeeded in blowing up a large and important road bridge.

The lateral mountain road between Kalambaka and Yannina through the historic Metzovo Pass was systematically destroyed by Captain Harker and bands of both ELAS and EDES, working separately. Every culvert was blown up; every bridge destroyed; and, wherever practical, the cliff-faces of cuttings were mined and embankments were cut away. This was a separate and deliberate operation, to undertake which I had obtained the permission of SOE (Cairo). Knowing that Sicily, and not Greece, was to be invaded in July, I anticipated that the ultimate invasion of Greece would be mounted from the heel of Italy, and would take place on the west coast of Epirus. The Kalambaka–Yannina road was the only lateral one, north of the coastal road between Athens and Messolonghi, by which the enemy could bring reinforcements from the east of Greece to the west coast. It was therefore of particular importance to destroy it now, before the enemy began to put strong garrisons alongside it.

Through Epirus, where Tom Barnes had carefully prepared a most comprehensive plan of sabotage, the results of his and his several officers' untiring leadership night after night were so brilliantly successful, and the consequent disruption of communications was so complete, that the enemy came to the conclusion that the west coast of Greece was already in imminent danger of being invaded by the Allies.

In Evrytania, young Themie Marinos, with some bands of Zervas under the command of a Dr. Houtas, kept the road between Agrinion and Arta almost continuously cut for several weeks.

Apart from the Peloponnese, only in Eastern Roumeli were results rather disappointing. Even there Arthur Edmonds got one band of ELAS to help him carry out a successful attack upon a railway bridge near Dereli, in the hills to the north of the Sperkhios river. It was destroyed just as a train was travelling over it, and the resultant wreckage took many days to clear.

At the same time as all this was going on, telephone wires were cut by the andartes throughout the mainland of Greece.

The enemy sent reinforcements from Athens towards Epirus, and ordered two of their divisions to move south into Greece from Yugoslavia, where they were already fully occupied against the Partisans. Not until some days after the Allied landings in Sicily were these reinforcements turned about and despatched through Italy to the main battle-front. Some of an enemy column, who were taken prisoners by Dr. Houtas' bands in South-western Epirus, said that they had left Athens no less than seventeen days before. From this it can be well judged how completely communications throughout Greece were being disrupted.

On 30th June, when our activities were at their height and by no means finished, I received a signal from the three Service Commanders-in-Chief in the Middle East requesting me to convey to all British ranks their congratulations and appreciation of the magnificent efforts which had dislocated enemy maintenance arrangements and troop movements in the Balkans and which would embarrass the enemy even farther afield. I sent back an appropriate reply, thanking them on behalf of all ranks, at the same time informing SOE that we had by no means finished.

Sabotage continued unabated until 11th July, when we received the glorious news that Sicily had been invaded the previous day by the Allies, and that a successful foothold had been obtained. I was instructed by Cairo to stop all further sabotage activity. I sent out a pre-arranged code word by wireless, re-transmitted by Cairo, to all stations in Greece, and within a couple of days sabotage ceased as instantaneously as it had begun.

In this account I have done bare justice to the tireless and gallant work of all ranks of the British Mission; not only officers and NCOs engaged on sabotage, but wireless operators, who often left their sets and actively assisted them, and who worked long hours under trying and dangerous conditions, keeping Cairo and myself informed of their officers' and local andarte bands' successes. I pay tribute to them all. In addition, I pay tribute to all those andartes who assisted and co-operated with them, and who loyally executed the instructions of the Middle East Command. Apart from large ambushes, disruption of telephone communications and many minor blockages, a total of forty-four cuts of the railway and roads were carried out on the mainland of Greece, no less than sixteen of them on the railway, before a halt had been called to our activities.

Only in the Peloponnese did we achieve virtually no useful contribution towards the invasion of Sicily. Here the problems of the development of Resistance differed from that in Northern Greece for two main reasons. Firstly, the country did not lend itself to guerilla warfare. The natural strongholds in the mountains were small because they were intersected by a network of roads, by Greek standards well developed. Secondly the Peloponnese was in a sense the front line of the Germans, especially after they had lost North Africa. The enemy therefore maintained more troops there than in Northern Greece, and they were particularly sensitive about their security. Their headquarters was in the centre of the peninsula, and this involved constant policing of the central mountain plateau.

At the end of February, when the Mission was reorganised with the object of preparing for widespread sabotage in the summer, I had informed SOE that I did not see how I could effectively control the development of Resistance in the Peloponnese. As a result of the great stress Cairo laid upon that part of Greece, I had planned to send Denys Hamson there, to make a start. As may be remembered, however, before a guide arrived for him, he had to be diverted to accompany Vlakhos and the remnants of Saraphis' National Bands to the Pindus. Some weeks later a Greek officer, known to us as Minis, was dropped on the mainland. At that time we knew little about the local situation in the Peloponnese. To develop the forces of Resistance, we therefore accepted Zervas' nominee, who was reputed to control a thousand andartes, scattered all over the peninsula. After having been fully briefed, Minis set off on foot with Zervas' guide to the Gulf of Patras. From there he crossed over to the Peloponnese in a small boat.

Soon after his arrival, Minis tried to arrange for the direct reception of other British parachutists by the andarte bands in different areas. But he had been unable to take a wireless set with him on his long and difficult journey from my headquarters on the mainland, and communication with Cairo through Athens was a slow business. Finally, in May, 1943, a British team under command of Major Reid jumped blind into the area. Simultaneously three other attempts were made by parties from Cairo to contact different bands which every andarte organisation claimed as its own. Of the three parties, two Greek and one British, the Greek ones established themselves in the Tripolis area. The British one, under

Commander Cumberlege, whose primary task was to block the Corinth Canal, was caught. Minis eventually got in touch with one of the Greek teams.

The situation which both Minis and Reid reported independently was not very encouraging. Zervas' nominee turned out to be rather a characterless leader, incapable of holding his own against two other rival andarte organisations which, unbeknown to me at the time when Minis set out, were already in the field.

One of the rival organisations in the Peloponnese was called the National Organisation of Officers, or EOA; it was nationalist in character, and was formed by officers from Athens who recognised the Royalist Government in exile. The other—no great surprise to us—was EAM/ELAS. But what was a surprise to us was its rapid development.

Until the spring, when we started encouraging Resistance Movements in the Peloponnese, EAM had paid little attention to their organisation there. But, as soon as they realised our interest in the area, they rapidly made amends. Early in July Aris sent one of his most forceful subordinates with a hundred andartes across by sea from Roumeli to the peninsula. Based upon their already carefully established network, EAM/ELAS developed bands all over the peninsula with lightning rapidity, usually liquidating or absorbing the bands of rival organisations in their customary way. Immediately before the invasion of Sicily, therefore, such few bands as might have contributed useful sabotage were fully occupied avoiding or fighting ELAS.

Subsequently I was often asked how many andartes had actually taken part in the operations on the mainland. It was difficult to make an accurate assessment. Indirectly, practically every andarte band of ELAS, EDES and EKKA had contributed towards them; for, even in districts where they did not actually carry out the destruction of telephone lines, bridges, enemy convoys or trains, the fact that they were in the district afforded the essential freedom of movement and security to British officers and small parties of picked andartes engaged upon tricky sabotage work.

Virtually all the thirty odd British Liaison Officers then under my command were continuously engaged for the three weeks preceding the invasion of Sicily. By night they were often attacking one target, and by day on the move over the mountains to a fresh one. Tom Barnes personally supervised the attack on, and destruction of, three different bridges, each separated by the best part of a day's march, in the space of five nights. His personal contribution was outstanding. In Northern Thessaly, ELAS bands under the direction of Lieut.-Colonel Hammond and Captain Johnson achieved excellent results. In Valtos, in straightforward fighting, some EDES bands, under one of Zervas' officers called Major Agoros, were conspicuously successful. This officer's ability and power of leadership were outstanding, and, in proportion to their numbers, his andartes probably accounted for more enemy killed in action than any others during the period of these intensive operations.

The day after the Allied landings in Sicily I sent a message through our wireless stations to the andarte bands of all organisations on the mainland. I asked the leaders to convey my congratulations to all ranks under their command and to thank them for their successes in the recent operations throughout Greece. These operations, I said, which had been carefully timed by the Middle East Command and loyally executed by all andartes, had contributed, and were still contributing largely towards the success of the Allied armies in Italy. The Axis had been led to believe that an Allied attack on the Balkans was imminent. Reinforcements otherwise destined for Italy had been sent to Greece, thus distracting the enemy's attention and assisting the unmolested passage of our large sea convoys in the Mediterranean. I realised that these operations had not been undertaken without much suffering by innocent civilians in Greece, which I deeply regretted.

I asked the andarte leaders to convey to all civilians my great appreciation of their loyalty to the andarte and Allied cause and their large contribution towards our final victory.

The war, I said, was progressing deliberately and relentlessly towards its certain end. The exact date when Greece would be invaded by the Allies was not yet known. All I asked, which I knew all Greeks would give, was their continued confidence and unswerving loyalty to the Military Commanders of the Allied Armies of the Mediterranean, one of whose armies was the Andarte Army of Greece. I requested them to continue to serve under their orders until the great day when Greece was liberated, and even longer, until the Axis' unconditional surrender.

CHAPTER XIV

Politics Predominate

MY TOUR of Thessaly and Macedonia in June, apart from the urgent business of getting ELAS to the post for widespread sabotage, had other interesting aspects. I talked with many people, most of them supporters, but some in suppressed fear, of ELAS. I soon gathered almost conclusive evidence that, until the early spring of 1943, there had been many independent bands in that part of Greece. During the previous March and April, however, EAM had swept them all from the field, with the threat of death to their leaders if they refused either to join up their bands with ELAS, or to disperse them to their villages. By the time I arrived on the scene, EAM/ELAS held an undisputed monopoly; there was literally no other organisation in the field in that part of Greece.

On 19th June I had followed GHQ ELAS from Avdela to Bohorina, the ELAS headquarters in Macedonia. I walked on foot for the first three hours only; after that I travelled by car all the way. I had a warm reception in the comparatively large country town of Grevena, and in several other villages through which I passed on my way. The country in that part of Macedonia was much kinder than the rugged type to which I had grown accustomed in the Pindus and in Roumeli. There were rolling grass-covered hills, with few forests to interrupt the view. Cherries were ripening in quantities on the trees. The more open scenery was delightfully refreshing.

A day or two after my arrival at Bohorina, I was laid up with a

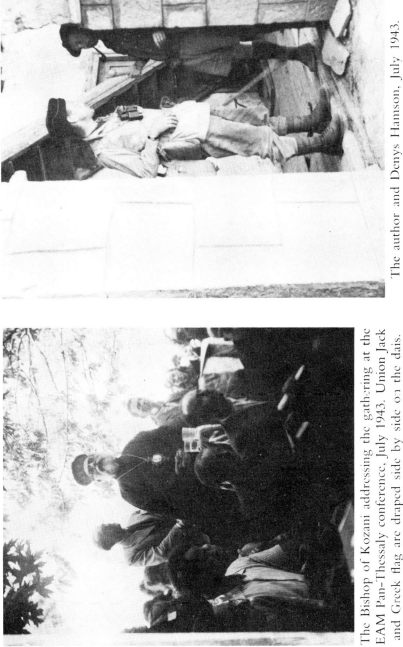

The Bishop of Kozani addressing the gathering at the EAM Pan-Thessaly conference, July 1943. Union Jack and Greek flag are draped side by side on the dais.

The author and Denys Hamson, July 1943.

Left to right: Yani, an escaped Cypriot P.O.W.; Kokinos, Zervas's EDES representative; Woodhouse; Jerry Wines, senior American OSS officer; Nikolopoulos, EAM/ELAS representative; at Woodhouse's H.Q.

A group of ELAS andartes.

mild fever. Meanwhile Evmaios was away on the Yugoslav frontier. He returned on 28th June with a representative of Tito and an andarte of the Albanian Left-wing Resistance Movement, LNC, which had aims somewhat similar to those of EAM. The following day a conference was convened by Evmaios at a nearby village named Tsotyli, at which both the ELAS leaders and the visiting partisan representatives spoke to a gathering of local ELAS andartes. I was invited to attend and to speak. I did both.

The most interesting feature of the different speeches was the reference by the Yugoslav Partisan—a lawyer called Svetoza Voukmanovitch—to the possibility of a Pan-Balkan Andarte Movement. There seemed to be considerable response from the rank and file of ELAS to this suggestion; sufficient to make me feel that their support of it was not wholly spontaneous, and that they had been primed about it beforehand by the political leaders of their bands. Another point which I recorded in my diary was the Yugoslav's suggestion during the luncheon interval that there should be an independent Macedonian Resistance Movement. This idea was received somewhat frigidly by the Greeks, who apparently had no desire to give up any of their country to a Macedonian movement. One of them jokingly pulled the leg of the Albanian representative, Tzortzius—who came of simple mountain stock—with the remark: "All right; if Yugoslavia divides up Greece, let us divide Albania. You"—pointing to the Partisan representative—"take the north, and we will take the south."

The Albanian did not think this a joke at all!

In the afternoon Evmaios spoke. He remarked quite openly that EAM's past intolerance of other Resistance Movements had been wrong and that now they must all co-operate. To get such an admission, made in public, was indeed a good omen for the future. I signalled the gist of these conversations to Cairo and added that there was an appearance of great friendliness, but little trust, between the Albanians, Yugoslavs and Greeks.

One of the results of the visit of the Partisan from Tito's head-quarters was a request by GHQ ELAS to me for a wireless set for them to open up direct contact with Tito. I applied to Cairo for a set; but, before I received one, ELAS had succeeded with black-market material and their own experts not only in making a set, but, supposedly without my knowledge, in establishing contact with Yugoslavia.

On 2nd July, when our sabotage operations in conjunction with the invasion of Sicily were in full swing, I left Bohorina for the south, accompanied by my new interpreter, Nasso Zaphirides,[*] who had recently arrived from Athens. Shortly before nightfall we reached the Aliakmon river. The bridge across it had been destroyed during our withdrawal in 1941. We stripped to the waist, waded across and camped for the night in the open, not far from the river. The following morning a car arrived to take us on southwards.

In the evening we reached Kastania, a little village at the foot of the Pindus Mountains, a mile or so to the south of the Kalambaka-Yannina road, where Karayioryis had recently moved his ELAS headquarters in Thessaly. There I found Sheppard, as well as all three members of ELAS GHQ. The Yugoslav and Albanian Partisan representatives were still with them.

On 7th July there was another ELAS gathering, similar to the one I had attended at Tsotyli in the previous month. At it I was again called upon to speak. The Bishop of Kozani, an impressive, heavily bearded Greek over six feet in height, who had been with ELAS for many months, said in his speech that the Greek Communist Party now formed the basis of EAM. This was later hotly contradicted by Evmaios, and I discovered that after the meeting

---

* In 1948 Nasso joined Markos' rebellion. It was subsequently discovered that he had been a Communist for some time. It was even suspected by some that he was a Communist agent whilst acting as my interpreter. Although I must admit I may have been completely fooled, I always thought he served me honestly.

was over, the Bishop was severely reprimanded for saying "such a stupid thing". Aris' speech at this meeting was an interesting one. He had not been present at Tsotyli. He stressed the wish of the Greek people, in fact their determination, to stand alone at the end of the war, and no longer to hang on to the apron strings of any Great Power. He admitted that the Communist Party had started EAM, but said that it was not a Communist monopoly and that EAM wanted all parties to join it. Commenting on a prevalent accusation that the Andarte Movement had started too soon, causing unnecessary suffering, he said that their casualties would never reach the figure of the thousands who had died of starvation in Athens in the winter of 1941.

Whilst at Kastania I received from Cairo the gist of an important extract from a broadcast made by the King of Greece to his people, on 4th July:

"As soon as Greece is free," the King had declared, "you will decide by popular and free vote the institutions with which Greece must endow herself to take her place in Europe. As soon as military operations allow, free and general elections will be held for a Constituent Assembly, in any case within six months. I am sure that no Greek, least of all myself, will fail to respect the Assembly's decision. Until then the monarchist constitution of 1911 * will be in force. As soon as the seat of Government can be transferred to Greek soil, the present Government will resign, in order that a fully representative Government may be formed, whose composition will guarantee the freedom of the elections."

My immediate reactions to this speech were full of optimism.

---

* The monarchist Constitution of 1911, which was a revised version of the 1864 Constitution, had been replaced by a republican Constitution in 1927. On the restoration of the monarchy in 1935, the 1911 Constitution was restored, subject to revision by a Constituent Assembly, which had not yet been carried out. (See C. M. Woodhouse, *Apple of Discord*, p. 118, and Bickham Sweet-Escott, *Greece, A Political and Economic Survey, 1939–1953*, p. 20 and n. 1.)

EAM, however, were quick to find a flaw in it. They pointed out that the King—they invariably called him 'Glücksburg'—said that there would be a period of six months between the arrival of the Government from the Middle East and the elections. Meanwhile he would be on Greek soil, the Royalists would arrest members of EAM/ELAS and the elections would then be rigged. No! They would not allow the King back to Greece until a plebiscite as to the constitution had been held. Until then they would not lay down their arms.

The same day I learnt from a usually reliable source that the Yugoslav Partisan representative was trying to persuade EAM to sever relations with the Middle East. At that time the Western Allies, who had already been supplying Tito for several months and who had hitherto given official backing, although meagre material support, to Michailovic, had not yet made public their decision to forsake Michailovic because of his co-operation with the enemy against the Communists. But the Partisans' offer of weapons and other war material from their surplus captured stocks was apparently insufficiently attractive to EAM to induce them to forfeit their supplies through our Mission. It is only fair to add that I never managed to obtain confirmation of the truth of this report.

A few days later I informed Cairo about the reactions in the mountains to the King's recent broadcast. I began by pointing out that the recent naming of an American gift cruiser to the Greek Navy, *King George*, had been received by EAM with a cold shoulder. I believed that the maintenance of the 1911 Constitution could only be made possible by the immediate restoration of confidence of the Greek people in their King in some further way.

I explained that EAM's viewpoint appeared to be that the King was prepared to make any sacrifices, except those concerning himself. Although it was not my business as a soldier, I humbly stressed once more that the sooner the King openly stated that he would not set foot in Greece until he was asked for by the common vote of the people, the better would be the chances of internal peace for the country.

During the period just before the final 'Military Agreement' was signed, EAM was seriously considering establishing a provisional Left-wing government in the mountains; a government which, in authority, would vie with the official one in the Middle East. But I was certain that virtually none of the leaders of the old political parties in Athens would join EAM.

Meanwhile every effort was being made by the different authorities in Cairo to broaden the Greek Government in exile in the Middle East. I had been asked to do my best to get politicians of moderate, as well as Left-wing, views to leave Athens for Cairo with this object in view. But the extreme Left-wing politicians were unwilling to do so because they were already in with EAM. The more moderate ones were unwilling apparently because they did not know which way the cat would jump after the liberation of Greece. They knew that there was considerable sympathy for the Resistance Movements among the people in the large towns and an equal lack of sympathy for the Government in exile among those in the Resistance Movements. They apparently felt that, if they left Athens and joined the Government in Cairo, in subsequent elections after the liberation of Greece they might lose a large number of their supporters.

The representatives of the old Liberals in Athens, like most other Greeks, had no longer any doubt in their minds about the eventual outcome of the war. But, because of the intensity of their mistrust of the Government in exile and because of the importance which they attached to their own post-war political struggle, they unfortunately never realised that their refusal to make their Government in exile more representative not only prolonged its weakness but was liable to lead later to general political chaos. They did not foresee that the resultant instability would aggravate post-war disorder, and would delay their country's realisation of both peace and prosperity.

For many months I had been steadily becoming more involved in political problems and had been sending back a great deal of political and semi-political information in my otherwise operational signals, not because I had any wish to get mixed up in political affairs, but because, in the maintenance of military control over the various Resistance Movements, in particular over ELAS, political problems were the greatest ones which faced me. I had had no previous training whatever in politics, and my sole political adviser, admirable as he was, was Chris, whose full-time services I required as my second-in-command. Early in June, however, I had been asked by Cairo if I would accept on my staff a specially trained officer to act as a representative of the Foreign Office, whom the latter wanted to send into the mountains in order to obtain a first-hand impression of the political aspects of the different Resistance Movements. The signal was couched in rather diffident terms, as if I might have been unwilling to accept such an officer. I welcomed an official representative from the Foreign Office, and had immediately signalled back to Cairo accordingly. A few weeks later this officer, Major David Wallace of the 60th Rifles, was dropped at my base headquarters in the Pindus. It was mid-July before I first met him.

Not more than thirty years of age, keen and straightforward, I liked the look of him from the start. During his first fortnight's stay in Zervas' area he had obviously been favourably impressed; but his next fortnight, amongst ELAS, was equally obviously a great shock to him. It seemed that neither he, nor the political authorities in either Cairo or London, had any idea that EAM and its armed forces, ELAS, had such an extensive grip on the people in the mountains, and such extreme Left-wing political control. He appeared surprised at the way that, time and again, I had turned a blind eye to their misbehaviour, when it had not critically affected operational plans, in order to remain in their confidence and to get the best value militarily out of them.

A few days after we met, David started sending back by signal long reports for Mr. Leeper,* the British Ambassador to Greece, containing his views on the political situation as he then found it in the mountains. He showed me them all. They were accurate and on the whole I fully agreed with the views he expressed. On more than one occasion he made minor amendments to them at my request.

I invited him to accompany me henceforth as my political adviser.

* Now Sir Reginald Leeper, G.B.E., K.C.M.G.

CHAPTER XV

Andarte Joint GHQ

THE FIRST meeting of the newly established Andarte Joint GHQ took place at Pertouli on 18th July, in a delightful, but then deserted, summer villa which I had appropriated as my own headquarters. Saraphis and Aris attended as the military representatives of ELAS; Evmaios made up the usual triumvirate as their political adviser and representative of EAM. Gikopoulos represented Zervas.

For the purposes of controlling activities on the mainland, Pertouli was well situated. A tortuous road, with a most indifferent surface, linked it at Porta with the better roads in the Thessaly plain; on it there was only one major bridge, which was prepared for demolition and could be blown up comparatively easily if we were ever severely pressed by the enemy. Three thousand feet high, in the summer it had a delightful climate; in the winter it should not be cut off by deep snow. Situated in the middle of the Pindus Mountains, it was as central a place as any for controlling the Resistance Movements on the mainland. Desirable as it was to make our permanent headquarters there, it was obvious, however, that sooner or later the enemy would come to hear of it, and, if they couldn't get at us overland, they were sure to bomb us savagely. Fortunately, as in peace time it was a small summer resort for those who lived in the hot plains, it had few permanent inhabitants. Even so, I decided to move out of the village itself as soon as possible.

There was a saw-mill nearby; and, having procured some bolts and nails off the black market from the enemy-occupied town of Trikkala, Ross Bower enlisted some local Greek carpenters to build us a log cabin, to our own design, in the fir forest a few hundred yards from the outskirts of the village. It had four bedrooms, a central conference room with a large table in the middle of it, round which the members of Andarte GHQ could argue in comfort, and a pleasant shaded veranda, on which we often whiled away the evenings playing cards.

On 20th July Colonel Psaros of EKKA, accompanied by a Greek called George Kartalis, arrived at Pertouli from Roumeli. Kartalis, who was Psaros' political adviser, had only recently left Athens. About forty years of age, tall, well built, with straight black hair neatly brushed back and dressed in a grey pin-striped flannel suit, he looked far too tidy to be in the mountains. I soon discovered that he was both cultured and intelligent.

Psaros had been summoned by me as a result of a report from Arthur Edmonds that, just before the 'National Bands Agreement' was signed by ELAS, one of Aris' bands had attacked some of Psaros' men a second time. I was determined to have Aris 'put on the mat' for this.

At a special meeting of our Joint GHQ Evmaios quickly admitted that a "serious mistake" had been made by the local ELAS commander, who had acted contrary to Aris' instructions. In retribution he recommended that not only should the damage to EKKA be made good, but that EKKA should be invited to send representatives to Andarte Joint GHQ. These proposals suited my purpose well, but I insisted that ELAS be penalised for their action, that EKKA should be armed by us up to a strength of a thousand andartes before ELAS in Roumeli received any more supplies of war material from us. This was agreed. And so it came about that within a day of their arrival Psaros and Kartalis signed the 'National Bands Agreement' and attended the future meetings of Andarte Joint GHQ.

I became particularly fond of Psaros. But he was too straight-forward a soldier to be involved in the perpetual wrangle between rival political movements in the mountains, and far too honest to be successful at it. EAM/ELAS soon began trying to persuade him to join up his bands with ELAS. They even offered him the post of C.-in-C. of the andartes of ELAS and EKKA throughout Roumeli. What Aris thought about this offer I never discovered. It certainly came to nothing while I was in Greece.

The andarte forces which GHQ now theoretically controlled had recently increased considerably in strength. ELAS had a force of approximately sixteen thousand andartes in arms, considerably less than half of whom had been provided with weapons by us. It had roughly another sixteen thousand self-armed village reservists, who normally continued their essential livelihood in the mountains and were only embodied for local emergencies. Those who had not been armed by us had weapons captured from the enemy or unearthed from hiding-places where they had been put when the Greek Army dispersed to its homes after the surrender in 1941.

Zervas' embodied forces in EDES then consisted of about five thousand, with about the same number of village reservists. We had armed approximately four thousand of his embodied force: a higher proportion than in ELAS, largely because in the first few months of 1943 the only ELAS bands with which we had been in contact were those under Aris in Roumeli.

Psaros' andartes in EKKA, seldom more than a few hundred strong, reached their peak strength of about a thousand in August.

When the final 'National Bands Agreement' was signed, ELAS was in virtual control of four-fifths of the mountain areas on the mainland. Zervas' domain was confined to Epirus and Evrytania. Where his bands were contiguous with those of ELAS there was often friction. Since the winter he had consistently been trying to expand his relatively small area. In the north, where both his bands and those of ELAS had taken part in the destruction of different sections of the Kalambaka road, immediately the operation was over, clashes had restarted. Farther west, near Filiates I had already been forced to send Chris with EDES and ELAS representatives to restore order and to stop the threat of widespread bloodshed.

Along the eastern edge of Zervas' area the River Acheloos formed a natural boundary and, to a large extent, prevented incursions or excursions by the competing factions. In the south, however, in Evrytania, where Papaiannou had already once been disarmed, and in Roumeli, where EKKA bands under Psaros had also suffered a similar fate, there was for ever trouble. Only a few days before the signing of the Agreement by ELAS, I had heard that stores which had been specifically dropped for Papaiannou's bands had been seized by the local ELAS leader. I had ordered Evmaios to summon him to our headquarters for court martial.

The moment EAM/ELAS were given an opportunity to carry out an act of aggression against another organisation out of sight of a British officer, they would do so, rather than attack the enemy. On the other hand, to be fair to EAM, it should be added that, as soon as the backs of the British officers were turned, some of their lower level rivals in EDES, knowing they could count on our moral support, seldom missed an opportunity of tormenting ELAS into such acts of aggression. Our British officers were still so thin on the ground that they often had to hurry hither and thither, keeping the peace; sometimes, as they did so, suffering rebuke, and even insults, from the EAM political advisers in ELAS. For high-spirited officers who had volunteered for hazardous sabotage work, the tasks which I had to give many of them called for the greatest efforts in patience and tact. All of them behaved magnificently.

Chris and I realised that the only thing which would ensure fair play throughout the mountains of Free Greece was to have so many British Liaison Officers—BLOs—that it would be virtually impossible for bands of one organisation to torment or attack those belonging to another without being observed. In this way we would be able to institute immediate reprisals upon the guilty leader or band by cutting off supplies to them. Our thirty to forty BLOs were closely grouped around about a dozen different wireless stations. I informed Cairo that we must at least double this number of officers and wireless stations in order to ensure the smooth running of the Resistance Movements.

At the first few meetings of Andarte GHQ we discussed such matters as regulations for the forming of new andarte bands, financial support to the different andarte organisations and the allotment of areas. We issued copious resolutions or instructions, based upon our lengthy discussions.

Zervas was quick off the mark after the signature of the new 'National Bands Agreement'. He recruited such a large number of new bands in Thessaly that his successes were soon embarrassing EAM. In order to prevent any Tom, Dick or Harry forming bands wherever and whenever they pleased, and to absolve the Joint GHQ of the responsibility for automatically having to arm them, we passed a resolution that new bands should only be formed after the agreement of the existing andarte commanders in the area, and that they would not be supplied with arms until they had been in existence for three months, and then only up to a maximum strength of fifty andartes if they belonged to a fresh organisation.

As regards financial support, we decided in conjunction with SOE (Cairo) to pay to the respective local andarte organisations one gold sovereign per month for each armed and permanently embodied andarte, in order to assist in the purchase of grain from the plains, both for the andartes and their families, and for the Greek people in destitute areas. It was open to the different organisations to use the money given to them as they chose. Zervas paid the families of his andartes a regular amount of money; ELAS had no such system. In fact, in some areas I discovered that ELAS was handing its gold sovereigns over to EAM, and giving credit notes to the Greek people in return for the theoretical purchase of grain for them.

On 23rd July we held a court of inquiry on the local ELAS leader Yerodimos' action in seizing arms belonging to Papaiannou's bands of EDES. The BLO in that area was an excellent young Greek army cavalryman called Kitso, who held a British war-time commission. It was undesirable for us to have a Greek officer in a tricky area where bands of both ELAS and EDES existed. But at the time there was no one else available.

From the stories we heard it was palpably evident that Yerodimos could give no excuse for his action. At the same time I was practically certain that he was merely carrying out instructions which he had received from his superior officer, Aris. Anxious to retain the confidence of EAM/ELAS, instead of insisting on Yerodimos being convicted and punished, having pointed out the 'conclusive' evidence of his guilt, I then went on to blame myself for having sent a Greek as BLO, even though he held a British commission, to such a potentially troublesome area. I said that, provided EAM were prepared to issue instructions to have Papaiannou's arms returned, I would overlook the matter.

My laxity had the desired effect; Evmaios thanked me genuinely for my "broadminded interpretation" of the situation, and assured me that my request would be granted. Such acts as this, which some may interpret as weakness on my part, reaped a large dividend in return. I had impressed upon EAM the fact that, if they were prepared to make determined efforts to abide by the terms of the recently signed 'Military Agreement', I was only too anxious to let bygones be bygones and to continue to give them material support. I thereby retained a large measure of Evmaios' confidence and trust, which I always respected. As a result, both he and Saraphis tended to regard me as an impartial arbitrator in all disputes and I strengthened my own hand by acting in such a way. In fact, as I saw it at the time, there was no other method of maintaining the military co-operation of EAM/ELAS.

I had now received clear instructions from SOE (Cairo) about our future activities in the mountains: to lie low during the ensuing months; to train up the andartes to the highest possible pitch; to limit their activities to minor sabotage, sufficient only to instruct recruits, and to maintain the morale of the different bands; and to carry out fresh reconnaissances with a view, when the time came for the invasion of Greece itself, to carrying out another series of widespread sabotage operations, similar to those recently completed.

In view of the internal political difficulties which I foresaw in trying to meet the requirements of the Middle East Command, and in view of the imminent collapse of the Italians, with the resulting possibility of obtaining a large quantity of arms from them, I decided to call in all my senior officers for a co-ordinating conference: to hear their particular problems and views, to give them a directive for the future and to ensure that we all spoke with the same voice throughout the country.

Between 18th and 20th July, officers of the British Mission in the mountains of Free Greece converged on Pertouli from all over the country. In spite of my many journeys backwards and forwards in the mountains, a few of these officers I was meeting for the first time, having previously only been in communication with them by runner or wireless. Most of the members of our original party had not met each other for months. All were inwardly glowing with modest satisfaction over the success of their recent widespread sabotage. I was well pleased with what they had already done, and proud to be in command of them. I told them so. 'Waffles'—the code-name for the conference—was a happy union, or reunion, for us all.

Unwilling to wait any longer for Nick Hammond, my senior BLO in Macedonia, who had not yet arrived, I held the first discussion with the remainder of my officers on 20th July. I outlined the requirements of the Middle East Command. I explained the internal political problems as I saw them and the general methods by which I wanted them kept under control. We had already been approached by one or two Italian garrison commanders, putting out feelers about surrender. I stressed the importance of getting formed bodies of troops to surrender to us unconditionally. I authorised my officers, in accordance with instructions from SOE (Cairo), to negotiate with the Italians in order to obtain the surrender of as many as possible with their arms. With each officer individually I then went over his own particular troubles, and solved as many of them as I could.

Nick Hammond did not reach Pertouli until 26th July. He had been delayed by having to spend a week in Salonika, meeting the leaders of a movement, PAO—Pan-Hellenic Liberation Organisation—which, a late starter in the field, was now demanding material support from us with fantastic claims but little to show for itself as an efficient andarte organisation. Its underground organisation in Athens had, however, procured some useful intelligence for the Middle East Command.

Nick had travelled into and out of Salonika by bus, dressed as a shepherd. On his return journey he had had the misfortune to sit on the only broken seat, which persisted in collapsing each time the bus turned a corner. He became the hilarious centre of attention of all the passengers, amongst whom were two German soldiers! Fortunately he spoke fluent Greek, but with a slight 'Cambridge University' accent!

On the night of 27th July, in answer to an earnest request by me, Zervas paid his first visit to our joint GHQ. The following morning we met privately; our meeting lasted four hours. Zervas accused me of deserting EDES in favour of EAM. I countered by

225

pointing out that this was his first visit in person to our Joint GHQ, where we would be only too glad for him to make his permanent base. He then argued with me that 'my' policy of continuing to support EAM/ELAS was detrimental to Greece's future and tantamount to handing arms to the Communists, who would unquestionably use them at a later date to spill Greek blood in their bid for power.

I replied that, apart from the fact that I was only carrying out the instructions of the Middle East Command, I was fully aware of the character of EAM and of the dangers of the policy which we had been ordered to pursue. I pointed out to him, however, that our first task was to win the war, and to achieve this we were bound to support all Resistance Movements who were prepared to assist us. I explained that the rank and file of ELAS were in no way different from those of EDES, and that, on the liberation of Greece, our Government had already promised to ensure free elections; that when we said "free" we meant "free"; and that we would not tolerate any attempt by the Left to impose a dictatorship with British weapons given to them to fight our common enemy.

At one period during our talks it looked to me as if Zervas was considering backing out of the final 'National Bands Agreement', which stipulated the establishment of a Joint GHQ, and that he intended to carry on on his own. But I did not give way. I informed him that, provided he fought the enemy, I would ensure that he was maintained with war supplies to the best of our ability. I was determined, however, to keep my own headquarters at the Andarte Joint GHQ in Pertouli. In the end Zervas, with his invariable charm and good grace, gave in to my wishes.

"Well, my dear Brigadier Eddie," he said, "I am older than you are, and I believe I know what is good for Greece. I believe that what you are doing is wrong for my country. However, I realise that you are only obeying your orders. I admire you as a soldier, and as a soldier I will always obey the representative of the Commander-in-Chief of the Allied Forces in the Middle East."

Wc shook hands.

It was about this time that I became embarrassed by a number of quite senior Greek army officers and politicians, with tainted, if not clearly 'pro-quisling' records, who were leaving Athens for the mountains, rather like rats leaving a sinking ship, and were arriving, one after the other, at my headquarters, offering me their services. Most of them had guilty consciences and were anxious to end up, even at this late hour, on the right side. A few, however, were genuinely patriotic Greeks who had been doing what they could for their country in Athens, and who now saw an opportunity of lending a hand in the mountains.

Unfortunately my own particular problem in dealing with them was not made easier by the fact that EAM demanded the arrest of practically all of them, on grounds of past collaboration with the enemy. Many of them were Royalists, or ex-Royalists by repute, and I knew what their fate would be at the hands of EAM. Although I had little sympathy for some of them, because they hadn't come to offer their services earlier, I was anxious for them all to be given a fair trial at the end of hostilities, and not to be shot out of hand. Also several of them could continue to obtain valuable information for us through their past positions and connections in Athens. Zervas came to our assistance in finding employment for a number of them.

Towards the end of July we received news of fresh clashes between EDES and ELAS bands in Northern Epirus. Andarte GHQ decided that Zervas and Aris would together investigate the trouble on the spot. Well do I remember seeing them set off together from Andarte Joint GHQ at the head of their andartes, arm in arm. How well this augured for the future, I thought.

CHAPTER XVI

Delegation in Cairo

AT THE time of our recent operations in conjunction with the invasion of Sicily there had been no central co-ordination of the different andarte movements except through me. Few, apart from Chris and myself, had known of the widespread nature of the operations, either in their planning stages or during their execution, and it was not until afterwards that the extent of our activities became known to all in Greece. The leaders of ELAS, however, had had a shrewd suspicion, to say the least, that Greece was going to be invaded. But I had told them that I had not been informed that this was so, and that immediately I was told anything to this effect I would pass on the information to them. For all these reasons, when news of the successful invasion of Sicily reached the people in the mountains of Greece, there was relatively little disappointment that Greece herself had not been invaded by the Allies. With news of the Allied successes in Sicily daily reaching us, the country people felt that it was only a matter of weeks, if not days, before their turn for liberation arrived.

When I heard that we were to lay off all further large-scale activity until the actual invasion of Greece took place, I immediately signalled to Cairo and asked them when they expected this to be. I was gravely concerned when I received their reply: "Not before the winter of 1943; possibly early 1944."

I had no idea that the capture of the remainder of Italy would take precedence over the liberation of Greece. Until then I had not considered in any detail the possibility of having to go through another winter with these Resistance Movements on my hands. Ever since the previous March, when I had received the signal telling me to get ready for widespread sabotage operations that summer in conjunction with an Allied invasion across the Mediterranean into both the Dodecanese and Sicily, I had always assumed that the mainland of Greece, even if it was not to be the actual point of assault, would be liberated, or evacuated by the enemy, within a few months of the invasion. I had accordingly planned to bring the activities of the Resistance Movements to a peak by the summer.

Apart from the all-important question of the morale of the civil population, on which the Resistance Movements depended, the problem of feeding the andartes through another winter was an extremely serious and worrying one; for the enemy had planned to seize all the crops in Greece as soon as they were gathered, and only to hand back to the country people in well-behaving districts the barest requirements of grain for their existence—in this way preventing, so they hoped, any grain reaching either andartes or the civil population in andarte-occupied areas.

Besides the broader aspect of morale and this important problem of food, there was the effect on the leaders of EAM/ELAS to be considered. By the terms of the final 'National Bands Agreement' the whole status of the Resistance Movements, and in particular of EAM, was raised. This was useful, perhaps essential, in order to keep them in check. If the leaders of EAM/ELAS could be imbued with a belief in the ever-increasing importance of their armed forces, and of their contribution towards the war effort, I had a chance of keeping a measure of control over them. If, however, their belief in their importance to the Allies was at any time to wane, the extremist leaders would take even less interest in the requirements of the Middle East Command, and would concentrate correspondingly more on their political aims. If, coupled with this, the andartes had to be maintained in a state of relative inactivity for many months on end, it would be almost impossible for me to stop widespread clashes occurring between the rival movements.

I signalled all this to Cairo, and stressed the grave concern with which I viewed the prospect of relative inactivity by the andartes continuing for many months more. I urged them to reconsider their decision and to plan for the invasion of Greece from Italy, across the Adriatic, at the earliest possible moment.

In a signal which Chris sent me through Cairo whilst he was away from my headquarters, he stated that he was becoming increasingly disturbed by the possible post-war use of the weapons being provided for the andartes. SOE (Cairo) commented that post-war considerations were not to be allowed to prejudice the success of future operations, for which the maximum effort would be required. But post-war considerations were always uppermost in the minds of the extremists in the Resistance Movements; the problem was how to control them. Although John Stevens was already on his way back to the Middle East, I was so concerned about the many problems that I told SOE (Cairo) that I considered it was necessary for me to come and discuss the future with them at the earliest opportunity, and I requested that arrangements should be made for my evacuation by caique.

SOE replied that they would on no account consider my making the journey to Cairo in such a hazardous way; but they endorsed my suggestion that I should visit them, and recommended that I should come out by air.

For some time past we had been looking around Greece for a natural air-strip, a thousand yards long, which would be suitable for a single-engined aeroplane. All attempts had so far failed, except in one place, near Denys Hamson's headquarters at Neraida, in the foothills a few miles south-west of Karditsa and the Thessaly Plain. Here Denys had discovered a long, wide and level area on a plateau some three or four thousand feet high on which, we later discovered, the Greeks themselves had planned to build an aerodrome shortly before the war. It was heavily cultivated; but it was well over a thousand yards long—nearly two thousand, in fact. When Cairo received Denys Hamson's report on it they gave up the idea of sending a single-engined 'plane and made the project more ambitious. They asked us to prepare a landing ground eighteen hundred yards long in order that a Liberator or Halifax could be landed on it.

Early in July Denys commenced the work of clearing the ground with a large labour force of Greek villagers. He estimated that he could make the air-strip in about a month.

At the conference with my officers at Pertouli in July I gave all my original party the opportunity of leaving Greece when Denys' airfield was working. Only Denys asked to leave as soon as possible; Nat Barker requested to go at a later date; the others elected to stay and see through to the end what they had begun so well.

On 24th July I travelled by car to pay Denys Hamson a fleeting visit, to inspect the progress on his airfield and to attend an EAM rally nearby.

In peace-time Neraida was a summer resort for people from Karditsa; it consisted mainly of well-built villas. Situated over three thousand feet high on pine-clad foothills, with the mountains just behind it, in the summer it had a delightful climate and its surroundings were ideal for holiday-makers from the hot malarial plains only five miles away.

Denys Hamson had appropriated the summer villa of General Plastiras. Out of a parachute he had silk pyjamas made for me by a seamstress from Karditsa. There was a geyser in his house and I enjoyed the luxury of a hot bath each day I was with him.

Wandering about Greece from station to station that summer, always in uniform, I had lived alternatively in luxury and in the utmost frugality. One night I would spend in comparative comfort, enjoying eggs and chicken, indeed sometimes a more lavish diet than that on which our families at home were living. The next night I might be sleeping in the open, passing between two enemy-occupied areas, feeding on maize-bread, cheese from goat's milk and black olives. The following one I might be in a cottage belonging to the poorest Greek, who, however poor he might be, invariably entertained with the greatest generosity and hospitality. On occasions like this, tired as I usually was after a long day's travelling, I often had to wait several hours after getting in before having my evening meal, for which I was ravenous, whilst my host literally killed the fatted calf and prepared an unnecessarily sumptuous repast. British officers were always given the best bedroom, unless there was a sick person in the house or cottage. We only offended the Greeks if we refused their offers and denied them the spontaneous pleasure with which they invariably gave us not only their best, but often their meagre all. This treatment was liable to make an Englishman feel vain; but it showed up the qualities of the Greek mountain people. The anti-British propaganda, with which the political leaders of EAM never ceased attempting to poison their minds, invariably appeared to have had no effect in our actual presence.

Between the bigger towns in the Thessaly Plain, which were heavily garrisoned by the enemy, and the mountains all around, in which the andartes moved unmolested, there was a belt of no-man's land. In the villages in this belt, one day armed andartes might be roaming freely in the streets; the next, the enemy might be in them. The large country town of Karditsa was a place such as this. I remember Nat Barker recounting how once he had been having a cool drink in a café when a Greek had rushed in through the front door to say that two German armoured cars were just approaching. Nat, finishing his drink, had walked out through the back door as the Germans walked in through the front.

I was extremely pleased with Denys' progress on the airfield. He had set up a huge organisation which included well over a

Mission H.Q. at Pertouli.

Camouflaging a Dakota in the mountains.

An andarte band of EDES.

Three ELAS andartes. The youthfulness of ELAS andartes compared with those of EDES is strikingly noticeable in these two photographs.

thousand Greeks, many of them women, working two shifts a day throughout the hours of daylight. Each shift was organised in small gangs under an overseer. The Greeks were employed upon filling in ditches, cutting down crops and removing obstacles, not least of which was flattening out a veritable hill at one end of the runway to give a clearer approach. I gave Denys full marks for the progress he was making. The work, however, was by no means completed and he assured me that it could not be finished before the first week in August. Cairo had intimated that they were prepared to send an aircraft any day after the end of July. We therefore signalled to them asking for the 'plane to come on 8th August.

The RAF were doubtful if the surface of our landing ground and approaches would meet their requirements. They had sent us specifications, reduced to simple ground tests which we could carry out with an ordinary motor-car. One of these was that the car should be comfortable to travel in at both twenty and forty miles per hour; another that from twenty miles per hour it should free wheel for more than a hundred yards before stopping. We carried out all these tests, and I signalled back that I was entirely satisfied with the results. In spite of this the authorities said that they must send an RAF officer to supervise the actual landing and take-off arrangements for the aircraft. I naturally raised no objections, being delighted to have all the technical assistance possible.

Denys was quite rightly concerned over the fact that, as the landing ground took shape, so its very shape became extremely obvious to enemy aircraft which flew high overhead almost daily, apparently on one of their regular mail or passenger schedules. He had only solved the problem the day before I arrived. He had decided to fell large numbers of fir-trees in the adjoining forests, and to bring them down—hundreds of cartloads of them —to the landing ground, where he had their cut stems replanted in a few inches of the top soil. He had them planted irregularly, scattered about both singly and in quite large groups. This work was in hand when I visited him. He also broke up the long and unnaturally straight line between the edges of the cleared landing-strip and the undisturbed crops by projecting his clearing here and there into the adjoining fields.

On the whole I thought the results were most satisfactory, and I told him so. They were excellent, considering the rudimentary facilities available. He received indirect recognition of his efforts in an unexpected way. About a week before the aircraft was due, the RAF, without warning us, sent over by day a high-flying air-craft from the Middle East to take photographs. These were duly developed and interpreted in Cairo, and we were sent a full report by signal. The gist of this was that we were congratulated on our progress, but it was pointed out that the landing ground was still covered with a number of obstacles, which looked like haystacks, and that the "shrubbery" must all be cleared.

The haystacks had been groups of camouflaged farm-carts, and the "shrubbery" was Denys' carefully replanted trees! We con-gratulated ourselves on Denys' efforts at camouflage. They had completely taken in the air-photography interpreters back in Cairo, who in due course apologised for their mistake and con-gratulated us.

The day after my arrival at Denys' headquarters I attended a big EAM rally. It was the most ambitious EAM gathering I ever saw. Karayioryis called it "The Pan-Thessaly Conference". No less than three thousand people, not only men and women, but many boys of EPON—the EAM Youth Movement—from all over Thessaly, were gathered together. It was a masterpiece of organisation, which went off without a hitch; but it gave both me and Denys Hamson the jitters, because the place chosen for the meeting, an interesting old monastery called Koroni, was only two miles from Denys' air-strip. When we heard where it was going to be held, we tried to get it changed. But it had been too late for Karayioryis to alter his arrangements. He did, however, forbid any of the Greeks at the gathering from going any nearer to the air-strip. Even so, thousands of them must have come to hear about it. The Greeks, however, used to call all of our ordinary dropping grounds "landing grounds", and so, when the Germans heard that a landing ground was being built at Neraida—and it is hard to believe that they did not—in all probability they thought that this was just another dropping ground.

The Pan-Thessaly Conference lasted for two days. I attended it only on the first day, as I had to get back to Pertouli to complete the briefing of my four senior BLOs as soon as possible after Nick Hammond's arrival from Macedonia. It was a gloriously fine day. Many rows of benches had been set out under some fir trees close to the monastery. A large wooden dais had been built for the EAM leaders to sit on; in the middle of it there was an elaborate rostrum for the speakers. Draped over it, moreover, were the Greek flag and the Union Jack, sewn together side by side. Immediately in front of the dais, facing the audience, sat over a dozen EAM journalist reporters, who took copious notes of every speech made. It was purely a propaganda meeting for EAM. Of the many speeches, David Wallace took notes for me on the more important ones.

As usual, I was invited to speak. Because of the size of the gathering, I prepared my speech particularly carefully and got David Wallace to vet it. As I delivered it sentence by sentence in English, my interpreter, Nasso, read it out in Greek from a previously prepared and checked translation.

I will not bore the reader with the text of this long speech. It had two main aims; firstly it was designed to make it more difficult for EAM to misbehave, by showing that the basis of their anti-monarchical and anti-British propaganda was false; secondly it was directed towards the unarmed masses without whose support resistance would have been impossible, the maintenance of whose morale was therefore so important, and from whom I planned to obtain carefully timed, well organised and widespread revolt in conjunction with the liberation of Greece by the Allied armies.

Colonel Gikopoulos, the EDES representative at our Joint GHQ, was also invited to attend this conference. His presence, and the fact that he made a speech, created what then appeared to me to be a promising atmosphere, in harmony with EAM's efforts to present a broader-minded outlook. But Gikopoulos later joined ELAS, no doubt under duress. Chris told me he never saw anyone, not even Saraphis, look more sheepish under an ELAS hat badge.

Late in the evening of 26th July, David Wallace and I returned by car to Pertouli. In due course we sent a full report to Cairo on the Pan-Thessaly Conference.

Until a few days before my visit to Denys, I had not mentioned to a single Greek the fact that I intended visiting Cairo. I had simply told the representatives of EAM that we were making an airfield at Cairo's request, in order to facilitate personal liaison visits between the Middle East and the mountains. With the time drawing near for my departure I realised, however, that I must inform the andarte leaders about my future plans. I told Evmaios about my projected trip a day or two before my visit to Neraida. He immediately asked me if he could accompany me. Knowing that it had been approved by Cairo as long ago as the previous March that representatives of EAM could visit the Middle East to explain their political and other views, I told him that I would be delighted for him to accompany me provided there was room, and I informed Cairo accordingly.

It was my original intention to take with me only three others: David Wallace, to assist me in political discussions; Stan Smith, my senior wireless operator, to arrange direct wireless traffic between our stations in Greece, thus cutting out the delay of retransmitting messages through Cairo; and Denys Hamson, who wanted to be evacuated.

A signal from Cairo, announcing the fact that there would probably be room for eight passengers on the aeroplane, arrived at Pertouli while I was away at Neraida, whereupon Chris had informed Evmaios that there would definitely be room for him. Evmaios had asked Chris to send a signal on his behalf to the Central Committee in Athens, telling them that it was his intention to visit the Middle East, and requesting the Central Committee to send representatives to the mountains as soon as possible, to brief him before his departure.

As soon as Zervas learnt that I planned to visit Cairo in a few days' time, and that I was taking Evmaios with me, he asked if he might send his second-in-command, Komninos Pyromaglou, with me too. I signalled to Cairo, who readily agreed.

When, in turn, Kartalis learnt of my projected trip he asked if he might represent EKKA in my talks in the Middle East on the future of the Andarte Movements. Again Cairo agreed that he should come. The eight seats in the aeroplane were now all allotted: David Wallace, Stan Smith, Denys Hamson, Evmaios, Komninos, Kartalis, myself and the RAF officer who was being specially dropped to arrange the ground control for the aeroplane, and who had to be got back to the Middle East as soon as possible.

A few days later I was concerned to learn from Cairo that there was probably only going to be room for four people in the aircraft, and that presumably therefore I would be bringing with me only Evmaios and Komninos, besides the RAF officer.

In answer to this I signalled the next day that I considered that the whole future of Greece might be bound up in this visit, and that we had it in our power to prevent civil war. It was vital, therefore, that David Wallace should accompany me to support me at all political interviews.

SOE (Cairo) replied that there would, after all, be room for eight passengers.

A week before I was due to leave for Cairo, after considerable thought I discussed with both Chris and David Wallace my method of approach to all the problems which had to be solved during my visit with the andarte representatives of EAM, EDES, and EKKA. I foresaw that, if I didn't present a clear-cut plan to these three organisations before we left, their representatives would be separately briefed for their own particular ends, and we would waste days, if not weeks, in talking, and possibly achieve nothing. I planned to be in Cairo for no more than a fortnight.

With the probability of many more months' delay before the liberation of Greece, the main question was how the Resistance Movements could continue to survive without civil war breaking out. The most effective solution would have been to keep the andartes busy fighting against the enemy. But the Middle East Command required them to maintain a state of relative inactivity in order to make surprise and widespread sabotage action again possible when Greece was actually invaded. Meanwhile Cairo wanted the andartes to be trained, and to become more proficient as a fighting force. For this to be possible, we agreed that both moral and material stimulus were necessary and that the different Movements must be developed. We decided that I should recommend development in three distinct but progressive phases.

Firstly came the all important matter of an incentive which would prevent the different organisations fighting one another. It was agreed that I should try to get the andartes officially recognised by the authorities in Cairo as part of the Greek armed forces. We wanted to prevent any further large increase in their overall strength which was liable to take place as a result of competitive expansion. We agreed therefore that the best way to achieve the requirements of the Middle East Command was to limit the different Resistance Movements to selective recruiting, but at the same time to provide them with light artillery and other supporting arms. In this way the andartes would be raised both in status and in quality, rather than in numbers, and the necessary stimulus to train would be provided. We agreed also that I should seek the agreement of the Greek General Staff in Cairo to the attachment to it of andarte liaison officers.

Secondly came the problem of civil administration. Most of the Greek members of our Joint GHQ were experienced regular or reserve officers, or civilians, who had had considerable political experience. Both the military and civil elements were politically minded to a degree only to be found in Greece. Around the large table in our newly constructed log-cabin outside Pertouli they all discussed any and every problem. The military leaders dealt with political matters as often as the political advisers discussed military ones; both discussed administrative matters of a military and civilian character.

With the raising of status of the andarte forces it was desirable that purely civil administrative matters, and with them as much as possible of the andarte politics, should be dealt with by the civilian or political members of our headquarters, whilst purely military matters were left to the soldiers. There was much to be gained, therefore, by trying to divide our headquarters into two elements, one military and the other civil, which, though they might remain interdependent, would work separately.

If the Greek General Staff would accept military liaison officers from the andartes, it was agreed to recommend that their Government should accept civil liaison officials. The latter would be in a position to give invaluable advice on the particular problems and needs of the people in Free Greece.

Lastly, in view of the unrepresentative character of the Government in exile and because of the extent to which it was out of touch with, and apparently lacked the confidence of, the people in the mountains, in particular of EAM, it was realised that something was necessary to overcome the dangers of a sudden change-over from andarte law to constitutional government on the liberation of Greece.

We then imagined that Greece would eventually be invaded from Southern Italy, and therefore that the west coast, close to some of the EDES strongholds, would be liberated before Athens. We decided that I should recommend that one or two officials of the Greek Government should in due course be transferred to the mountains of Free Greece so that they could smooth the way for the return of the Government, by providing a measure of continuity in civil control, and a means of absorbing the civil organisation of the Resistance Movements within the national structure.

Before my departure from Pertouli for Neraida I talked separately to Komninos Pyromaglou of EDES and George Kartalis of EKKA on the above lines, and obtained their wholehearted agreement to the decision that we should mutually recommend these three phases of development of the Resistance Movements. Evmaios had already left to be briefed by the representatives of the Central Committee from Athens, who were expected at Karditsa shortly before his departure. On 5th August I myself set off for Denys Hamson's headquarters to carry out a final inspection of the airfield and then await the aircraft which was due to take us to Egypt three nights later.

A nine hour journey, on a characterless but comfortable grey pony which Saraphis had recently presented to me for my personal use, brought me that evening to Pyrgos, a small village nestling under the hills on the southern edge of the Thessaly Plain. Here I inspected a new ELAS cavalry unit. It possessed about a hundred horses, some of them first-class animals. It was used for reconnaissance and occasional sabotage in the plains. I was quite impressed with what I saw of it, and particularly with its general spirit of keenness. Many horses, however, had bad galls through lack of saddle-blankets and of dubbin for the maintenance of their harsh, army saddlery. I promised the ELAS commander that, on my arrival in Cairo, I would try to obtain the necessary additional equipment for him.

The following evening I reached Neraida. The RAF pilot-officer, Freddie Rotherham, for ground control on our air-strip, had been dropped by parachute the previous evening. He had unfortunately sprained his ankle on landing. I carried out an inspection of the landing ground, and was more than satisfied with the job that Denys had done; so was Rotherham.

At midday on the 7th, David Wallace, Stan Smith, my chief wireless operator, Komninos and Kartalis, arrived from Pertouli. Evmaios had not yet turned up; apparently he was still waiting at some secret rendezvous for his confederates from Athens. Late that night a message arrived from him asking me if we could postpone our departure for twenty-four hours, because the representatives of the Central Committee had not yet arrived. I agreed to do so and we signalled to Cairo accordingly.

On the evening of the 8th Evmaios turned up at Neraida, accompanied by Yioryios Siantos, Secretary of the Greek Communist Party, KKE, Elias Tsirimokos, leader of the small independent, Socialist political party called ELD or Popular Democratic Union, and two others, Petros Roussos and Constantine Despotopoulos, both of whom were Communists. They were all members of the Central Committee of EAM. Within a few minutes of their arrival, I was asked to meet them. I discovered that Siantos, their leader, was under the impression that Tsirimokos, Roussos and Despotopoulos would be able to accompany Evmaios and me to Cairo. I asked him upon what grounds he assumed this, since all along I had only agreed to take Evmaios with me. He replied that he had received a signal from my headquarters, through Cairo, to the effect that there would be room in the aeroplane for as many representatives as the Central Committee chose to send. I hotly denied this, and was about to accuse Evmaios of misrepresenting the situation in the message which, in my absence, he had asked Chris to forward to Athens, when Siantos produced out of his pocket the actual signal which he had received. He read it out. When it was translated to me I immediately realised that with a considerable and—for EAM—convenient stretch of the imagination, it could have been read to mean that there were going to be seats on the aeroplane for additional representatives of EAM. I had no reason to disbelieve that this was the actual signal sent by Chris on behalf of Evmaios. Months later I discovered that it was in fact, word for word, the signal which Evmaios had handed to Chris to be relayed through Cairo to the Central Committee of EAM in Athens, and that Evmaios, therefore, was entirely to blame for any misunderstanding. I told Siantos I was prepared to believe that there had been a genuine mistake. Even so, I added, as no doubt Evmaios had already warned him, it would be impossible for me to take these three additional representatives. Siantos thereupon replied that he was very sorry, but either all four went, or none of them; he could not allow Evmaios, whom he now conveniently classified as a member of ELAS, to go alone without EAM representation.

I pointed out that if there was not room on the aircraft for all these people and if he refused to allow one of them to go, it would mean that EAM would not be represented in Cairo during talks of far-reaching importance. After endless wrangling, I could not get Siantos to give way, and I finally agreed to send a signal to Cairo informing them that four EAM representatives, not one, wished to visit the Middle East. I told Siantos that I was unlikely to get a reply from Cairo by the following evening, but that provided the pilot of the aircraft agreed to take the three additional passengers, I would not object. If for any reason he refused, then I would do my utmost on my arrival in Cairo to have another aeroplane sent for the four of them the following night. To all this Siantos readily agreed, and, late in the night, we parted.

The following morning, 9th August, I had a conference with Siantos and the other representatives of the Central Committee, in order to lobby them in the same way as I had already done with the EDES and EKKA representatives, about a common approach to our problems in Cairo. After a most satisfactory discussion, which lasted two hours, Siantos agreed that his representatives should tackle the problems in exactly the way that was wanted.

The aeroplane was due at ten o'clock that night. Rotherham told us that it was going to be a Dakota, which would not need more than half the length of the air-strip we had prepared. Shortly before dusk Denys and he went down to the air-strip to rehearse the special party of andartes, whose job it was to light up the edges of the air-strip as soon as the aircraft came in to land. Because of the undesirability of having many lights clearly defining the air-strip for one moment longer than absolutely essential, in case an enemy 'plane might be in the vicinity, a strict light-dousing drill was necessary. At nine o'clock in the evening no reply to my signal about the additional EAM representatives having been received, I followed on down with all the andarte delegates.

A few minutes before ten we heard an aircraft in the distance. Two bonfires, a few hundred yards away from the landing end of the air-strip, were the only pre-arranged signals visible from the air. The aircraft drew nearer, still at a considerable height. We could not restrain a cheer as it flashed the correct signal towards the ground.

With an Aldis lamp, Rotherham immediately answered back. Shortly afterwards he signalled the strength of the wind and some other details regarding the weather and the runway. The aircraft gave an O.K. and started losing height. It made one complete circle of the air-strip and then flew off to make its final approach. As it turned away Rotherham signalled with his Aldis lamp down the air-strip. Each of the twenty-four andartes who were lying on the ground at about a hundred-and-fifty yard intervals along its edges, twelve on each side, almost simultaneously lit up the oil lamps which they had in front of them. The air-strip was now clearly defined, and I prayed that for the next quarter of an hour we might be free of interference from enemy aircraft.

We were all gathered together at the landing end of the ground. The Dakota glided in; its black shape suddenly loomed large out of the darkness; it appeared to be overshooting; two hundred and fifty yards from us it touched down to make a perfect landing. As it passed up the air-strip so the well drilled andartes doused their lamps behind it, and, when the aircraft finally stopped, all the remaining lights, except for Rotherham's red Aldis lamp, went out. I breathed freely once more.

The aircraft had turned half-way round preparatory to taxi-ing back to us, when we heard the pilot rev up the engines. As bad luck would have it, he had chosen to turn right over one of the ditches which Denys' men had filled in, and one of the wheels stuck in the soft ground; fortunately only momentarily, and by racing his engine, the pilot managed to get clear. Back to us the aircraft lumbered, and, when opposite us, it turned again and came to a halt, with engines still ticking over, ready for the take-off. As the aircraft stopped I looked at my watch. It was one minute past ten, one minute late.

Within the next eleven minutes we had unloaded a party of new arrivals and some stores brought in by the Dakota; the pilot had informed me that he could easily take the additional three EAM representatives, and we had all clambered in. At twelve minutes past ten we took off, and, within a few moments, our course was set for Egypt. Just under six hours later, after an uneventful journey, we landed at an aerodrome outside Cairo.

It was strange to feel the sand under my feet once again as, with staff officers of SOE, we walked across to the aerodrome buildings to have a cup of tea. Half an hour later we moved on into Cairo, the andarte delegates to go to a house which had been reserved for them in Maadi, a garden suburb of Cairo, and I to the private flat of Lord Glenconner, the Head of SOE (Cairo).

After revelling in a delicious hot bath, I put on a dressing gown and went out on to the shady veranda of my host's comfortable flat, where he—and breakfast—awaited me. The noise of the distant trams and other traffic in the crystal brightness of that early Egyptian summer morning, still cool and refreshing, sounded strange after a year in the rugged mountains of enemy-occupied Greece. The past year seemed real enough. But the present comfort and security was like a dream.

For the first time for almost a year I relaxed completely.

CHAPTER XVII

Cairo and London

IT WILL be remembered that, in the early days, Resistance in Greece was nominally directed by an Anglo-Greek Committee in Cairo. When, in the spring of 1943, the Greek Government in exile and the King moved from London to Cairo, and its members thus became readily available for direct discussion, the Committee sat less frequently. As the political hue of the Andarte Movements was gradually established to be predominantly Republican, the Royalist elements at the head of the Greek Government became steadily less enthusiastic about the Resistance, and less interested in its day to day control. Before I arrived in Cairo, the Anglo-Greek Committee had already ceased to function. By August, 1943, assistance in the direction and control of the Andarte Movements had in fact largely slipped away from the Greek Government, and had almost entirely passed into the hands of the British. As a result of this the Government in exile had become considerably out of touch with events and developments in the mountains of Free Greece.

The Greek Government, moreover, still largely consisted of Royalists. All of its members had been out of physical touch with their people for two years. In an attempt to make it more representative, some Royalists had been replaced by such few leaders or members of the old Liberal, or Republican, parties as happened to be available in the Middle East. Even so, it still remained unrepresentative; for, in Athens, there had meanwhile arisen under the Axis yoke new Republican parties, around some of which Resistance Movements had formed.

The leaders of the old Liberal parties in Athens were mainly conservative in their views. But, as I have previously indicated, they appeared to think that, until the King made an unequivocal declaration regarding a plebiscite, they would lose the bulk of their following to the new Republican or Resistance leaders if they showed any leanings towards the Government in exile. In general, therefore, they held back their support to both the Resistance Movements and the Government in exile. Meanwhile, there were Royalists in Athens, many of them senior army officers or rich industrialists, who were playing with both the German-sponsored Government and the Greek Government in exile. But few of them would have anything to do with the Resistance. I received further reports that Royalist agents in touch with the Middle East advised them to lie low until Greece was liberated, and discouraged them from going into the mountains. Eventually, in order to meet the Government in exile half-way, the Venizelist Liberals had despatched a M. Exindaris to Cairo to represent their views. It so happened that he arrived only a few days before my delegation from the mountains.

At the end of July, anti-Royalist disturbances—mutinous, by our standards—in the Greek Brigade, then in Palestine, and the consequent internment of agitators, had increased the troubles of the Greek Government to such an extent that, when we arrived in Cairo, it was seriously considering resigning. For all these reasons, the Republican members of the Government were more than ready to listen to the delegates from the mountains, to obtain the real facts about their country and their people.

Soon after my arrival I discovered that no programme had been prepared for the andarte delegates. It had not even been decided whether they would be allowed to see members of their own Government. It was not long, however, before their arrival was known in all Greek circles in Cairo, and the Republican members eagerly sought permission to interview them.

247

I submitted to Lord Glenconner the plan upon which we had already agreed in the mountains to base the presentation of our problems. He readily approved it, and within twenty-four hours permission was obtained for the delegates to come into Cairo and to be interviewed by their own Government. The second day after our arrival they were officially received by them, before any discussions had been held between them and the British authorities.

Whilst the representatives of Zervas and EKKA, Komninos Pyromaglou and George Kartalis respectively, behaved tactfully and correctly, the EAM delegates cast aside the joint proposals on which we had previously agreed and came straight to the political issue uppermost in their minds. They submitted that ninety per cent of the people of Greece were against the King's return, and they demanded a statement from the Government that he would not be allowed to return until a plebiscite had shown that the majority wanted him back. Their case was strengthened by the full agreement and support of M. Exindaris. They quickly obtained not only the ears but the sympathy of practically the whole of the Greek Government, and they carried the other andarte delegates with them. Within four days of our arrival, only the Prime Minister, M. Tsouderos, and one or two others stood by the King. At that time relations between SOE (Cairo), GHQ Middle East and the British Embassy to Greece appeared cordial, and it seemed to me that there was a large measure of agreement between all the British authorities concerned in Cairo that, if the King made a further suitable declaration, there was an immediate prospect of solving the problems which had been seriously troubling the Greek Government immediately prior to our arrival.

On my second day in Cairo Mr. Leeper, the British Ambassador to Greece, took me to see the King of Greece. He told me beforehand that I could speak quite frankly and that I was at liberty to tell the King all that I had already told Mr. Leeper about the anti-monarchial feeling in the mountains.

Although I never recorded my impressions of him at the time, I remember the late King of Greece as of slightly above average height, grey haired, clean-shaven, and with a big, thin-lipped mouth and a somewhat glassy smile. Although long past middle age he carried himself well for his years, but tired bespectacled eyes, a sallow complexion and a heavily lined face betrayed a possibly dormant illness. He spoke English fluently with hardly a trace of a foreign accent.

In the talk which I had with the King, as tactfully and as politely as I could, I explained to him the situation as I then saw it inside his country. It was my humble opinion, I said, that, if he were to go back to Greece at the head of his forces, EAM would separate themselves from the national group of guerillas which had been formed, and would declare themselves openly against him; Zervas would align himself alongside the King, and the result would probably be immediate civil war. I pointed out that he would be in serious personal danger, unless protected by British forces; that, should he go back to Greece under our protection, EAM would regard it as interference by the British in purely Greek affairs; and that this, again, would cause their open revolt.

On 13th August, after a dinner-party at the house of the Deputy Minister of State, Lord Moyne, I had another private conversation with the King of Greece. I asked him, in all seriousness, if he would consider visiting us in the mountains, in order to restore the people's confidence in him. He thought he was too old to undertake this. In answer to my suggestion that he might possibly stay outside Greece as his country's Ambassador during peace negotiations, and until the plebiscite as to his future had been held, he replied that he considered he must return with his army. His many friends in England would consider that he was shirking his duty if he remained behind.

Until I had been sent a political adviser, the British Embassy and the Foreign Office had to a large extent relied for their information on the trend of political affairs inside Greece on extracts on political matters from the many signals I and my officers sent back to SOE (Cairo). But, from the time of David Wallace's arrival, the British Ambassador should have been able to receive political reports, in which he would have full confidence, even though they came through my wireless channels and the cipher departments of SOE. For the first fortnight that he was in Greece, however, apart from sending a signal asking for some personal kit which he had lost on the night of his arrival by parachute, David had sent no messages. He had been busy interrogating Greeks and forming his own opinions. During the second and last fortnight before he came out with me, he had sent off to Cairo in cipher many long reports, addressed personally to the British Ambassador. On his arrival in the Middle East, he discovered to his consternation that the majority of these reports were still being deciphered by SOE. For over a month I myself had been drawing Cairo's attention to the delay in receiving replies to my non-priority signals. At that time sometimes many days, even weeks, elapsed before replies were received.

The result of all this was that, when my delegation arrived in Cairo, the British Ambassador was not as prepared as he might have been for the political situation which almost immediately arose. He ordered a full enquiry into the reasons why SOE had not delivered his personal signals from David Wallace. It was discovered that the delays were almost entirely due to the unforeseen and rapid expansion of wireless traffic all over the Balkans. This had caused great overloading of the cipher staff. Reinforcements had been demanded, and they were already on their way, both from England and South Africa; but none had yet arrived.

Whilst SOE (Cairo) got its broad, para-military directives from the headquarters of SOE in London, it got its local directives from the C.-in-C.'s Committee, of which both the Chief of Staff and the British Ambassador to Greece were members. It thus owed its loyalty to more than one master, and its charter was of necessity somewhat elastic. Although its staff consisted mostly of war-time soldiers, its head, Lord Glenconner, was an able civilian. This was an excellent arrangement whilst Resistance was in its early stages of development and remained clandestine; but when, as in 1943 in Greece, it had developed into widespread and overt guerilla warfare, the task of directing a veritable Resistance Army necessitated closer co-ordination with our military strategy and many dealings with branches of GHQ, Middle East.

On the political side Lord Glenconner had at that time no advisers of his own; none, in fact, closer to him than the British Ambassador to Greece, who owed his allegiance firstly to the Foreign Office. At the daily meetings which he had to attend with both soldiers of the General Staff and officials of the Embassy, he therefore stood at a considerable disadvantage. Much depended upon the fitting of personalities and on mutual confidence. When it is realised how interwoven politics had become with Resistance in Greece, and how, in the early periods of their clandestine work, the officers of SOE had been trained to shield the identities and activities of those who were working for them in the field, it can be seen that, even without such an incident as that caused by the delay in delivery of David Wallace's signals to Mr. Leeper, there were latent seeds of misunderstanding and discord even among the most broad-minded authorities concerned with the then largely overt forces of Resistance in Greece.

In war, however good wireless communications are, liaison officers are still necessary to paint a complicated picture to distant commanders. The picture in Greece was as complicated as any. SOE (Cairo) had managed to send John Stevens in to me in March, 1943. But, after a slow journey by caique from the east coast of Greece, he had been delayed in Turkey and he had not yet got back to the Middle East. He did not actually reach Cairo until ten days after my arrival. Consequently, not one liaison officer had yet got back to the Middle East for the whole eleven months since my original party had been despatched.

Whereas I discovered that most of those with whom I had to deal in SOE (Cairo) were quick to realise the problems which faced me in connection with the future Resistance in Greece, I found several in GHQ, Middle East who, although sympathetic, had no conception of the seriousness of the overall situation. Some of our soldiers, who had witnessed the masses at the funeral of Metaxas, and the loyal support of the people of Greece to their King and Government when their country was in danger in 1941, could not understand the complete change of opinion which I now reported; nor could they believe that it was genuine. They were not taking into consideration, and for the most part did not understand, the factors which made such a thing possible. They had forgotten, or did not know, that in 1924 the Greek people had overwhelmingly voted in favour of a Republic rather than for a Monarchy, and that in 1935, only eleven years later, King George II of Greece was restored to the throne by a vote of ninety-seven per cent in favour of his return. Even allowing for some local 'arrangement' of these figures, there would appear to have been a complete change of opinion.

The British Government itself appeared to be unprepared for the sudden alignment of the majority of the Greek Government alongside the fervent, anti-monarchical elements of EAM. When, therefore, on 22nd August the Greek King telegraphed Mr. Churchill and President Roosevelt at the Quebec Conference asking what action he should take, it is perhaps not surprising that he was advised by both not to act hastily or unconstitutionally. Both apparently considered that if he had acceded to the EAM demands, he would virtually have been signing his own abdication, and his Prime Minister, M. Tsouderos, would also have had no other course than to resign. There would have been none, other than a handful of young members of the old Republican parties, and the andarte delegates, available from whom to choose successors in the Government. Moreover, as the andarte delegates and M. Exindaris only spoke for about a quarter of the people of Greece, the Foreign Office was far from certain that they were really representative of the present opinions of the Greek people as a whole; and it was naturally considered premature to anticipate opinions after the liberation of Greece, when the Resistance Movements would have ceased to exist, or been absorbed within the peacetime structure.

SOE (Cairo) thought the available information indicated that a representative government might have been built up around the remaining members, but the British Government disapproved of such an unconstitutional solution of a major problem whilst Greece was still under the Axis yoke. Apparently it was feared that the abdication of the King and the resignation of M. Tsouderos' Government would result in any new government becoming the tool of EAM, the most powerful and influential Resistance Movement, created and predominantly led by Communists. It was also rightly argued that EAM had not recruited most of its following; it had largely conscripted it; and even with its following, it was only representative of one-eighth of the Greek nation. The only feasible alternative to handing over power to EAM would have been the dissolution of all constitutional government and the temporary institution of a purely military set-up. This would have meant that Greece would have no one with political authority to represent her in international affairs, when the country was finally liberated.

Whilst approving all attempts to broaden the Government in exile constitutionally, the British Government therefore regarded any other method as highly dangerous. They considered that the support of the monarchy until a national plebiscite could be held under conditions of tranquillity provided the only certain way of maintaining a constitutional government. This appeared to be the main reason why, at this critical period, they gave their full support to the King, and used all their influence to prevent the resignation of the Greek Prime Minister and his Government. When therefore, a few days later, the EAM delegates impatiently overplayed their hand and, without any previous indication, demanded that they should be given three seats in the Government, it was not difficult to understand why they were met with stern resistance from the Greek King and M. Tsouderos and even from other members of the Greek Government who until then had been backing the EAM delegates.

Relations became strained between SOE (Cairo) and the British Embassy under its firm new directives from the Foreign Office. I and my superiors were blamed for bringing the andarte delegates to Cairo with such drastic proposals, without first having prepared the way. Lord Glenconner pointed out to Mr. Leeper that his people could hardly be held to blame for what Greek nationals discussed with their own Government and that, anyhow, the majority of the Greek Government and of the people in Free Greece—and others in Cairo—had appeared to be in favour of the delegates' earlier proposals.

When the British Embassy passed on instructions to SOE (Cairo) that the delegates were to be sent back to Greece as soon as possible, I became thoroughly alarmed about the consequences. I requested an interview with Mr. Leeper and warned him frankly that it would appear to EAM that, by turning them away, and by supporting the King, the British intended to reimpose him when the country was liberated. This would in turn give EAM the very propaganda which they wanted for further expansion in the mountains, and might ultimately expose the people of Greece to the danger of a dictatorship of the Left.

I pointed out to the military authorities that the 'Military Agreement' would break down, and that the value of the forces of Resistance would probably be lost in internecine strife. Lord

Glenconner also warned them about the repercussions there might be amongst sympathetic or subversive elements in the Greek armed forces in the Middle East; further, that, if we ignominiously dismissed the andarte delegates, we ourselves would in all probability find ourselves at war with EAM when Greece was liberated. But the British Government stood firm, and insisted upon the solution of the Greek governmental crisis by constitutional methods. As the military factors were considered to be of secondary importance, the C.-in-C., General Wilson, although in sympathy with my problems and almost entirely in agreement with my views,* was in no position to overrule the instructions which the British Embassy received from London.

It was my intention all along that the Greek delegates should not be in Cairo for more than about two weeks. On 14th August they had had a satisfactory interview with the C.-in-C. But, whilst I was lunching with them five days later, they told me that, as a result of the impasse on political matters and the instructions which I had been ordered to pass on to them not to force an issue, and because of the resultant delay in the solution of the major problem about the King's return to Greece, the military aspects of their problem had hung fire. They said that they could not complete all the necessary discussions before their departure, which was being planned for three days hence.

I did what I could to have their departure delayed. With Lord Glenconner I saw the C.-in-C., the British Ambassador and Mr. Casey, the Minister of State; but we failed to get their departure postponed. Pending a decision on the all-important political matters, we suggested that the delegates might temporarily be 'got out of the way' by sending them on a battle-field tour; but this recommendation was likewise turned down.

On 21st August a farewell meeting of the delegates was arranged

* *Vide* Field Marshal Lord Wilson of Libya, *Eight Years Overseas*, pp. 166–168, 180.

with Mr. Casey. It lasted about an hour and a half. However, possibly because of my instructions to the delegates not to make any forthright demands and to be tactful, at the end of it not one of the six had voiced what was uppermost in their minds, their objection to being made to return to Greece with their political mission so rudely rejected, and their military one uncompleted.

They were due to leave the following afternoon. Although I had told them about the plans for their departure, no one, as yet, had told them to their faces that they must go; no one had asked them to stay. The Minister of State was already shaking hands with them and wishing them good-bye. With his permission I then spoke out and, in front of the delegates, told him that three days ago I had been informed that, if the Greeks stayed on in Cairo, they might cause the resignation of their Government, with the result that M. Tsouderos might not be able to form another one. The C.-in-C. therefore wished the delegates to return temporarily to Greece, pending the King's decision about their recommendations regarding his future movements and their ideas submitted for broadening the Greek Government by including representatives of the Resistance Forces.

This gave the Greeks the opportunity they needed to unburden their minds, a move they had been too polite to make until that moment. For the next twenty minutes they ably gave the reasons why they wished to stay in Cairo until a decision had been reached regarding the future movements of the King and the composition of a national government. They said that they had delayed all other discussions pending a decision on these points, to which they had been asked by me not to press for an immediate answer.

Mr. Casey, however, was unable to accede to their request, and he ended up by thanking them for the most interesting talk he had had with them and advising them to act in accordance with the C.-in-C.'s wishes.

Despondently, after shaking hands with him once more, the Greeks filed out.

Immediately afterwards I explained to Mr. Casey the disaster which I feared would follow if the six delegates went back to Greece in such a disappointed frame of mind. Lord Glenconner supported my contention. But Mr. Leeper, who was also present, considered it more important that the Greeks should go back. Mr. Casey said that he saw no way of allowing them to stay; and so we parted.

The next morning the C.-in-C., with Mr. Leeper at his side, said good-bye to the delegates. They pleaded with him to be allowed to stay. But this was no longer purely a military matter, and the C.-in-C. was not in a position to give way. This was a tragedy; but I had done all I could to see that their case was fairly presented. A little later, with their bags packed ready to leave for the aerodrome I learnt that one of them had asked a senior SOE staff officer whether, as they were Greek subjects and they were under the impression that the Greek Government did not wish them to go, they could visit their Prime Minister on their way to the aerodrome.

They were told that they could not be prevented from doing this, but that, at the same time, they must understand that an officer of SOE was not in a position to advise them to do so. It was up to them to do what they thought was right.

On their way to the aerodrome they did, in fact, visit M. Tsouderos. What actually transpired during that visit I have never discovered. A few hours later, though, M. Tsouderos asked our Embassy to delay the departure of the delegates. The British Ambassador agreed and their aircraft was cancelled.

During the next week I attended daily conferences with the delegates and staff officers of SOE (Cairo) on purely military matters. By the end of it we had covered all the points we wished to tackle. In the middle of September, the delegates returned to

Greece, accompanied by Colonel Bakirdzis, a Socialist, who had earned a D.S.O. in the 1914–18 war, and who wished to join EKKA in the mountains. A few days before their departure Lord Glenconner and I set off by air for London; but not before the first American officer—Captain Ehrgott—had been sent into Greece to join our Mission which, with an ever increasing number of Americans, soon became known as the 'Allied Military Mission'.

I had regarded David Wallace, my political adviser, as an officer under my own command. But after my first week in Cairo it was difficult for me to see him. From the day of our arrival he was ordered to base himself on the Office of the British Embassy to Greece and to take his orders from Mr. Leeper, no longer from me. Later he went sick and was confined to his house with what he described to me as gout. He was eventually sent home to England to report to the Foreign Office several days before I followed him home. I missed his advice and support tremendously.

Even after three weeks in Cairo I was still far from sure that the political authorities were yet fully briefed as to the exact situation inside Greece, or that they realised the full implications of sending the delegates back empty-handed. I therefore sat down and wrote a long report, in which I traced the development of the Resistance Movements and events which lead up to the present situation. I completed it just before my departure for London and arrived in England armed with several copies of it, which were distributed to the various Ministries.

On arrival in London I was convinced that in the course of a few days, if I were given the appropriate interviews, I would be able to make the present situation inside Greece quite clear to all concerned. My first few days were occupied chiefly in seeing different officers in the War Office, for the most part amplifying my report. I saw the Directors of Military Operations and of

Military Intelligence and was interviewed by the C.I.G.S. I was congratulated on the part which we had played up to date in assisting the Allied cause and I formed the impression that the War Office still required the maximum military contribution from the andartes for the general prosecution of the war.

After a talk with the Joint Planners in the Cabinet Offices, I discovered to my great disappointment that it was the intention of the Allies, when the time eventually came, only to send the minimum force to liberate Greece. Apparently no more could be spared. I was told that this small force would be despatched only when the Axis forces were about to withdraw either because they were required as reinforcements elsewhere, or because Greece became outflanked by our advance up the mainland of Italy. I immediately raised the question of the maintenance of law and order, and pointed out that the return of the Greek King at the head of his army under these conditions was a virtual impossibility.

I had more than one talk with representatives of the Ministry of Economic Warfare on the serious economic crisis, particularly in regard to food, which faced Greece on her liberation.

Virtually out of touch with David Wallace, I had no means of obtaining an introduction to anybody in the Foreign Office. I formed the impression that no one there wished to question me and that, for political information, they were quite content to rely upon David. But, although he had spent three years in Greece before the war and he spoke Greek fluently, he had only been with us in the mountains for a month; he could not know as much about my problems as I did, and I felt it my duty to tell the Foreign Office all that I knew. At the end of my first week, therefore, I got in touch with David and asked him to arrange an interview for me on whatever level he thought appropriate. As a result, on 16th September, I was interviewed by Sir Orme Sargent, the Permanent Under-Secretary of State. He began by telling me that the Foreign Office considered I was responsible for putting the andarte leaders up to the idea of asking for portfolios in the Greek Government. I firmly refuted this allegation and we got on to a discussion about the problems which faced us. It was decided that it would assist the officers under my command if the full story of the King's loyal support to the Allies in 1941 was published and if a simple brief could be given to me for them all.

Sir Orme Sargent then pointed out that in my report I had stated that less than a tenth of the total number of andartes in the mountains had actively contributed towards the sabotage in conjunction with the invasion of Sicily. Why, then, was it necessary to go on arming the andartes, thereby increasing the political difficulties for Greece on her liberation? I pointed out that the British saboteurs, though they sometimes acted alone, on many occasions required the active assistance of andarte bands; moreover, that their freedom of movement and security in the mountains depended indirectly upon far larger andarte forces than were necessary for carrying out any particular act of sabotage. In addition, I stressed the fact that enemy reprisals against innocent civilians were so heavy that, unless their morale was maintained by the knowledge that there was widespread indigenous resistance in the form of armed andartes, it was possible that it might crack, with the result that the movements of British officers and small Allied sabotage parties would be betrayed by enemy agents able to operate in the mountains. I also pointed out that without a continuous stimulant to the andartes, there was a serious risk that political differences between the various andarte Movements would cause internecine strife to the detriment of the war against the common enemy. It was already our intention, however, to arm the andartes qualitatively rather than quantitatively in the future, by giving them supporting arms instead of more rifles and light automatics.

Two weeks after my arrival I was asked to give a talk in the Curzon Cinema to a large gathering from the different Ministries.

I was given no brief for my talk. I could easily have recounted a 'blood-and-thunder' story of the many experiences of my past year in enemy-occupied territory. Because, however, of the impression I had formed that many people still did not realise either the involved nature or the seriousness of the problems which faced my Mission in Greece, I decided to explain once again what they were and how they had arisen.

The reactions to my talk were immediate. It was made clear to me that I had put SOE (London) in an embarrassing position *vis-à-vis* the Foreign Office. In short, I was afterwards told that I ought not to have spoken as I had done on political matters. They were no concern of mine—how I wished they were not!—and I should have confined myself purely to an exciting story of my year in the mountains. It was a pity no one had told me so beforehand. Re-reading the text of my talk now, more than ten years later, it is easy to see how youthfulness and over-anxiety led me beyond the bounds of diplomacy and how I must have given the Foreign Office the impression that I thought I knew how to do their job better than they did.

After my talk at the Curzon Cinema I was summoned on two different occasions to Buckingham Palace; the first time for an interview with Sir Alan Lascelles, Private Secretary to the King, and the second for a twenty minutes frank fireside talk with His late Majesty himself. I had the satisfaction of being asked for, and being able to state quite openly, the situation as I saw it. I confined myself purely to facts. I found His Majesty extremely well briefed and most interested in all I was able to tell him.

Following these two visits, I was interviewed briefly by Mr. Eden in the Foreign Office and later, at length, by Mr. Churchill at Chequers. I pointed out to both that, although our policy might be a just and fair one, we had left all public announcements on Greece to the Greek King and Government and that our silence, particularly after the return of the andarte delegates with their aims so unfulfilled, would be interpreted by some inside Greece as determination on our part to enforce the return of the King. Although I knew this to be untrue, those inside Greece did not, and I felt that it was up to us to explain our policy in order to defeat such counter propaganda.

During my visit to Chequers, while sitting round the table after lunch with a good cigar—I was given an additional one to take away—Mr. Churchill discussed with me many aspects of the Greek political situation and of my problems. I took the opportunity of telling him politely that I thought a part of his recent speech at Quebec, in which he had said he looked forward to the return of the Greek King to Greece, had made my task more difficult. Our frank and friendly conversation lasted well into the afternoon; it was five o'clock before I took my leave. "God bless you," were Mr. Churchill's parting words. "Don't let the Greeks prejudge the issue about their King. I want to see him have a fair deal."

I was now becoming most concerned lest the Foreign Office should order me to sever all relations with EAM/ELAS, not least because the withdrawal of our liaison teams from their bands would have been most hazardous to my officers and men concerned. I was seriously handicapped by the fact that the Foreign Office still would not take me into their confidence. It was clear they considered that SOE had exceeded its charter in that it had, so they believed, pursued a dangerous political policy of its own without keeping the Foreign Office informed. At the same time they obviously thought that I was to no small extent responsible for the political crisis which had recently arisen in Cairo. As a result any recommendations I was permitted to make were regarded with suspicion and I could make no progress.

By the beginning of October a firm policy had not yet been given me by the Foreign Office. I had already been away from Greece far too long and I was unwilling to delay my return to

Cairo any longer. On 8th October I broadcast a message of good cheer to the andartes from the BBC. After a short introduction by myself, David Wallace,★ who spoke Greek, broadcast on my behalf. In this speech, at Mr. Churchill's request and quoting his authority, I said that in future we would help the people more and more. But I was not authorised to say anything that would allay EAM's fears of our interference in Greek political affairs.†

The next day, having at length obtained agreement that a directive would be sent on to me in the Middle East as soon as possible, I left for Egypt.

I got back to Cairo on 10th October to learn that the situation inside Greece had deteriorated and everyone was in fear of the imminent outbreak of civil war on the mainland. But, as I thought that EAM would take no irrevocable step until they had heard the result of my visit to London, I sent a message to Chris that I was delaying my return for a few more days in order to come back with a definite policy and plan as a result of my two months' absence. "I feel certain", I wrote, "that the Foreign Office will give me some cards with which to return after my interview with the Prime Minister."

I had wrongly appreciated the situation. The Italian collapse which had already resulted in several thousand additional weapons being brought into the mountains within grasp of ELAS; clever German-planted information that Zervas was co-operating with them; equally clever rumours initiated by the Germans that they

★ This was the last time I ever saw David Wallace. Several months later he returned to Greece as Chris' Foreign Office representative. Shortly afterwards he was most unfortunately killed by a stray bullet in an andarte engagement with the Germans.

† As is indicated in Bickham Sweet-Escott's *Greece, A Political and Economic Survey, 1939–1953*, p. 27, n. 1, it was not, I think, until 9th November, 1943, when Mr. Churchill denied categorically in the House of Commons that His Majesty's Government had given any undertaking as to the future status of the King of Greece, that any further move was made to undermine EAM's main propaganda weapon.

were leaving Greece; the failure of EAM's delegates in Cairo; and my failure, so far, to return; all apparently indicated to EAM that now was their second chance of seizing power.

I was at the SOE Training School in Haifa when on 19th October an officer, who had just arrived from Cairo, gave me the depressing news that civil war had broken out and that I would probably not be returning to Greece. I hurried back to Cairo, to discover that Chris had already been informed that I was not returning, and that in his capacity as temporary commander he had been asked to submit a full report on the situation, and his recommendations for our future policy towards the andartes, in particular EAM.

Whether or not the British Embassy expected to get original views from Chris, now that he no longer owed any allegiance to me as his commander, I do not know. But Chris' report, which was brought out by air, entirely supported my interpretation of our past instructions, and he stated that he saw no possibility of adopting any new policy in the future. Whether I came back or not, the past one was now the only possible one to follow.

A day or two later I heard that Lord Glenconner was remaining in London, and that both he and his two immediate subordinates were being replaced. But, before one of them, Colonel Tamplin, was relieved, he died suddenly in his office, as a result of a stroke probably brought on by continuous overwork.

In an interview with General Scobie,* then General Wilson's Chief of Staff, I gathered that the C.-in-C. was still trying to get permission for me to go back to Greece to try to stop the civil war, because, he said, all andarte organisations had confidence in me. But I also gathered that there were political objections because of "my pro-EAM policy".† To this day I maintain that I

---

* Now Lieutenant-General Sir Ronald Scobie, K.B.E., C.B., M.C., retd.

† I heard that the King of Greece had threatened to abdicate if I were sent back to Greece.

never had a policy other than that of every soldier, namely, to obey orders and to obtain the maximum contribution towards the war effort. I told General Scobie that I did not see how I could succeed unless the Foreign Office, as well as the C.-in-C., had complete confidence in me. Because our military activities were so bound up with politics, I must be told what the Foreign Office actually wanted. Otherwise I would prefer them to find someone else.

Several weeks of depressing inaction, uncertainty, frustration, and worry followed. It was almost with relief that late in November I heard that Chris had been officially appointed as my successor and that I would definitely not be returning to Greece. But at heart I was miserably disappointed because I was being denied the opportunity of completing the task which I had begun among a people whom I had grown to love and whom I believed I understood.

(See Appendix, p. 285, for more detailed accounts of visits to Buckingham Palace, the Foreign Office and Chequers)

CHAPTER XVIII

More EAM/ELAS Bids for Power

AFTER THE EAM delegates returned to the mountains from Cairo frustrated and without me, Chris was faced with ever-increasing difficulties trying to maintain the shallow accord between the rival factions which had been achieved after months of effort shortly before my departure.

The first serious dispute arose in connection with the Italian collapse. There was keen competition for the privilege of looking after those of our late enemy who would surrender, in order to obtain their military support. At first ELAS were determined to take care of their arms for them. As a result, the Italian commanders did their best to negotiate only with officers of the Mission, were prepared to surrender to EDES, but shied away from ELAS. Chris eventually obtained Saraphis' agreement that the Italians would be allowed to keep their arms and it was decided that the fostering andarte organisation would in each case be the one nearest to the garrison of the surrendering Italians.

Twelve thousand Italians gave themselves up, mostly in small parties all over Greece. The only large-scale surrender came from the Pinerolo Division which was located in ELAS-occupied areas. Seven thousand of them joined us in formed bodies and shortly afterwards fought a most successful action alongside ELAS defending Porta, at the entrance to the Thessaly Plain, from quite a large scale and determined German attack.

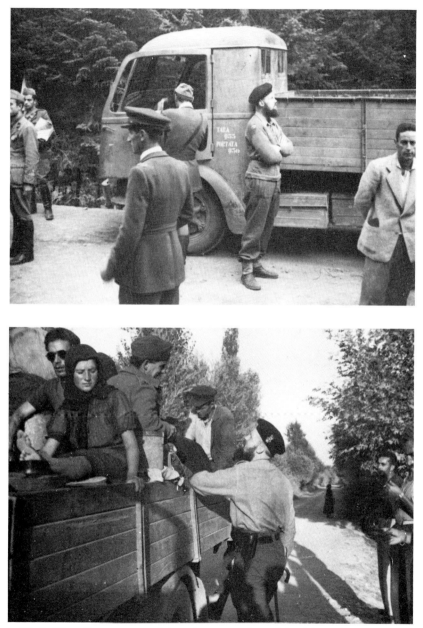

Chris Woodhouse supervising the surrender of the Pinerolo Division near Porta, September 1943.

'General' Saraphis (ELAS), General Infante (Pinerolo Division) and Chris Woodhouse, with Ross Bower behind.

General Zervas (*left*) and his Cretan Adjutant, Captain Michalli Miriadakis, in 1943 when Zervas was presented with the ribbon of his O.B.E. by Chris Woodhouse for his part in the Gorgopotamos Operation.

The luxury of harnessed spring water outside Theodorina, which also boasted of its own generated electricity, both rare luxuries in the mountains.

Aris (*left*) in convivial mood, with his bodyguard and BLOs.

EAM/ELAS quickly realised the danger to themselves from having a large, well-organised and effective force of Italians in their midst and they now began to take systematic steps to break up its cohesion which its commander, General Infante, had so far preserved. Desertions were encouraged by Communist propaganda; whole units were ordered to be detached for remote purposes; and equipment was 'borrowed' and never returned. In spite of Chris' efforts on Infante's behalf to preserve its identity, the Pinerolo Division as such soon ceased to exist.

The end of this episode came towards the middle of October, in the course of the most disastrous week in the history of the Mission. Simultaneously with the disarmament by ELAS of every co-belligerent Italian unit in Greece "as a precautionary measure to forestall a Fascist plot", ELAS forces attacked the followers of Zervas throughout the country "because he was collaborating with the enemy".

Days of chaos followed. In the course of the fighting, a New Zealand officer, Lieutenant Hubbard, was killed by ELAS and a question was asked in the House of Commons as to why we should continue to support a Resistance Movement which killed British officers. No one knew what would happen to the Resistance Movements, to the Mission, to the Italians or to Greece. On 19th October the Germans occupied Metsovo, almost without opposition. The biggest drive in the history of the occupation was on, and the thin fabric of our eleven months' patient work crumbled so quickly that there was nothing to oppose the enemy. In the course of a few days the military effectiveness of the andarte Movements in Greece had been reduced almost to nothing.

Within a few weeks Zervas' andartes were driven west by ELAS as far as the Arachthos River. There, only, were they able to hold their ground against all but local penetration, until they counter-attacked back to the line of the River Acheloos. Throughout the civil war sufficient material was dropped to Zervas to sustain his forces, and, with the knowledge that ELAS was getting virtually no war supplies, to maintain morale in EDES. The number of Greek lives taken by other Greeks did not reach large proportions. In the three months of fighting perhaps only a few hundred were killed. During the conflict EKKA unwillingly and passively sided with EAM, ultimately only to be attacked themselves by ELAS a few weeks after the fight against Zervas had ended. As a result, therefore, not only was Zervas confined to a fraction of the area that he had previously held, but the identity of EKKA was almost completely lost, together with several capable and gallant leaders of this organisation, ultimately amongst them Colonel Psaros, who was killed by ELAS in a fresh outbreak of fighting nearly a year later.

During all this time, however, the Allied Mission was not withdrawn from EAM. At the height of the civil war Allied officers in EAM areas continued to receive supplies of medical equipment and other essentials for distribution. In one area in Northern Macedonia, where ELAS continued to fight against the enemy—there were no andartes of other organisations to fight against in the vicinity—the local bands received uninterrupted supplies of ammunition. When, therefore, EAM/ELAS belatedly realised that they were not powerful enough to sweep the board, the Mission still remained largely non-partisan; and Chris, after much patient work, was able to induce Zervas and EAM to come to terms. In February, 1944, a truce was signed at Plaka, whereby it was agreed that, if Zervas would in future confine himself to the relatively small area in the southern Pindus then still under his control, ELAS would leave him unmolested there.

Stage by stage the Allied Mission managed to persuade ELAS, first in one part of Greece and then in another, mostly in areas distant from that under Zervas' control, to take up arms once more against the Germans. As soon as bands did so they were rewarded with supplies to carry on their fight against the common enemy. Thus it came about that, by the beginning of 1944, although there still was sporadic fighting on the perimeter of Zervas' area and although no formal peace had been signed, the civil war had practically come to a stop.

But from then onwards nothing could make it possible for EAM and Zervas, with or without EKKA, to be united. Blood had been spilled in open conflict. Hatred had become too deep and too bitter between the rival movements. If the Middle East required any effective military assistance from the andartes in the future a new line of approach would be necessary. ELAS would have to be kept entirely separate from Zervas' movement. Such an irreconcilable separation of the andarte movements gave rise to grave forebodings of future bloodshed on the liberation of Greece, when the conflicting organisations would have to be absorbed within the peace-time structure of the nation.

The catastrophe which I had striven so hard and for so long to avert had occurred.

Towards the end of January, 1944, I left the Middle East to take part in the invasion of Western Europe. Before I departed I sent farewell messages to my own officers, ELAS GHQ and Zervas. ELAS GHQ sent me their good wishes. "My thoughts", Zervas wrote back, "turn to the cave on Giona, from where together we started our struggle for the freedom of the individual and the liberation of my country. You must always regard the soil of Greece as your own. May we meet again in happier circumstances in a free world for whose freedom you have always striven."

One of the last interviews—which I requested to be arranged—was with the King of Greece who summoned me to bid me fare-well. I will always remember our parting words. "Good-bye and good luck to you," he said in his perfect English. "Thank you, sir," I replied, "and may I, with humble respect, wish you good luck, also." A smile spread across his face as he thanked me and I withdrew. I did not feel like smiling; for I feared that if he persisted in his intention to return to Greece the moment it was liberated he faced certain death.

Throughout 1944 there was incessant manœuvring for political power between the three main factions actively involved; EAM, based upon Athens and spread almost throughout the whole of Greece; the old political parties, or what remained of them, in Athens; and the Government in exile in Cairo. Zervas' andarte movement, although potentially an important factor, was at that time on the defensive and could not be counted as a fourth faction. As a result of continuous efforts in Cairo, in the summer of 1944 the Government in exile was successfully broadened into a 'Government of National Unity' including representatives of the old political parties, EDES and, ultimately, EAM.

Meanwhile the officers of the Allied Mission, working under the able leadership of Chris and his American second-in-command, Jerry Wines, were preparing an extensive sabotage programme for the time when Greece was to be invaded by the Allies. It was much on the same lines as that prepared for the cover plan for the invasion of Sicily, but it was a more difficult proposition because this time the Mission and the andartes had to make real trouble for the Germans, not just to create the illusion that trouble was coming.

This sabotage was therefore a grimmer business. Apart from the Peloponnese where the civil war left in its wake conditions which played straight into the hands of the Germans and allowed them to thin out their troops unmolested by the andartes, the fighting was fiercer, the destruction greater and the casualties heavier. No precise estimate of the cost to the enemy can be made, nor can the proportion be fixed between the contribution of the Mission, the andartes, specially trained American and British Regular Army detachments sent to augment the andartes, and of the Balkan Air Force operating from Italy. It would not be an exaggeration to estimate the damage at about a hundred locomotives destroyed, five hundred vehicles destroyed or captured, and five thousand Germans killed. But it cannot be denied that, even at a high cost, the Germans fulfilled their principal intention of extracting the bulk of their forces intact, leaving only the outlying garrisons of a few islands to keep Allied forces busy, and to delay rehabilitation until the final surrender of Germany.

On 18th October, two days after the official entry of Allied troops, the Greek Government reached Athens—without the King. Their authority was at once respected and, apart from clashes in the Peloponnese between ELAS and Security Battalions, order prevailed everywhere.

Meanwhile the leaders of EAM/ELAS were far from idle. While the Germans were leaving Greece, many bands of ELAS, if only a comparatively small fraction of their total numbers, were marching south on Athens. They marched under the orders of EAM; they obviously marched to propagate its cause. But, although it is not unreasonable to suppose it, I have yet to discover conclusive proof that they marched to achieve a *coup d'état* involving action against British as well as Greeks, should there be an attempt by Right-wing elements to do them down. In fact, the evidence available indicates that EAM believed we would be bringing to Greece such an overwhelmingly strong force of combat troops that a *coup d'état* would be impossible. Not until EAM discovered the smallness of our numbers and the weakness of our dispositions did they realise that they now had yet a third chance of seizing power.

The spark which relit the civil war came soon after the Government had ordered the disbandment of all andartes. The EAM members of the Government immediately resigned, or were forced to resign by the threats of their confederates. EAM argued that, if the andartes were disarmed and the Greek regular forces—

the Mountain Brigade and the Sacred Battalion—were left untouched, they would be handing over armed authority to Greek forces which had already been politically combed of all Republican elements,* and which would be used by Right-wing extremists to defeat the Republican Movements. The Greek Police, they also argued, was still the same force which Metaxas had organised; they claimed that it was full of quislings and that it ought to be purged.

Meanwhile unofficial extreme Right-wing elements had been openly hostile to EAM and their demonstration of political strength; in fact some EAM supporters had been murdered by members of a secret Royalist organisation in Athens before their leaders resorted openly to force. EAM allegedly feared that the promise of free elections counted for nothing. They knew how often such promises had been defeated in past Greek history. They stood firm. A mishandled demonstration on 3rd December gave them their excuse to take up arms in defence of their cause. Typical of Balkan internecine strife, it quickly developed into a barbarous, venomous and bloody affair. Into it on the side of the constitutional government and law and order British troops were tragically but inevitably drawn. They soon found it a grim and dirty business.

As soon as the fighting began in Athens, General Scobie sent Chris to Yannina to ensure that Zervas' andartes behaved correctly. On 21st December, EDES was attacked by very large forces of ELAS. Seriously short of ammunition—because a few weeks previously he had been ordered by SOE to hand over a large amount to ELAS bands to enable the latter to harass the Germans withdrawing in Eastern Greece—Zervas was forced to fight a withdrawing action from Epirus to the west coast. He soon held only a small area around Preveza. By the end of the

---

* In April, 1944, as a result of mutiny in the Greek armed forces in the Middle East, some pro-EAM agitators had been removed from the Brigade.

month the Royal Navy had evacuated him and his loyal followers to Corfu.

Until reinforcements arrived by air, the situation of the British forces in Athens and Piræus was almost as precarious. From a force already dangerously weak to combat the sudden attack by ELAS, General Scobie had to form several fresh detachments to guard his scattered depots. But had we stood aside or withdrawn from Greece, either action would have been tantamount to handing over complete power to EAM, and would have resulted in the most ghastly and widespread massacres by EAM/ELAS, immeasurably greater than those which they subsequently perpetrated on their hostages. Powerful though EAM were, we had to stay and fight it out with them. There was then no alternative. To save Greek from Greek it now had to be so.

On 30th December, 1944, after nearly a month of bitter fighting in Athens, it was announced that the King was resolved not to return to Greece until he was "summoned by a free and fair expression of the national will", and the Archbishop of Athens was appointed Regent. Thus at last was this vital announcement made. The tragedy lay in that its object was now not to prevent civil war and bitter bloodshed, but to bring it to an end.

CHAPTER XIX

Retrospect

> " neither that nor any other policy could have completely succeeded."
> C. M. WOODHOUSE, *Apple of Discord*.

IN MOST enemy-occupied countries during World War II, where the Forces of Resistance received the active support of the Western Democracies, and there were at the same time Communist-inspired Patriot organisations, the political pattern of Resistance was much the same. The Communists, in pre-war years a political minority, in some cases having struggled underground for their very existence, made the most of the opportunity of enemy occupation to organise widespread Patriot Movements and People's Fronts, with the ultimate object of assisting or achieving their political aims on the liberation of their countries.★ At the best there was mutual agreement between them and other Movements to tolerate each other; at the worst there was open conflict between them, to the detriment of the war against the common enemy. It happened to a certain extent in France and Belgium; to a large extent in Poland and Yugoslavia; it happened in Malaya and in China. It was much the same in Greece. Metaxas, by declaring the Communist Party illegal, had, in 1936, driven it underground. The advantages which Greece gained from the four years of his dictatorship were too short-lived for his appointment by King George II of Greece and his stern measures to be overlooked by

---

★ Subsequent history has shown that it is the strategy of the Communists always to work through a small minority. This is what they were trying to do throughout the occupation of Greece and in December 1944.

the Greek nation suffering under the Axis yoke. The King's act of setting up the Metaxas dictatorship in 1936 gave the leaders of EAM their biggest political weapon five years later.

Towards the end of 1941, when EAM began forming armed bands of ELAS, many young Greeks and a considerable number of older men of every political opinion throughout the Greek countryside, voluntarily joined ELAS in order to continue the fight against the enemy. At that time there were only a few independent bands and there was no other national organisation for them to join. Most Greek country-folk were in full accord with the publicised aims of the 'People's Movement' of EAM, and of its armed forces, ELAS. Many did not then know that EAM owed its inception to Left-wing extremists, who might have ulterior motives; they did not know that most of the pre-war politicians in Athens had given the Movement a frigid reception and had refused to have anything to do with it; nor, in their true patriotism, would they have cared much had they known it at that stage in the war, when Russia was fighting gallantly as our ally. All they wanted to do was to carry on the fight against the enemy; all they wanted to know about EAM/ELAS was whether this organisation would help them do so.

EAM's original policy was to concentrate and control all Greek Resistance under the guise of a harmless 'progressive' political banner; to build it up, outwardly, on the broadest possible national basis; to fight against the occupying powers as and when practicable; and to develop ELAS' potential, but to demonstrate neither its true Communist character nor its full strength until the day of liberation approached. The policy of avoiding large-scale clashes with the enemy's armed forces suited its leaders' political ends; it also happened to be the correct method of carrying out guerilla warfare in such a small country as Greece.

From 25th November, 1942, when the Gorgopotamos viaduct was successfully demolished, until the 1st November, 1944, when

275

the last German soldiers left Greek soil, considerable publicity was given to the andarte struggle against the occupying Power. For two years Allied propaganda floodlit the activities of Greek Resistance to friend and foe alike.

For the maintenance of continuous overt guerilla warfare, extensive undeveloped areas are necessary to provide safe bases from which armed bands can operate. Unless these areas are sufficiently large, the whole countryside is liable to be combed by the enemy and devastated by their reprisals, and the toll of wasted and innocent lives is liable to be not only excessive, but out of all proportion to the military value of the Resistance.

In the middle of the war there were vast expanses of undeveloped country behind the lines in Russia; from them Russian *franc tireurs* successfully waged guerilla warfare. French Resistance, about which much has been written, was, it is true, magnificent; but, until 'D' Day, because of the few suitable guerilla bases, its activities were largely clandestine. Even the mountains of Yugoslavia were barely large enough for Tito's Partisans, whose existence caused not only the cruellest suffering to the civil population, but cost them over a million dead.

The mountains of Greece are considerably less extensive than those of Yugoslavia. To ask the local inhabitants to allow their homeland to be made into a base for overt guerilla warfare for two years was indeed asking great and cruel sacrifices of them. To expect guerilla forces to exist quiescently for a further eighteen months after their activities had reached a peak—for the invasion of Sicily—was expecting the impossible, without tragic cost to the local population.

Not until Chris' visit to Athens in January, 1943, did we establish beyond doubt the utter inseparableness of EAM and ELAS and the full Communist character of their direction. But, as a result of an earlier decision by the Anglo-Greek Committee in Cairo—advised by Greek agents in Athens—not to give unilateral support to ELAS, a leader of more moderate political opinion was sought in the spring of 1942 to co-ordinate guerilla warfare against the enemy. It was some little time before any such leader was found. Andarte struggles were nothing new to the people of Greece, who had inherited from their forefathers the lessons of great and historic klepht struggles born in the mountains. Several potential leaders who were contacted in Athens considered that, without greater material support than that which the Middle East Command indicated would be possible, the frightful cost to the Greek people would be out of all proportion to the military benefit to the Allies. In the end Zervas, having refused an EAM offer to become C.-in-C. of ELAS, convinced of the importance of the Allied requirements, took to the mountains in the early summer of 1942, and formed his own Resistance Movement, largely independent of EDES in Athens. The knowledge that he would receive material support from the Allies similarly influenced Colonel Psaros in his decision to leave Athens in 1943, and to form active forces in the field around EKKA, a Movement with political views somewhere between those of EDES and ELAS.

EAM viewed the formation of new Resistance forces with contempt and mistrust. Why, they asked, should the Allies persuade other Greek leaders to take to the mountains and form rival andarte organisations, when all that was wanted was one big national Movement? Why should they be rewarded with gold for doing so? Why should they receive material support from the Allies out of proportion to their numbers? What was the matter with EAM and ELAS, which had been formed solely as a result of their own initiative, unaided by the Allies? Why did the Middle East Command want to make difficulties for them with these additional organisations in the field, which sooner or later were bound to come into conflict with them?

Such questions as these would all have been reasonable had EAM themselves pursued a broad-minded policy of moderation;

had even the leaders of the 'old' political parties in Athens sunk their differences and joined up with EAM. But, early in 1942, months before our first party of British officers had been dropped into Greece, the refusal of the politicians in Athens to have anything to do with EAM had already made its leaders over-anxious. From the spring of 1942, both in Athens and in the field, EAM/ELAS began to spoil their case by intolerance—brutal by our standards—of any competitors in the field, and by giving their post-war aims too much attention in relation to their fight against the common enemy. They assumed and behaved as if all those who were not actively with them were against them.

If it had been possible for the leaders of EAM to keep throughout to a moderate political course, soon after the liberation of Greece a Republic might have been established without bloodshed. But the Movement was under control of extremists. Their bitter memories of Right-wing dictatorship and their evergrowing fear of external interference to assist in its re-establishment at the end of the war, led them to make mistakes similar to those often repeated in Greek history; it lost them an opportunity of achieving by constitutional means what they subsequently failed to achieve by force. Their political rivals, seeing on which side their bread was buttered by the Western Democracies, seldom missed an opportunity to taunt them and to take advantage of their own favoured position. This, coupled with cleverly planted enemy propaganda, only hastened the long sequence of EAM excesses, which ruined their case and ultimately played it straight into the hands of their political opponents.

The leaders of EAM were not the only ones to make mistakes. Historians have recorded many people's wars, both clandestine and overt. A long time ago Clausewitz summarised the principles of fighting them and recently Cyril Falls has given us a succinct review of their characteristics and worth in his "Hundred Years of War". I must admit, however, that until I became engaged in this type of warfare, I had not closely studied it. I believe that I was no exception and that when we began to support guerilla activity in Greece, most of us were in ignorance of the obligations with which we were saddling ourselves until the end of the war, and of the snowball which would eventually roll down from the mountains through the very gates of Athens.

Whilst Allied strategy on the main battle-fronts was defensive, every act of sabotage, almost every bang, in enemy-occupied territory reaped a moral reward out of all proportion to the military gain—great even though the latter often was by itself—and fully justified our policy. When the Allies changed over to the offensive, however, morale-raising bangs and propaganda were comparatively unimportant; the strategical effect of every act of sabotage was what really counted. But by then it was too late to try to send back to their homes the many thousands in the guerilla forces and to reduce overt guerilla warfare to selective sabotage by a few small clandestine groups. There were three reasons. Firstly, in so many cases their homes had been burnt by the enemy. Secondly, because the Greek Resistance was to such a large extent inspired from within and self-armed, the great majority would not have agreed to lay down their arms; in ELAS they certainly would not have been allowed to do so. Thirdly, the consequent loss of a visible stimulant and morale amongst the Greek people would have seriously handicapped such sabotage groups as remained in operation. Any diminution of Allied support to the Resistance could justifiably have been regarded by the andarte organisations as tantamount to betrayal; and it is reasonable to suppose that EAM/ELAS would have done their best to persuade the people in the mountains that they had been betrayed by us. In fact, because of the ever increasing scale of enemy reprisals, once we had given material support and encouragement to the guerilla forces in a small country like Greece, we were morally bound to go on supporting them until the end of hostilities almost regardless of the strategic value of their actions against the enemy.

Throughout the period of the Axis occupation of Greece the military object of the Allies remained constant. It was to get the maximum contribution towards the war effort out of the Greek Resistance. In spite of the temporary civil war in 1943, this policy was never altered, until the country was liberated and EAM/ELAS forced the British to accept battle against them.

Soon after its occupation, Greece became of considerable strategic importance to the enemy. Not only was the country bled white to provide the maximum local produce, but its ports, in particular Piræus, were used both to supply the enemy's island air bases in the Eastern Mediterranean and to slip supplies across by sea to North Africa.

In the autumn of 1942 just as we broke out of the El Alamein line, the destruction of the Gorgopotamos viaduct resulted in the only railway to Athens being cut for six critical weeks, during which the enemy was unable to use Piræus to reinforce his troops in North Africa with more than such small reserves as already happened to be in Southern Greece. The widespread sabotage of communications in June and July, 1943, temporarily diverted two German divisions from the main battle-front in Sicily. It contributed to no small extent towards the overall cover plan, the success of the landings and the capture of the island. It has been estimated that between 1941 and 1944 over twenty-five thousand casualties were inflicted upon the enemy by the andartes. It is known that over one hundred and fifty locomotives were damaged or destroyed. Over a hundred bridges were blown up. Over two hundred and fifty ships of about sixty-eight thousand tons in all were sunk or damaged by sabotage. During 1943 andarte action necessitated the retention of thirteen Italian divisions in Greece. After the Italian capitulation, the Germans were forced to keep six divisions there. Had the enemy weakened his army of occupation before civil war broke out in the mountains, they would have run serious risk of a nation-wide Greek rising against them. All this was no small material dividend, apart from the consideration of morale.

It is worth considering what might have happened had we supported none of the Greek Resistance Movements.

But for British persuasion, it seems unlikely that such an out-standing and gallant leader as Zervas would have taken to the mountains. Without him there would have been no effective rival organisation to EAM/ELAS. In fact, had we given no material support whatsoever to guerilla activity, what happened to the many small independent bands in Macedonia in the spring of 1942 before we arrived on the scenes would have happened to others throughout Greece. They would all have been incorporated by EAM/ELAS or liquidated. By the end of 1943 at the latest, EAM/ELAS would have had a clear field; and at the end of the war, this movement, dominated by Communists, would have been in an immeasurably stronger position to achieve its political aims.

Had the British refused from the very beginning to give any support whatsoever to EAM/ELAS, what would have happened? ELAS, the army of EAM, had already been in existence in many parts of Greece more than six months before the arrival of the British Mission in August, 1942. Moreover it was already fighting against the enemy in a manner which suited EAM's political ends. It was fighting with its own weapons and ammunition, obtained from the places where they were hidden when the Greek army dispersed to its homes in 1941. As time went on, it captured more arms from the enemy. It obtained a particularly big windfall from the Pinerolo Division after Italy's collapse. By 1944 less than a third of the arms of ELAS' permanently embodied force of fifty thousand men had been supplied by the Middle East Command. If the armed village reserves of ELAS, another force of about fifty thousand, are taken into account, less than one sixth of their arms had been provided by us. Although shortages of automatic weapons and of ammunition in general would have prevented EAM/ELAS from carrying out frequent and large scale activity against the occupational forces, there certainly would not have been any shortage of arms or ammunition for a *coup d'état* at the end of the war, even if we had supplied them with nothing.

Had we given all our support to Zervas and none to ELAS, we would have been unable to hold ELAS in check in the winter of 1942. Able to muster far stronger forces from other parts of Greece than Zervas possessed in Valtos—before he had received any large quantity of weapons from us—they would almost certainly have attacked him that winter. At the worst Zervas' movement would have been liquidated. At the best it would have been confined to his small mountain stronghold and limited recruiting area, within reach of which there were few sabotage targets of military importance and from which he would have been unable to interfere with the long-term plans of EAM/ELAS.

The fact that we were not certain about the character and aims of EAM/ELAS until five months after our arrival in the mountains is relevant here. It would have been unreasonable for us to have shunned them until January, 1943, at the earliest. The time when we could have broken off relations with EAM/ELAS was in the spring of 1943, when Zervas was strong enough to stand up against them. I advised this action as a temporary measure until they behaved themselves. SOE did not agree with me, largely because of conflicting reports from Sheppard who was with ELAS on Mount Olympus and who was not yet under my command. But it appears probable that however much or little support the Allies had given to the different Resistance Movements, the Greek Government in exile would have been faced with a great political problem due to the Greek Communist Party, EAM/ELAS, and the reaction to the Metaxas regime, when it eventually returned to liberated Greece.

From the spring of 1943 onwards, when it was decided that we were not to break off relations with EAM/ELAS in spite of their misbehaviour, there was probably only one way of saving Greece from internal bloodshed; it consisted of two complementary measures. One was to knock away the main pillar of EAM's propaganda and strength—the avowed fear that a dictatorship of the Right would be re-established at the end of the war with the aid of British bayonets—before it would be too late for its removal to have effect. The other was for adequately strong British forces to drive the enemy out of Greece soon after the invasion of Sicily, when Resistance was at its peak, when co-operation between rival Movements was at its best and before there had been any serious clash between them.

One must have a large measure of sympathy for King George II of Greece who to many—including, at the time, myself—appeared to be behaving unnecessarily stubbornly. But by the spring of 1943 he knew full well the type of people who were behind EAM. Small wonder that he hated us having anything to do with them; and that, once reassured by Mr. Churchill and President Roosevelt, he persisted in his refusal to announce that he would defer his return to his country until a plebiscite had been held. The British Government, moreover, cannot be blamed for standing by the King of Greece—their loyal ally in 1941—whilst still the constitutional head of his country.

With regard to an earlier liberation of Greece, not until the Quebec Conference in August, 1943, was it finally decided to be impracticable. No one more than Mr. Churchill wanted to witness the earliest possible liberation of Greece. But the Americans were unwilling to weaken our forces on the decisive battle-fronts.

To sum up. Between 1941 and 1944 the root of the Anglo-American problem in Greece was that, in spite of all our efforts to make both the Resistance and the Government in exile more representative, so as to reduce Greece's troubles when she regained her freedom, our short-term military policy of supporting EAM/ELAS—by far the strongest Resistance Movement—turned out to be in direct contradiction to our long-term political policies. In trying to get the best of both worlds, both inevitably suffered. Our anxiety over the premature political issue in the summer of 1943 unfortunately strengthened EAM's false case against us; and it nearly ruined all further military contribution from the Resistance.

For Greece, our gallant Ally, fate played its hand harshly. Before our arrival there in 1942 the cards had already been dealt for serious post-war disturbance. It was tragic that we did not seize the passing opportunities we had of minimising her troubles. Historians may ultimately conclude that it was impossible for us to have done so.

Postscript to Chapter XVII

*More Detailed Accounts of my Visits to Buckingham Palace,
the Foreign Office and Chequers*

I WAS first summoned to Buckingham Palace on 28 September
1943. I understood that I was going to see the King. I arrived
in a car driven by a woman M.T.C. driver in uniform. At the
Palace gates no one asked me for my pass or my name. We
drove across the forecourt to the east wing entrance in
accordance with instructions. An A.R.P. warden outside took
no notice of us. There was no bell and no one else about. I
opened the door and walked in. There was no one in the
passage. I found a door on the right with an official inside,
who did not know I was coming. He took me along to the
study of the Equerry, Sir Alan Lascelles.

   It soon became apparent that I was not going to be seen by
the King. But I had an interesting hour long conversation with
Sir Alan and another person who I believe was Sir Godfrey
Thomas. I found Sir Alan extremely well briefed. He kept on
asking me highly pertinent questions to draw out my views of
the situation inside Greece and the prospects of the Greek
King. We then discussed the visit of the Andarte delegation to
Cairo. After I had evaded answering several particularly
pointed questions, Sir Alan said, 'You can say what you like
to me. I don't belong to the Foreign Office and we are

completely neutral here'. I eventually admitted, I hope with due diffidence, that I didn't think the situation had been well handled by Mr Leeper.

A week later I heard that the Palace staff thought that the prospects of the Greek King returning to Greece were remote.

I was summoned again to the Palace at noon on 30 September, this time to the Inner Courtyard entrance, obviously to be seen by the King. On arrival I was met by an A.D.C., who led me to the King's private study. I spent half an hour alone with him there, both of us comfortably seated in fireside armchairs. After ten minutes of questioning by him on local colour and the general situation inside Greece, the King settled down quite freely to ask the questions he obviously wanted to put to me about the prospects of his cousin King George's return to Greece. I told him frankly about the situation as I saw it. Amongst other things I explained to him how the Greek people did not look upon their King as we looked upon him. 'At the moment', I said, 'there is only a small Royalist group, virtually a political party, which favours his return. These Royalists regard their King more as the leader of their party, under whom they would attempt to intrigue, protected by British bayonets, in order to regain power inside Greece, rather than as we look upon you, Sir, as our Constitutional King.' The King asked me if I had told his cousin about this when I saw him in Cairo. I replied that I thought I had, but that if I had not, in all probability the King already realised this was so. 'Ninety per cent of the people of Greece at present appear to be Republicans', I continued, 'and feared this intrigue by the Royalists. It was for this reason that they were so opposed to the return of the King until there had been a free expression of the people's will.' I explained the subtle difference between what the Greek King had suggested and what the great majority wanted. 'The King had suggested', I said, 'that he should come back to Greece at the head of his Army and he had assured his people that within six months free elections would be held. The Republicans feared that during those six months clashes would break out between them and the Royalists protected by the British Army and that the leading Republicans would be locked up, particularly the more leftist ones. The King had said that the elections would be for a Constitutional Assembly, which would then decide his future. The people mistrusted this, as they thought that these elections would be rigged after the arrest of their leaders. They wanted all the people to vote first of all about the return, or not, of their King.'

Later he said, 'I saw my Secretary of State yesterday and told him he ought to see you. He must get this sort of information first hand from the people who have seen for themselves. Obtaining it from subordinates who have seen you is not good enough.' Shortly before I departed he said, 'See that you see my Secretary of State.' I replied, 'It is a little difficult for me to arrange such an interview. I feel that it ought to be done from the other end.' He agreed. 'Yes, I suppose that this is so.' We parted cheerfully over a light-hearted joke, which I failed to record.

I noted afterwards that I was impressed by the King's deep interest and his obvious sincerity: also by the relaxed way in which we talked to each other after the first few moments when he had difficulty in getting some of his words out.

The next day, 1 October, I was not greatly surprised to be summoned to see Antony Eden, but only for twenty minutes. I recorded that 'he was short of time, but all smiles, polite and certain that he was perfectly briefed, but obviously ill-briefed, by his subordinates. He told me about the Greek political situation as he saw it and what he wanted done regarding our wholehearted support of the Greek King. He omitted to tell me how it could be achieved. I hardly opened my mouth during the whole interview.'

By then I was deeply shocked and frustrated by the generally prejudiced attitude in the Foreign Office and their refusal to face up to unpalatable facts. 'One exception', I noted, 'was Mr Dixon, who at the time was unfortunately too busy with Italian affairs to devote much time to the Balkans, which he apparently understood well. It was not until I got to Chequers that I found a great man to whom I could talk freely and who was prepared to listen.'

My records continue, 'I arrived at Chequers shortly after 1.15 p.m. on 2 October. At about 1.30 Mrs Churchill joined me. Churchill's personal assistant, a naval Commander, and Churchill's brother, a nice old country gentleman, were also there. At about a quarter to two, the Old Man, having at last got out of bed, where he had been working all the morning, dressed in his one-piece dungarees, joined us with his Secretary, Peck. He greeted me and immediately entered into quite a long dissertation about S.O.E., which was carried on as we almost straight away walked into the dining-room. 'Ah, yes,' he said, 'your organisation has been meddling in the work of my Foreign Office and, if it had not been for me, they would have gone under. They must not try to run things their own way. We are the people who do that. Don't you get mixed up in politics. Leave that to the politicians.'

'I sat down to lunch between Mr and Mrs Churchill. Whilst Mrs Churchill talked to me on social topics, Churchill often simultaneously talked on the highest level about confidential matters, even when the servants were in the room. I found myself having to talk to Mrs Churchill about the A.T.S., the contribution of the women of Britain to the war effort, and gardens, whilst listening to Churchill as well. Every time Churchill and I got into a deep discussion, Mrs Churchill would try to steer the conversation away onto a more social subject. But as the Old Man appeared quite at ease talking about confidential matters in front of the servants, I soon began to put in my say too.'

'I said that I felt certain that our policy towards Greece was a just one, but that we had left all public announcements to the Greek King and Government, and that our silence, particularly as a result of the Andarte Delegation's return with their aims so unfulfilled, would be interpreted by those inside Greece as determination on our part to enforce the return of the King. Although I knew this to be false, those inside Greece did not; and I felt it was up to us, by tactful propaganda, to explain our policy.'

'After lunch, sitting round the table, smoking a good cigar – Churchill insisted that I pocketed another one to take away with me – I showed him photographs, which had recently come out of Greece, of the Italian General Infante and his surrender with seven thousand of his troops. I also showed him a stereoscopic pair of aerial photographs of the Asopos railway viaduct, lying at the bottom of the gorge it had spanned, after we had blown it up at the beginning of our widespread demolitions in conjunction with the invasion of Sicily. He chuckled delightedly.'

'I told him that I thought his recent speech at the Quebec Conference, in which he had said that he looked forward to the Greek King's return to Greece, had made my job more difficult. Surely, I said, what happened to their King is a Greek affair and it is not for us to interfere. He asked me what he had said at Quebec and I produced an extract of his speech from my attaché case. He looked it through and then politely said that he agreed with what he had said; so I left it at that.'

'I then produced a draft of the broadcast over the BBC, which I was proposing to make to the andartes before I left

London in a few days time. It contained a message of good cheer as from Churchill. It was entirely non-political and had already been approved by S.O.E. and the Foreign Office. Churchill read it through in silence and at the end said, 'Well, that's all right, perfectly harmless. Would you like me to add a little pep to it?' I said I would be delighted if he would, whereupon he got out his fountain-pen filled with red ink and slowly started scratching away. Afterwards I was handed what he had written to read and comment. I found that he had added a paragraph almost exactly on the lines I had suggested at lunch, affirming and justifying our policy towards Greece. It read as follows: 'The Greek people must be masters of their destinies. They alone can decide their future form of govern-ment. England, always their friend, will never interfere in their home politics and will always champion their sovereign rights. We have obligations of honour to King George because he fought for the Allied cause. These we must discharge. They do not in any way affect the full freedom of the Greek people to settle their own affairs once conditions of tranquility and orderly politics are re-established.'

He gave the amended draft to his Secretary to be retyped and went off to his study; Mrs Churchill took me for a walk round the garden. It was then about half past three. About half an hour later I returned to Mr Churchill's study. The retyped draft of my broadcast was brought in. Mr Churchill read it through. He soon started altering it a little bit and eventually became firmer, calling for his blue pencil. He then began striking out whole sentences of what he had written. 'No,' he said, 'It is too risky. I don't want to say anything in the wrong way.' I stressed that if he would allow me to make a statement which would give confidence to the Greek people that we had no intention of interfering with their affairs, it would be of the greatest help to me. 'Yes,' he replied, 'but I don't like it being done in this way. The Americans are very interested in this and I don't want to say anything over the heads of my colleagues. No, I don't like any of this, it's too risky.' And his blue pencil went through all he had written. 'No,' he continued, 'I'll say this in the House in the proper way. You just say what you have written.'

I did not argue further and my draft again went out to be retyped, almost as it had been originally, but with a few words of Churchill's added here and there, improving the English and deleting superlatives, which, he said, weakened the force of good English, not realising that the speech was to be translated into Greek.

One point I could not get into Churchill's head was that the andartes were not 'bandits', but that they represented all types of Greeks as well as many Republican leaders. Sarafis had been Military Attaché in Paris; Tzimas had been a Communist Deputy; Kartalis had been Finance Minister in more than one Greek Government; Colonel Psaros was one of the most capable soldiers I had ever met. There were many others. They were not just 'Tom Wintringhams',★ which Churchill had more than once called them. I could not convince him that I was in touch not only with the andartes and the mostly poor people in the mountains, but with virtually every element and every thinking body inside Greece, including those in all of the big towns.

When I said earlier that I thought between eighty and ninety per cent were Republicans and no longer Royalists now, he replied, 'Yes, that's what you say or think. I am not sure you

---

★ Churchill was presumably referring to Captain Tom Wintringham, military correspondent of the *Daily Worker* and commander of the Saklatvala Battalion of the 15th International Brigade during the Spanish civil war. During World War II he wrote articles for *Picture Post* on guerilla warfare.

are right'. I told him I had been accused behind my back of political prejudice and that this was entirely false. Everything that I had said was based on considerable evidence and what I knew to be true. Throughout our discussions he had treated me with respect and as his equal. I found that I could speak to him in a straightforward manner, in spite of the fact that he wanted to do a lot of the talking himself. He congratulated me on my work in Greece and before I departed he invited me to get in touch with him direct, should I find myself faced with apparently insuperable difficulties in obeying my orders. He twice rose to say goodbye to me. He respectfully gave me God's blessing. 'Don't let them pre-judge the issue about the King,' he concluded. 'I want to see him have a fair deal. I won't be stampeded by a lot of "Tom Wintringhams."' When I replied that our prolonged silence about our policy might be interpreted as weakness or an attempt at interference to restore the King and that the more leftist of the Republican elements might turn towards Russia for support, he retorted, 'I won't be blackmailed by these bandits! If they want to go to Russia, let them. When Greece is freed, who is going to save them from starving? We are. And they oughtn't to forget that. You see that the King gets a fair deal.' I replied that I would do my best.

As I went out with Churchill's personal assistant through the front door, he said, 'The Old Man is a bit muddled.' I asked him if he thought I had made my points clear. He thought I had done so. I asked him to do his best to put over to Churchill once again that the andartes were not just 'Tom Wintringhams', but that they represented a large section of the people of Greece today.

I left at 5 o'clock, already late for an appointment in London. I was pleased with my visit. I had almost achieved a tremendous success in obtaining an unequivocal statement from Churchill about our non-interference with the future of the Greek King. I felt that my failure to do so was only of a temporary nature. As a result I believed that we would soon be able to obtain a further contribution from the Greek Resistance forces towards the war effort and be given a chance, however slender, of saving Greece on liberation from civil war. What an optimist I was!

Long afterwards Chris Woodhouse said to me, 'You only made one mistake in Greece and that was to accompany the Andarte Delegation to Cairo. I feared at the time that you might never be allowed to come back to Greece.' But so much was at stake that, even now, I believe I was right to have reported personally on the many problems, paramilitary, civilian and political, which faced me as a result of the unexpected delay in the liberation of Greece.

Index

ACHELOOS, R., 117, 121, 126, 160, 195, 221, 267
Adriatic Sea, 230
Aegean, 122
Agoros, Major, 208
Agrinion, 65, 88, 151, 166, 203–4
Airborne Troops, 13 *ff*. See SAS.
Aircraft (for Special Operations). Dakota, 243–4
 Halifax, 123, 167, 231
 Liberator, 19, 25, 39, 43, 121, 123, 231
 See RAF.
 Enemy, 197 *ff*., 233
Airfields, Greek, 230 *ff*., 234, 236, 240, 243–4
 Middle East, 23–7, 167
Air Force, Balkan, 270
Air Force, Royal. See RAF.
Alamein. See El Alamein.
Albania, Albanian, 91, 152, 155
Albanian Resistance Movements, 123–4, 152, 211, 212
Albanians, Turco-, 152, 155
Alexander, Field-Marshal, 18
Aliakmon, R., 212
Allied strategy, 121 *ff*., 202, 228, 259, 279 *ff*.
Americans, 258, 270, 283
America. See U.S.A.
Amphissa, 46
Amvrakia, Gulf of, 98
Anagnostakis, 155–6
Anatoli, 168, 172, 181
Andarte Joint GHQ. See GHQ.
Anglo-Greek Committee in Cairo, 98, 100, 109, 246, 276
Arachthos, R., 267
Archibishop of Athens. See Damaskinos.
Aris Veloukhiotis. See Klaras.
Arta, 58, 88, 91, 96, 108, 111, 117, 152, 204
Asopos Viaduct, 17, 20, 27, 54, 170–86, 194, 202–3
Athanassiades, Tommy, 153–4, 156–8, 167, 175, 191, 197, 199
Athens, 17–18, 20, 50, 65, 72, 86, 88–90, 98, 102, 106–7, 114–20, 125, 135, 140, 144–9, 153, 169–70, 175–6, 178, 185, 187, 197, 199, 200, 203–4, 206–7, 212–13, 215, 219, 225, 227, 237, 240–2, 246–7, 271–3, 275–80

Atlantic Charter, 119, 190, 192–3
Attica, 17, 122
Avdela, 199, 210
Avlaki, 117–18, 125, 128, 130, 136, 147, 150–3, 159, 171

Bakirdzis, General (Colonel), 258
Baphas, 46–7, 51, 59, 76
Barba Niko. See Nikolaos Beis.
Barker, Nat, 22, 27, 42, 61, 66, 76, 91, 98, 107, 110, 113, 115, 142, 150, 161, 203, 231, 232
Barnes, Tom, 22, 28, 34–5, 61, 66, 67, 77–8, 80–2, 85, 91, 99, 110, 112, 113, 121, 124, 152, 154–8, 204, 208
BBC, 199, 263
Benghazi, 17
Bishop of Kozani, 212 *ff*.
Bliaux, Captain, 199
Bohorina, 210, 212
Bower, Ross, 151, 162, 165, 197, 219
British Ambassador to Greece, 121 *n*. See also Leeper.
British Embassy to Greece, 249, 251, 254–5, 258, 264
British Government, 108, 119, 188, 189 93, 226, 252–3, 255, 263 *n*., 283

Cabinet Offices, 259
Casey, Rt. Hon. R. G., 255, 256 *ff*.
Central Committee of EAM. See EAM.
Chiefs of Staff, Washington, 113
Chittis, Sergeant, 22, 42, 91
Chris. See Woodhouse.
Churchill, Sir Winston (Mr.), 184, 185, 252, 261 *ff*., 263, 283
Civil War, dangers of, 108, 128 *ff*., 189 *ff*., 226, 254, 259, 282 *ff*.
Commander-in-Chief (Naval), Mediterranean, 97
Commander-in-Chief, Middle East Land Forces, 16, 18, 37, 114, 126, 135, 185, 191, 193, 199, 227, 250, 255–6, 257, 264 *ff*.
Commanders-in-Chief, Middle East, 204, 209

Communist Party of Greece. See KKE.
Cook, Major John, 22 ff., 27, 50, 63–7, 76, 86, 91, 98–9, 124, 152, 155
Corfu, 273
Corinth Canal, 42
Crete, Cretans, 17, 19, 25, 43, 67, 70, 104, 144, 177
Cumberlege, Commander, 207
Cypriot(s), 165

Damaskinos, Archbishop of Athens, 169, 273
Demertzes, 104
Dimitriou ("Nikiphoros"), 65, 66
Denys. See Hamson
Deo, Aaron, Corporal, 62, 91
Dereli, 204
Derna, 167
Despotopoulos, Constantine, 241
Directives, SOE (Cairo), 19 ff., 96, 97 ff., 121 ff., 205, 228–30, 263
  Political, 189, 215, 263
Dodecanese, Plans to liberate, 122, 202, 229
Duffy, Lieutenant, RE, 156

EAM, EAM-ELAS, 89, 100–3, 105–6, 108–9, 114, 116, 120, 126–9, 132–3, 135, 140–8, 150, 152–5, 158, 163–7, 172, 175–8, 180, 187–96, 200–1, 207, 212–14, 216, 218, 220–5, 227, 229, 231–2, 234–6, 238–9, 242–4, 248–9, 252–5, 262–4, 266–84
  Central Committee of, 101, 106, 118–20, 126, 128, 137–41, 145–6, 149 ff., 153, 157, 166, 172–3, 175, 187–8, 192–3, 200, 237, 240–2
  Delegations, 128 ff., 236, 241, 246–58, 266
  Origins of, 100 ff., 274 ff.
  Youth Movement. See EPON.
Economic Warfare, Ministry of, 259
Eden, Rt. Hon. Sir Anthony (Mr.), 261
EDES, 102, 103, 106, 108, 113, 118, 126, 129, 152, 154–6, 166, 173, 195, 203, 207, 220–1, 223, 225, 226–7, 236, 238, 240, 243, 266, 268, 270, 272. See also Zervas.
  Origins of, 102, 277
Edmonds, Lieut.-Colonel (Capt.) Arthur, 22, 42, 61, 66, 91, 121, 124, 142, 143, 144, 150, 165, 167–8, 170–3, 180–1, 191, 194, 204, 219
Ehrgott, Colonel (Captain), 258
EKKA, 115, 144, 150, 173, 207, 219, 221, 237–8, 240, 243, 248, 258, 268, 269, 277. See also Psaros.
El Alamein, 13, 17, 21, 167, 280

ELAS, 76, 88–9, 100–3, 106–8, 114–16, 118, 125–7, 129, 132–8, 140–50, 152, 154–9, 161, 165, 167–8, 170, 172, 173, 175–80, 182, 188–9, 193–6, 198–200, 201, 203–4, 207, 210–12, 216, 218–23, 226–8, 236, 240–2, 263, 266–9, 271–3, 275–7, 279, 281–2
  First encounter with, 65
  GHQ. See GHQ, ELAS.
  Origins of, 101, 275
ELD, 101, 221
Embeso, 107
Engineer-in-Chief, GHQ, Middle East, 15, 21
EOA, 207
Epirus, 113, 124, 152, 154–8, 203, 204, 220, 227, 272
EPON, 234
Evmaios. See Tzimas.
Evrytania, 151, 173, 204, 220, 221
Exindaris, M., 247, 248, 253

Falls, Cyril, 278
Fascists, Fascism. See Italy.
Filiates, 221
Foreign Office, 151, 216, 249, 251, 253, 254, 258, 259, 261–2, 263, 265
  representative. See Wallace.
France, 102, 115, 274
Frangista, 167

Gardiki, 142–4, 168
George VI, King of England, 261
George II, King of Greece, 22, 98, 103–4, 119, 128–9, 146, 150, 188–93, 213, 214–15, 246–9, 252–6, 259–62, 263 n., 269, 271, 273–4, 283
Germans, Germany, 34 ff., 49, 100, 105–6, 117, 119, 120, 122, 143 ff., 144–5, 161, 164, 168–70, 176–9, 183–4, 189, 194–5, 197–8, 203, 205, 225, 232, 247, 263, 266, 267–8, 270–2, 280
GHQ, Andarte Joint, 77–8, 193, 195, 201, 218–21, 225–7, 236, 239
  ELAS, 175, 178, 180, 187, 191, 194–5, 196, 198, 199, 200, 210, 212, 269
  Middle East, 13, 17 ff., 19, 70, 100, 104, 110, 113–14, 116, 119–23, 126, 130–32, 136, 145–6, 148, 151, 156–8, 171, 173, 175–7, 187–8, 192–3, 195, 199, 200–1, 205, 208, 213, 215, 224–6, 229, 234, 236, 238, 242, 247, 248, 250–2, 258, 263, 264, 269, 277, 281
Gikopoulos, Colonel, 196, 198–9, 218, 236
Gill, Capt. (Lieut.) Inder, RE, 22, 64, 66, 91

Glenconner, Lord, 245, 248, 251, 254, 255, 257
Gordon-Creed, Major Geoffrey, 172, 178–83, 185, 194, 203
Gorgopotamos Viaduct, 17, 20, 54, 56 7, 60, 63, 66, 70, 72–86, 89, 97, 113, 121, 137, 142, 169, 275, 280
Greece, Liberation of, 108 ff., 128 ff., 189 ff., 228 ff., 238–40, 259
Greek Army, 120, 220, 227, 239, 247, 255, 271 ff.
Communists. See KKE.
Constitution, 119, 189, 213, 214
Government, 22, 98, 100, 103, 104, 109, 129, 146, 189–91, 207, 213, 215, 239, 246–8, 252–7, 260–1, 270–1, 282, 283

Hamilton, Lieut.-Colonel, 13–17
Hammond, N. G. L., 124, 165, 178, 208, 225, 235
Hamson, Denys, 22, 34–5, 37–8, 40, 52, 53, 55–6, 60, 61, 66, 81, 82, 91, 93, 121, 124, 128, 133, 134, 147, 150, 161, 206, 230–4, 237, 240–1, 243, 244
Harker, Captain, 203
Headquarters. See GHQ.
Hermes, 107
Hootas, 204
House of Commons, 263 n., 267
Hubbard, Lieutenant, 267

Infante, General, 267
Italy, Italians, 18, 34 ff., 41, 45–7, 51–7, 59, 62, 64, 65, 68, 85, 88, 91, 95, 104, 106, 111–12, 117–22, 127, 144, 152–3, 164, 169, 170, 203, 208, 228, 230, 240, 266, 267, 270, 281
Collapse of, 263, 266, 267, 280

Johnson, Captain, 208
Jordan, Bill, 95–7, 107, 110, 159 ff. 163

Kalambaka, 139, 199, 203, 212, 221
Kanellopoulos, Panyiotis, 98, 100, 108
Karadjopoulos, George, 179
Karalivanos, 36–8, 41 ff., 44 ff., 46, 59, 62, 63, 71, 76, 86
Karayioryis, 135–41, 199, 200, 212, 234, 235
Karditsa, 138, 139, 152, 230–2, 240
Karoutes, 34, 35, 38, 40, 46, 51, 59
Karpenisi, 64, 88, 118, 142, 167
Kartalis, George, 219, 237, 240, 241, 248
Kastania, 212, 213
Kastelli, 173, 174
Katsimbas, 35 ff., 39, 46

Khosepsi, 96, 154, 158, 159
Khuri, Sergeant (Lance-Corporal) Michael, 49, 60, 66, 91, 143, 181, 182, 185
King George VI. See George VI, King of England.
King George II of Greece. See George II, King of Greece.
Kitso, 151, 223
KKE, 101–2, 105, 119, 126–9, 140, 145, 212 ff., 241, 253, 274, 275, 281, 282
Klaras, Athanasios (Aris), 62, 64–5, 66–8, 70–3, 75–8, 80, 83, 86, 88, 99, 100, 102–3, 107, 110, 113, 116, 119, 121, 125, 137, 140, 144, 146, 171–5, 176–8, 191, 195–6, 207, 218, 220, 223, 227
Kleidi, 110
Kolokythia, 144, 145, 148, 150
Konstantinides, Major, 155–7, 158
Koroni, 234
Kostopoulos, Major, 114, 125, 134, 140
Koukouvista, 41, 42, 45, 144 ff., 174, 175
Koutsoyiannopoulos (Prometheus), 18, 20, 50, 52, 67, 86, 88, 98, 117, 120, 144
Kozakas, 125, 126, 130, 132–5, 137–8, 140–1, 145, 147
Kranias, 173–4, 176, 194

Lambrakis, Colonel, 96, 163
Lang, Lieut.-Colonel (Major) Derek, 24
Lascelles, Sir Alan, 261
Leeper, Sir Reginald (Mr.), 217, 248, 250, 251, 254, 257, 258
Liascovo, 195, 198
Liberals (Republicans or Venizelists), Liberal Party, 70, 103, 104–5, 114, 116, 215, 246, 247, 252, 272
L.N.C. See Albanian Resistance Movements.
Lockwood, Lance-Corporal Chester, 179, 180
Louros, R., 95

Maadi, 245
Macedonia, 102, 119, 124, 145, 161, 178, 196, 200, 202, 210, 211, 225, 235, 268, 281
MacIntyre, Major Henry, RE, 171, 179, 181–3, 185
Maclean, Billy, 155 ff., 158
Macromoni, 168
Malaya, 274
Marinos, Themie, 20, 22, 27, 64, 66, 76, 82, 87, 89, 90, 96, 97, 107, 110–13, 124, 132–4, 137–41, 144, 153, 204
Maund, Rear-Admiral L. E., 15

Mavrolithari, 69, 71, 75, 85, 90, 168, 172–3, 178, 188
Mediterranean, 93, 176, 202, 208, 209, 229, 280
Megalohari, 90, 96, 111, 113, 118
Merophilo, 133
Mesokhora, 133
Mesopyrgo, 113, 117
Mesounda, 133
Messolonghi, 108, 154, 203
Metaxas, General, 70, 103, 104–5, 145, 146, 154, 176, 177, 183, 184
Metzovo, 199, 203, 267
Michael Khuri. See Khuri.
Michailovic, 121, 214
Michalli, Captain, 67, 76, 79, 90–5, 99, 121
Micklethwait, Major, 152, 158
Middle East, Middle East Command. See GHQ, Middle East.
Military Agreements, 130–2, 135–6, 137, 140–1, 144, 146 ff., 156, 163, 176, 177, 187–8, 191–2, 194, 196, 199, 200, 201, 215, 219, 220, 221–3, 226, 254
Minis, 206, 207
Ministry of Economic Warfare. See Economic Warfare.
Morton, Sergeant, 142
Mouzaki, 138, 166
Moyne, Lord, 249
Mutch, Lance-Corporal Charlie, 181–2, 185

Naarfi, Jemal, 42 ff., 45, 49, 66, 91
Nasis, General, 154
National Bands, 114 ff., 116, 128–9, 130 ff., 137, 145–6, 148–9, 151, 161, 173–4, 176, 178, 188, 190–2, 195, 201
    Agreement. See Military Agreements.
National and Social Liberation Movement. See EKKA.
National Liberation Front. See EAM.
National Organisation of Officers. See EOA.
National Popular Liberation Army. See ELAS.
National Republican Greek League. See EDES.
Navy, British Naval Activities. See RN.
Nazis, Nazism. See Germans.
Neraida, 230, 231, 235, 237, 240, 241
"Nikiphoros" (Dimitriou), 65, 66
Nikolaos Beis (Barba Niko), 41, 45, 48, 51, 52, 58, 60, 61, 71, 84, 87, 121

Oiti, Mt, 56, 74, 83, 84
Olympus, Mt, 101, 116, 124, 125, 127, 137, 140–1, 161, 203, 282

Palestine, 247
PAO (Pan-Hellenic Liberation Organisation), 225
Papachristo, Dr, 90, 110, 112, 113, 118
Papadia Viaduct, 17, 18, 20, 53
Papaiannou, 151, 173, 174, 176, 180, 194, 221, 223
Parachute Training School, 17
Paramythia, 92
Parga, 90
Parnassus, Mtns., 45, 115, 125, 142, 144, 153, 154
Patras, 206
Paxos, Isle, 93, 94
Peloponnese, 102, 122, 124, 128, 180, 204, 205, 206–7, 270
Perivoli, 199
Pertouli, 218, 219, 225, 226, 231, 235–6, 237, 239, 240, 241
Phillips, Sergeant, 22, 64
Pindus, Mtns., 114, 122, 125, 128, 134, 141, 145, 149, 151, 160–1, 176–7, 218, 268
Piræus, 17, 18, 273, 280
Pisperis, Colonel, 154, 158
Pistolis, Costa, 57, 169
    Yani, 52, 53, 54–5, 56–7
Plastiras, General, 70, 102, 114–16, 142, 231
Platanousa, 154
Poland, Poles, 184, 274
Political Directives. See Directives.
Popular Democratic Union. See ELD.
Popular Party, Populists (Royalists), 103, 104, 106, 119, 127, 133, 214, 227, 246, 271 ff.
Porta, 134, 138, 218, 266
Preveza, 199
Prodhromos, 137
Prometheus. See Koutsoyiannopoulos.
Prophet Elias, 40, 46, 49, 51
Psaros, Colonel, 115, 125, 142, 172–4, 176, 180, 188, 194, 219, 220, 268, 277
Pyrgos, 240
Pyromaglou, Komninos, 79, 80, 81, 195, 237, 240–1, 248

Quebec Conference, 252, 262, 283

RAF, 17, 121, 160, 179 ff., 184, 233, 234, 237, 241
    aircraft. See Aircraft.
Rallis, 164
Reid, Major, 206, 207
Rendina, 141
Republican Party of Greece. See Liberal Party.
RN, 17, 273
Romanon Monastery, 96, 154, 156, 158, 159

Roosevelt, 252, 283
Ross. See Bower.
Rotherham, Flight-Lieut. Freddie, 241, 243, 244
Roumeli, 17, 65, 73, 87, 88–9, 101, 103, 110, 118, 124–5, 129, 135, 137–8, 140, 142, 149–51, 153, 164–67, 170, 173–4, 176, 189, 191, 196, 204, 207, 219, 221
Roussos, Petros, 241
Royalists. See Popular Party, Populists.
Russia, Russian, 102, 122, 198, 275, 276

Salonika, 17, 18, 202, 225
Sarandis, 135
Sarandoporon Pass, 203
Saraphis, Colonel, 114–15, 125–30, 132–7, 140, 142, 144–8, 175, 177, 178, 191, 195–6, 199, 200, 218, 224, 266
Sargent, Sir Orme, 259 ff.
Scobie, General Sir Ronald, 264 ff., 272
Scott, Captain, RE, 171, 179, 181, 182, 183, 185
Seferiades, Alexis, 19, 39, 41, 144
Serbian Resistance Movement. See Yugoslav Resistance.
Sheppard, Colonel (Major), 116, 124, 125–7, 137, 140, 161, 165, 178, 199, 200, 212, 282
Shugli, Osman, 42 ff., 45, 49, 91
Siantos, Yioryios, 119, 241, 242–3
Sicily, Invasion of, 121, 202–5, 207–8, 212, 228, 270, 276, 280
Skolikaria, 99, 110–12
Smiley, Colonel (Captain) David, 156, 158
Smith, Staff-Sergeant Stan, 160, 236–7, 241
Smokovo, 139, 141
Socialist Party of Greece, 101, 128
Spanish Civil War, 62
Special Air Service (SAS), 14
Special Operations Executive, SOE (Cairo), 13, 17–20, 22, 50, 86, 90, 93, 95–100, 106, 108, 110, 112–17, 120–30, 132, 140, 144, 146–7, 150–1, 153, 159–61, 163, 170, 177–9, 181, 188–9, 191, 193, 196, 200, 203, 205–6, 212, 215, 222, 224–5, 228, 230, 233–4, 236–9, 241–5, 248, 250–4, 257, 264, 272, 282
SOE (London), 13 n., 250, 261, 262
Training School, 264
Sperkhiadha, 167, 168
Spherkhios, R., 141, 167, 204
Spiliotopoulos, Colonel, 118 n.
Stevens, John, 151, 165, 230, 251
Stirling, David, 14

Stott, Donald, 142, 144, 179–86
Strategy. See Allied Strategy.
Stromni, 45–9, 52, 57, 60–3, 66, 71, 86, 172, 182
Suez Canal, 14, 16, 17, 21, 23, 27

Tamplin, Guy, 264
Tassos, Eleftherias, 144
Tempe Valley, 203
Theodhoriana, 153, 159, 160, 162–3, 165–6, 189, 197–8
Thessaly, 17, 102, 132–4, 137, 138, 140, 141, 150–2, 161, 164, 166, 178, 195, 196, 200, 203, 208, 210, 212, 218, 230, 232, 234, 240, 266
Tickell, General Sir Eustace, 21
Timfristos, 19, 180
Tito. See Yugoslav Resistance.
Tobruk, 17
Tom. See Barnes.
Tommy. See Athanassiades.
Trikkala, 135, 137, 219
Tripolis, 206
Tsirimokos, Ilias, 101, 241
Tsotyli, 211–13
Tsouderos, 252–4, 256–7
Tunisia, 122
Turco-Albanians. See Albanians.
Turkey, 13, 18, 117, 151, 251
Turnavo, 177, 194
Tzimas, Andreas (Evmaios), 119, 145–7, 149–53, 164–5, 173, 175–8, 187–8, 191–2, 194, 196, 200, 211, 212, 218, 221, 223, 237, 240–2
Tzortius, 211

Union of Popular Democracy. See ELD.
U.S.A., 283. See also Americans.

Valtos, 19, 67, 68, 86, 88, 90, 95, 102, 142–3, 166, 282
Varibobi, 135
Vathyremma, 134
Veloukhiotis, Aris. See Klaras.
Venizelists. See Liberal Party.
Vlakhos Major, 125–6, 128–9, 130, 133, 136, 147, 206
Voukmanovitch, Svetoza, 211
Voulgareli, 164, 197

Wallace, David, 216 ff., 235–8, 241, 250–1, 258–9, 263
War Office, 258 ff.
Wilmot, Sergeant Len, 22, 34–5, 40, 90
Wilson, Field-Marshal Lord (General), 185, 255, 264
Wines, Major Jerry, 270

Wingate, Lieut.-Colonel (Captain) Pat, RE, 171, 179
Woodhouse, the Hon. C. M., 19–23, 27, 40–43, 45, 46, 49, 51, 54, 57–60, 62–3, 65–6, 71, 73, 75, 77–80, 82–4, 86–7, 89, 90, 95–101, 106–8, 110, 114, 116, 117–20, 121, 124, 128, 130, 136–7, 144–5, 150–3, 159, 162, 164, 195–7, 199, 200, 216, 221, 228, 230, 236–8, 242, 263–8, 270, 272, 274, 276
Woodhouse's first meeting with Zervas, 66–8

Xyrokombos, 112

Yani. See Naarfi.
Yannina, 91, 95, 96, 154, 162, 199, 203, 212, 272
Yerodimos, 223

Yioryiades, 155, 158–9
Yorgo, 39, 46
Yugoslav, Yugoslavia, 145, 204, 211, 212, 274
   Resistance, Partisans, 204, 211, 212, 214, 276
      Serbian Movement, 121, 123, 214. See also Michailovic.

Zakhariadhis, Nikos, 119 n.
Zapharides, Nasso, 212, 235
Zervas, Alexis, 89, 154
Zervas, General Napoleon, 19–20, 50, 58, 65–73, 75–80, 82–3, 86–91, 96, 99–102, 106–8, 110–15, 117–21, 126–30, 132–8, 140–2, 144, 146, 148, 151-6, 180, 195–6, 198, 200–1, 204, 206–8, 218, 220–1, 222 ff. 225–7, 237, 248–9, 263, 267–70, 272, 277, 281, 282